Related Books of Interest

Developing and Hosting Applications on the Cloud

By Alexander Amies, Harm Sluiman,
Qiang Guo Tong, and Guo Ning Liu
ISBN: 0-13-306684-3

The promise of cloud computing is that centralization, standardization, and automation will simplify user experience and reduce costs. However, achieving these benefits requires a new mind set. *Developing and Hosting Applications on the Cloud* covers these aspects of application development and operation and provides practical guidance, giving numerous code examples and demonstrations of system utilities for deployment, security, and maintenance.

This title makes special reference to the IBM SmartCloud Enterprise, but the principles explained are general and useful to anyone planning to automate management of IT infrastructure using the cloud. Developers using cloud management application programming, architects planning projects, or others wanting to automate management of IT infrastructure will value this end to end story for why they would want to develop a cloud application, how to do it, and how to make it part of their business.

The Business of IT
How to Improve Service and Lower Costs

By Robert Ryan and Tim Raducha-Grace
ISBN: 0-13-700061-8

Drive More Business Value from IT...and Bridge the Gap Between IT and Business Leadership

IT organizations have achieved outstanding technological maturity, but many have been slower to adopt world-class business practices. This book provides IT and business executives with methods to achieve greater business discipline throughout IT, collaborate more effectively, sharpen focus on the customer, and drive greater value from IT investment. Drawing on their experience consulting with leading IT organizations, Robert Ryan and Tim Raducha-Grace help IT leaders make sense of alternative ways to improve IT service and lower cost, including ITIL, IT financial management, balanced scorecards, and business cases. You'll learn how to choose the best approaches to improve IT business practices for your environment and use these practices to improve service quality, reduce costs, and drive top-line revenue growth.

Related Books of Interest

The Art of Enterprise Information Architecture
A Systems-Based Approach for Unlocking Business Insight

By Mario Godinez, Eberhard Hechler, Klaus Koenig, Steve Lockwood, Martin Oberhofer, and Michael Schroeck
ISBN: 0-13-703571-3

Architecture for the Intelligent Enterprise: Powerful New Ways to Maximize the Real-time Value of Information

Tomorrow's winning "Intelligent Enterprises" will bring together far more diverse sources of data, analyze it in more powerful ways, and deliver immediate insight to decision-makers throughout the organization. Today, however, most companies fail to apply the information they already have, while struggling with the complexity and costs of their existing information environments.

In this book, a team of IBM's leading information management experts guide you on a journey that will take you from where you are today toward becoming an "Intelligent Enterprise."

The New Era of Enterprise Business Intelligence:
Using Analytics to Achieve a Global Competitive Advantage

By Mike Biere
ISBN: 0-13-707542-1

A Complete Blueprint for Maximizing the Value of Business Intelligence in the Enterprise

The typical enterprise recognizes the immense potential of business intelligence (BI) and its impact upon many facets within the organization—but it's not easy to transform BI's potential into real business value. Top BI expert Mike Biere presents a complete blueprint for creating winning BI strategies and infrastructure, and systematically maximizing the value of information throughout the enterprise.

This product-independent guide brings together start-to-finish guidance and practical checklists for every senior IT executive, planner, strategist, implementer, and the actual business users themselves.

Listen to the author's podcast at:
ibmpressbooks.com/podcasts

Visit ibmpressbooks.com
for all product information

Related Books of Interest

Enterprise Master Data Management
An SOA Approach to Managing Core Information

By Allen Dreibelbis, Eberhard Hechler,
Ivan Milman, Martin Oberhofer,
Paul Van Run, and Dan Wolfson
ISBN: 0-13-236625-8

The Only Complete Technical Primer
for MDM Planners, Architects, and
Implementers

Enterprise Master Data Management provides an authoritative, vendor-independent
MDM technical reference for practitioners:
architects, technical
analysts, consultants, solution designers,
and senior IT decision makers. Written
by the IBM® data management innova-
tors who are pioneering MDM, this book
systematically introduces MDM's key
concepts and technical themes, explains
its business case, and illuminates how it
interrelates with and enables SOA.

Drawing on their experience with
cutting-edge projects, the authors
introduce MDM patterns, blueprints,
solutions, and best practices published
nowhere else—everything you need to
establish a consistent, manageable set
of master data, and use it for competitive
advantage.

Mining the Talk
Unlocking the Business Value in
Unstructured Information
Spangler, Kreulen
ISBN: 0-13-233953-6

Is Your Company Ready for Cloud?
Choosing the Best Cloud Adoption
Strategy for Your Business
Isom, Holley
ISBN 0-13-259984-8

Get Bold
Using Social Media to Create a
New Type of Social Business
Carter
ISBN 0-13-261831-1

IBM Cognos 10 Report Studio
Practical Examples
Draskovic, Johnson
ISBN-10: 0-13-265675-2

Data Integration Blueprint and Modeling
Techniques for a Scalable and
Sustainable Architecture
Giordano
ISBN: 0-13-708493-5

Sign up for the monthly IBM Press newsletter at
ibmpressbooks/newsletters

Mobile Strategy

Mobile Strategy

How Your Company Can Win
by Embracing Mobile Technologies

Dirk Nicol

IBM Press
Pearson plc

Upper Saddle River, NJ • Boston • Indianapolis • San Francisco
New York • Toronto • Montreal • London • Munich • Paris • Madrid
Cape Town • Sydney • Tokyo • Singapore • Mexico City
ibmpressbooks.com

IBM Press Program Managers: Steven M. Stansel, Ellice Uffer

Cover design: IBM Corporation

    Associate Publisher: Dave Dusthimer
    Marketing Manager: Stephane Nakib
    Executive Editor: Mary Beth Ray
    Publicist: Andrea Bledsoe
    Senior Development Editor: Christopher Cleveland
    Technical Editors: Vijay Dheap, Christopher Pepin
    Managing Editor: Kristy Hart
    Designer: Alan Clements
    Project Editor: Jovana Shirley
    Copy Editor: Apostrophe Editing Services
    Indexer: Cheryl Lenser
    Compositor: Nonie Ratcliffe
    Proofreader: Jess DeGabriele
    Manufacturing Buyer: Dan Uhrig

Published by Pearson plc

Publishing as IBM Press

IBM Press offers excellent discounts on this book when ordered in quantity for bulk purchases or special sales, which may include electronic versions and/or custom covers and content particular to your business, training goals, marketing focus, and branding interests. For more information, please contact

    U. S. Corporate and Government Sales
    1-800-382-3419
    corpsales@pearsontechgroup.com.

For sales outside the U. S., please contact

    International Sales
    international@pearson.com.

The Library of Congress cataloging-in-publication data is on file.

Pearson Education, Inc.
Rights and Contracts Department
501 Boylston Street, Suite 900
Boston, MA 02116
Fax (617) 671-3447

ISBN-13: 978-0-13-309491-6
ISBN-10: 0-13-309491-X

Text printed in the United States on recycled paper at R.R. Donnelley in Crawfordsville, Indiana.
Second printing May 2013

To Phyllis and Bruce Nicol for teaching me perseverance.
And to my wife Joy and sons, Luke, Caleb, and Isaiah
for their love and support.

Contents

Foreword

"Mobile" is a topic that seems to have been with us for a very long time, yet it still seems very new. The excitement, the enthusiasm, and even the frenzy is obvious across the web, in newspapers and magazines, and in water cooler conversations in businesses. We take so much for granted now, features that didn't even exist five years ago, but we should also accept that we're only at the beginning of this revolution.

Why do I say "revolution" instead of the safer, more conservative "evolution"? Mobile is not just about the latest smartphone or tablet, or 3G vs. 4G vs. WiFi, or even how big your device's app store is compared to mine. The societal changes being driven by the significant use of highly programmable and interactive mobile devices with fast connectivity are affecting healthcare, banking, retail, mining, and almost all industries with which we engage. If you question this, just ask your local doctor or, even better, a teenager.

Many pieces had to come together to cause this great acceleration. First, of course, are the devices and their operating environments. These vary from very closed to very open depending on the provider, but they form the basis, the foundation, on which we can build.

Next are the apps. I'm not necessarily impressed with the sheer volume of the hundreds of thousands of apps that are out there because of the great redundancy and variable quality. However, they are showing us how the fundamental notion of "software application" has morphed. "Pick one thing and do it right" is not a bad motto for many app developers, at least at first. "Do something no one has ever done before" might follow, and "Change the way I live my life" might ensue. There are apps that do all this. I believe apps will change significantly over the next five years. How do you even begin to make sense of this revolutionary transformation?

Start with this book. I have worked with Dirk Nicol for many years as a colleague at IBM® and I believe he captures exceptionally well what you need to understand to do mobile right. Why do mobile at all? What value can it return to your business, your organization, your clients, or you? How do you handle security and manage those devices and apps? How do you decide how to build the best app for your intended use?

Dirk addresses all these questions and more. Use this book to quickly get yourself current on the state of the art for mobile, then start building those apps and services that will make you stand out successfully against your competitors.

—**Bob Sutor**, Vice President, Business Analytics and
Mathematical Sciences, IBM Research

Preface

For the past 20 years of my IT career, I have focused mostly on business strategy. I have played a key role in defining IBM's strategy around e-business, Java™, Web 2.0, cloud computing, Internet standards, developer communities, and most recently mobile. Over the years, I have honed my skills in strategy development and have applied these experiences to writing this book.

Of all the technology trends I have been involved in, mobile has had one of the most profound impacts on the industry and individuals. Unlike other technologies, mobile is personal. It has become part of our everyday lives. The mobile device is always with us helping get things done—helping us connect to friends and colleagues or simply entertaining us in our spare moments on the go. Because mobile technology has integrated into our daily lives, it creates a historical opportunity for businesses to interact, engage, and deliver new value to their customers and employees. As a result, mobile has become a top priority for business leaders today.

For the past several years, I have worked in the mobile arena educating customers, speaking at events, briefing analysts, and developing product strategies—almost universally, business leaders struggle with how to develop a mobile strategy. The challenge is due to the unique nature of the mobile industry. Mobile technology is in constant flux—there seems to always be a new set of technology or platforms to consider. Mobile is broad, touching almost every aspect of a business. The high-expectation for quality apps that are delivered quickly is unprecedented. Finally, security and privacy becomes a fundamental issue because the device contains a mixture of personal and corporate data. With all these challenges, the biggest strategic question I hear over and over is, "How do I get started?"

This is why I wrote this book. I wanted to apply my experiences in strategy development and mobile technology to help business leaders start developing their mobile strategy. I wanted to give them the tools to help answer the key strategic questions: What are all the capabilities and technologies I need to consider? How do all the pieces fit together? How do I get my app developed? How do I manage and secure my mobile business? How do I take full advantage of mobile technologies to transform my business? How do I prepare my mobile business for the future? I have pulled together the latest thinking and concepts in the industry today to help business leaders answer these strategic questions.

I hope you enjoy the book and can apply some of the concepts to help make your mobile business better. The mobile technology era is just starting, and there will be many new exciting technologies and innovation in the future. There is much more ahead of us and much more to learn. I would love to have a conversation with you to hear what you have learned. Please join me at my blog (http://www.dirknicol.com) and my Twitter account (http://twitter.com/dirknicol).

—Dirk Nicol

How This Book Is Organized

Each chapter follows a similar structure. There is an introduction that outlines the key market situation surrounding a topic. The bulk of the chapter defines key considerations for your mobile strategy and discusses key concepts and technologies. The chapter then concludes with a summary of key concepts. The overall structure of the book is designed to outline key trends in the industry, a framework for defining a mobile strategy, and a set of strategic considerations that help you define your mobile strategy. These use cases are supported by examples.

- **Chapter 1, "Introducing the Mobile Enterprise"**: This chapter provides an introduction to the overall mobile landscape and outlines the implications to consider when developing a mobile strategy.
- **Chapter 2, "Defining Business Value"**: This chapter outlines how to define the overall goals for your mobile strategy and how to deliver business value.
- **Chapter 3, "Mobile Business Challenges"**: This chapter outlines the challenges that businesses face as they adopt mobile technologies.

- **Chapter 4, "The Mobile Framework"**: This chapter defines an overall framework for defining a comprehensive mobile strategy.

- **Chapter 5, "Mobile Development"**: This chapter outlines the key considerations for building mobile applications and connecting them to back-end systems.

- **Chapter 6, "Mobile Security and Management"**: This chapter talks about how to manage and secure your mobile applications and devices.

- **Chapter 7, "Mobile Business Transformation"**: This chapter provides insight and direction as to how you can transform your business to take advantage of mobile technology.

- **Chapter 8, "Planning a Mobile Project"**: This chapter outlines the key steps and considerations for defining an overall mobile project.

- **Chapter 9, "SoCloDaMo (Social + Cloud + Big Data + Mobile)"**: This chapter describes the emerging new platform that brings together social networks, cloud computing, data analytics, and mobile and how you can leverage it in your mobile strategy.

- **Chapter 10, "International Considerations"**: This chapter brings a worldwide perspective to your mobile strategy.

- **Chapter 11, "Case Studies and Mobile Solutions"**: This chapter provides examples that can help you understand how other companies have delivered successful mobile solutions.

- **Chapter 12, "Moving Forward"**: This chapter concludes the book with a summary of key concepts.

Acknowledgments

I would like to thank Vijay Dheap and Chris Peppin for their assistance in reviewing the content of this book and providing great suggestions and insight. Vijay and Chris are experts in their field, so it was a privilege to have them contribute to this effort.

I also wanted to thank several of my team members at IBM who took the time to review sections of the book and provide thoughtful comments. Thank you to Todd Kaplinger, Miku Jha, Ron Favali, Girish Dhanakshirur, and Yonni Harif.

I would like to thank the team at IBM Press for the opportunity to deliver this book to you. Thanks goes to Chris Cleveland, Jovana Shirley, and San Dee Phillips for their help in bringing the best possible product to our readers. Thank you to our executive editor, Mary Beth Ray, for allowing us the opportunity to create this book on a flexible schedule.

I also wanted to thank IBM's Steve Stansel, the editorial program manager for IBM Press, for giving me the opportunity to write my first book.

I would like to thank Bob Sutor and Michael Karasick for giving me the opportunity to take a leadership role in driving our mobile product strategy at IBM.

Finally, I would like to thank my family, Joy, Luke, Caleb, and Isaiah, for supporting me in the ambitious undertaking of writing my first book.

About the Author

Dirk Nicol is the program director for IBM Mobile Strategy and Product Management at IBM. He has spent years helping IBM advance new and emerging technologies. He has held a variety of roles at IBM, which included semiconductor development, programming, hardware development, marketing, and strategy.

Dirk has worked extensively with helping to educate and build communities around new technologies. Prior to his current position, Dirk led IBM's cloud standards program and was a founder of the Cloud Standards Customer Council initiative. Dirk also conceived and led the development of the developerWorks® project—one of the largest worldwide developer communities. Dirk holds a master's degree in electrical engineering and an MBA degree in management and strategy at the University of North Carolina. He calls North Carolina his home but is often seen presenting about the latest technology trends and strategy around the world. When home, he enjoys time with his wife and three boys jogging along the North Carolina Tobacco Trail.

We are at the beginning of a new mobile era. The technology, best practices, and methodologies will continue to evolve. This book was designed to be a starting point on a journey. I would like to take that journey with you to learn and grow together. Check in from time to time to let me know what you have learned and how your mobile strategy is progressing.

Dirk's blog is at http://www.dirknicol.com

Follow him at twitter at: http://twitter.com/dirknicol

Linkedin: http://www.linkedin.com/in/dirknicol

I

Introducing Mobile Enterprise

Mobile devices, including smartphones and tablets, are transforming the way enterprises do business both inside the company and with customers and partners. The rapid growth in mobile device usage is fueled by a fundamental change in technology that has transformed the way individuals conduct their lives. People now have an always-connected, always-available computing device giving them a tool to complete their task with ease, efficiency, and effectiveness. Mobile devices have been integrated into our daily lives, making us more efficient, more social, and entertained whenever and wherever we want. This change in the interaction model creates both opportunity and risks for businesses. Enterprises see the tremendous opportunities in making their employees more productive, reaching new customers and improving customer satisfaction. This in turn leads to improving the bottom line and generating new business models never conceived of before. At the same time, mobile devices have expanded the power of the individual. In every interaction between you and your customer, the customer is armed with unprecedented computing power, information, and social and contextual insight at their fingertips. This power shift forces enterprises to rethink how they interact with their customers and empowers their employees to take better action in context of their task at hand.

Those companies that fail to change the way they operate run the risk of losing to their competitors. As a result, enterprises need a comprehensive mobile strategy.

Mobile Landscape

Although the mobile enterprise isn't a new concept, it has been transformed in recent years by significant change in technology. Mobile devices are more portable, more powerful, easier to use, and significantly less expensive. This has led to unprecedented levels of adoption, and today it is not uncommon to own multiple mobile devices, each tailored to a specific use.

Mobile technologies have transformed the way you live, which will continue for the foreseeable future. The mobile industry is at its early stages, with much more change ahead. It will be just as big of a trend as mainframes, PC, or even the Internet era (see Figure 1.1). In some respects, mobile is an evolution of technology that has been developing over time.

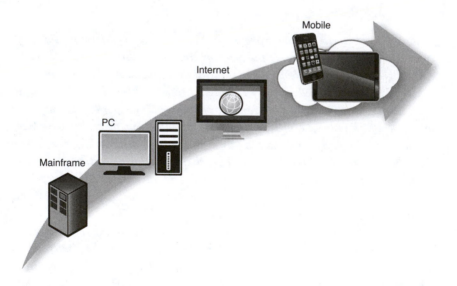

Figure 1.1   Mobile is the next era of computing.

The mainframe era brought computing power and intelligence to businesses to help them automate tasks such as bookkeeping and logistics. The mainframe enabled businesses to scale and free up individuals from performing manual tasks to perform more interesting and valuable services. This in turn enabled business to expand and become more profitable.

The PC era enabled computing power to enter into the homes and offices of businesses. Computing power was no longer confined to a data center where a select few had access—as it was in the mainframe era. When PCs entered into homes and offices, it began to impact your daily life—making you more productive, effective, and even entertained. The desktop PC also began to consolidate tasks and physical technology. Documents written on a typewriter or tasks performed on an adding machine were now done on the PC. Filing cabinets of documents were replaced by PC storage. The PC helped people to get tasks done and become more efficient while consolidating other tools into a single platform.

With the PC era, computing became accessible to the masses. With the Internet, information and connectivity became ubiquitous. You could send email, chat, join online communities, watch movies, and connect with anyone in the world. With an Internet accessible PC in everyone's home or office, the world could share information and store it in one place (the Internet). This provided a collection of information and knowledge that was easily accessible to anyone. The consolidation of the physical technology continued. Email replaced the interoffice memo and reduced the need to send physical mail through the post office. Blogs and online articles began to replace the magazine and newspaper. Music became digitized and distributed on the Internet replacing the CD and even record stores. Online stores replace traditional brick-and-mortar stores such as the bookstore, the toy store, the movie rental store, and the magazine store. The Internet continued the trend of the mainframe and PC eras of simplifying tasks making computing power accessible while consolidating real-world tools into software and hardware to help people be more productive.

The mobile era continues several trends of the past such as easy access to computing power and information—as you saw with the mainframe, PC, and Internet era. Mobile, however, is a fundamental shift in how people interact with businesses and each other. The mobile device enables people to perform tasks they could never do before or complete tasks more efficiently. Individuals now carry with them computing powers approaching that of a PC, including access to the Internet and connection to traditional systems, their social network, and other contextual services. Just as the PC made people more productive at home and work, the mobile device makes them productive at every other moment of their lives. As a result, they have ubiquitous and unprecedented information and resources in their pockets to help them at their moment of need. This is a fundamental shift in how computer technology and software interacts with your daily life and as a result is a shift of power to individuals.

At the same time, mobile is not just a turn of the crank. Mobile computing is fundamentally different in many respects. You carry it around with you, the location is relevant, and it is not quite the same as the '90s PC. The devices have new technologies that drive context. Location information is available via GPS and orientation via the accelerometer; and many include a compass for directional information. Mobile devices have both a camera and microphone, available for capturing and recording the environment around you.

Mobile technology is delivered in a much shorter technology cycle time. Many get new phones each year, upgrade the operating system monthly to take advantage of new features, and upgrade applications on a weekly basis. As a result, market leaders can change dramatically in the span of a 2-year phone contract. For example, in late 2009, Android had less than 10 percent of the U.S. mobile market, according to IDC. One year later, it was 45 percent. During the same period, BlackBerry's share dropped from approximately 45 percent to 25 percent.[1] It takes only a few years to completely change out the leading technology. With so many different mobile device platforms and leaders coming and going, the mobile ecosystem is complex and the technology is much harder to manage. You will have a hard time controlling which device your customer or employee will be using. As a result, supporting native applications (those mobile applications that are written for a specific device) across a wide variety of platforms can be expensive. In addition, the app store introduces a new distribution model that is much different than simply hosting a web page on a server. There are also concerns with security given new threats, lost or stolen devices, and the challenges of managing mobile devices originally designed for the consumer market and not the enterprise. As such, many enterprises are moving toward mobile middleware. *Mobile middleware* (or sometimes referred to as a Mobile Enterprise Application platform [MEAP]) is a set of capabilities that sit between the client device and traditional back-end or cloud systems. The Mobile middleware approach can help deliver cross-platform support and manage the complexity of a fragmented and rapidly changing technology landscape and help to connect to back-end systems.

Mobile is also a unifying technology to other major trends in the industry today. Cloud, social, and big data are all driving profound changes in the IT industry. Mobile, in many respects, is a unifying technology that provides the entry point and a user experience that brings these technologies together (also called SoCloDaMo—Social, Cloud, Big Data, and Mobile). This complementary set of technologies come together to deliver new value in the context of an engaging system. A mobile solution leverages the cloud for ubiquitous computing power, social for sentiment and peer insight, and big data to analyze and interpret the data in the context of the mobile experience based on time, location, and environment. Tying these trends to existing business processes and systems (systems of record) can deliver a differentiating mobile enterprise solution.

Mobile devices have already had a profound impact on the IT industry and will continue to do so for many years. This is just the beginning with tremendous opportunities for businesses to deliver significant value to customers and expand the bottom line. To capture this value, you need to consider how these smartphones and tablets have changed and delivered a disrupting influence on the industry.

The Disruption of Smartphones and Tablets

The mobile device has become a part of daily lives like no other technology in human history. In a *Time* magazine poll, 66 percent would rather take their mobile phone to work rather than their lunch, and 51 percent of all respondents said their mobile phone was more important than their PC or their laptop.[2] In addition, 20 percent said they check their mobile device every 10 minutes, and 30 percent said that being without their mobile device for even short periods leaves them feeling anxious. On a global basis, more people have mobile subscriptions than have clean water or electricity.[3] This makes the mobile device one of the most pervasive technologies in history.[4]

These statistics show that mobile devices are not just another technology trend but are truly shifting the way people live their daily lives, interact with each other, and get things done.

Catalysts for Disruption

What caused such a radical change in the industry and what were some of the key features of the smartphone and tablets that have had such a profound impact on the industry? There are a set of key features that drove their success and continue to drive the industry. These features enabled mobile devices to enter into your life, helping you solve problems at the right time (not just when you are behind a PC) by engaging you with contextual information and computing intelligence:

- **Engaging user experience:** The user experience is a critical element of smart mobile devices. The smartphone and tablets revolutionized the way people interact with the mobile device through multitouch and gesture interaction. This new interface enabled the end user to have a much more sophisticated interaction with the device. There was no need for a built-in keyboard, thus saving hardware space and enabling a larger screen size so that end users can select links and apps with just a touch of the screen. The ability to zoom in and zoom out, with just a pinch of the screen, enabled end users to view large content elements with a small screen. This opened up the entire World Wide Web to the mobile device in its original form.

  The responsiveness of the interaction was another critical element of the user experience. The transitions between screens, application responsiveness, and the startup of the device were extremely quick. The perception of instantaneous interaction and responsiveness further set these devices apart from traditional PCs and mobile phones.

  The user interface is also different from traditional mobile phones and PCs in that the interfaces are beautifully designed for simplicity and aesthetics. The interaction is extremely intuitive and simple. All the extra steps and options that you might see with a PC user experience have been removed. Given the small screen real-estate, only the essential interaction steps are available. This dramatically expands the adoption and use of the device, increases productivity, and simply makes it a joy to use. How many people have been startled to see 3 year olds become productive using a smartphone or tablet as they navigate through a set of screens to get to their favorite video or game?

- **Speed of innovation:** The smartphone and tablet industry delivers mobile devices at a dizzying speed. Entire new platforms are introduced every few months instead of over a period of years. This keeps new innovation and features entering the market at lightning speed, keeping customers coming back to buy new versions of the devices every few months or upgrading at the end of each carrier plan.

- **Feature integration:** The capabilities of the mobile device are highly integrated and provide a rich set of utilities. The mobile device provides a seamless user experience integrating web and native features onto the same device. Cloud-based apps such as Google G-Mail are integrated and provide a seamless experience. This greatly expands the scope of applications and utilities available to the mobile device.

- **Social interaction**: Because the devices are with you and easy to transport, they enable you to extend your personal interaction with others within the context of where you are. Social networks such as Facebook were popular before the advent of the smartphone and tablet; however, the smartphone and tablet have revolutionized social networks. Now you can send a text, take a picture, or share an experience in the moment instead of waiting to get back to your computer.

- **Battery life**: Advancements in lithium-ion polymer batteries enabled mobile devices to maintain their charge for an extended period of time. You can also recharge a lithium-ion polymer battery whenever convenient, unlike older technologies in which you had to completely discharge the battery. You can charge a smartphone once and have it last at least a full day or longer depending on use. Unlike the PC or laptop that keeps you tied to a power plug, the long battery life enables the mobile device to bring computing power with you wherever you go.

- **Instant on**: The smartphone and tablet turn on instantly. Unlike the PC where you wait for bootup, the mobile device is ready to assist you whenever you need it.

- **Always connected**: The mobile device is always connected to a network whether through a carrier cell network or a Wi-Fi connection. With a data plan, the mobile device delivers constant access to the Internet enabling continuous access to information and resources and tools to solve problems in context of a task.

- **Sensors and context**: The mobile device can sense the world providing contextual information and information to help people with their task at hand. Built-in GPS (Geo Positioning System) provides access to location information providing context. Knowing where an individual is located provides a wealth of information about the context of an engagement or navigation. An individual's task gets augmented by knowing where the individual is located. Bringing together the GPS with information about the nearest resource that may help with a task becomes critical. Is there a friend nearby or a resource that can help? If a construction worker is supposed to inspect a house, was he actually in the building? Perhaps security is enhanced or decreased as they enter or leave a particular region. The notion of triggering an event based on someone's location is referred to as *Geofencing*. Geofencing is a capability that uses the global positioning system (GPS) to define geographical boundaries. A geofence is a virtual barrier that allows the administrators to set up triggers so when a device enters or exits a geofence boundary an event is triggered such as a notification, email, or change in security level. The accelerometer provides a new way to input information. The accelerometer can allow the device to determine orientation or motion. This ability not only enables simple actions such as changing the screen from landscape to vertical, but also makes various business applications possible. You can "bump" a device to exchange money. Or perhaps shaking the device can signify a specific event such as erasing the previous data entry. You can even point the phone at the night sky, and with augmented reality, see the names of the starts overlaid on top of the image of the star in front of you. The compass enables information about orientation. This becomes important for navigation and knowing which direction the individual is facing. This may be useful for applications that require hiking or navigating across unfamiliar territory.

- **The mobile app:** The mobile app is a simple, easy-to-use, task-specific application. Most are free, whereas some apps cost just a few dollars. They are easy to access from an app store and install themselves. The mobile app helps you perform the task at hand or can change your device into any tool you need. In the same way that the PC replaced the typewriter and the adding machine, the mobile device is consolidating all sorts of other devices. The app can transform your mobile device into a calculator, compass, book, magazine, radio, flashlight, GPS, picture frame, camera, wallet, answering machine, alarm clock, calendar, to-do list, pedometer, musical instrument, and even a PC.

- **The app store:** The distribution model is also different, with the advent of the app store; individuals can go to a central location to download apps with just a few clicks. Updates to the app are provided directly from the app store. No need to search the Internet and hope for a download that is virus-free. For Apple's App Store, the submission of apps is reviewed to ensure the app is reliable and performs as expected. In addition, apps have star ratings and user comments—making it plain to see which apps are worth downloading. In addition, when an app needs to be updated, you are notified to return to the App Store to get a new version.

Finally, these factors all contributed to a mobile revolution that profoundly changed the personal lives of millions of individuals. They gave people tremendous amounts of productivity, fun, and enjoyment. This consumer revolution has now spread to the IT industry.

Implications of the Consumerization of IT

Consumerization of Information Technology (or IT) refers to the introduction of consumer technology and culture into the enterprise. In the past, driven by the high cost of technology and centralized control, enterprise dictated the tools and technologies that employees would use to do their jobs. Today, with the pervasive nature of mobile devices and cloud services, employees are taking more control and driving IT change such as Bring Your Own Device (BYOD) programs.

Historically, technology innovation originated in large companies and governments. Only large organizations had the R&D budget to finance new technology breakthroughs. They invented new products such as calculators, fax machines, or PCs. Over time, as these products sold to more people, the price dropped due to higher volume of sales. As the prices per unit dropped, it became possible for the products to be sold to the consumer market, often opening up a new market for the product.

With the advent of the Internet and the World Wide Web, a new pattern emerged. Companies such as Google began to offer free advertising-supported, cloud-based consumer applications such as Gmail for email and Google Docs for word processing, spreadsheets, and presentations. These applications became good enough to compete with traditional software such as Microsoft Outlook or Microsoft Office that had to be purchased and installed on a PC.

The mobile revolution took a giant leap forward in 2007 with the release of the Apple iPhone. Although smartphones had been around for more than a decade, Apple delivered on the promise of transforming the cell phone into a handheld computer. The release of the Apple App Store and the first Google Android smartphone in 2008 further accelerated mobile adoption into the consumer marketplace along with the rapid growth of cloud services. The result is that end users are no longer ignorant about technology. The simplicity and power of consumer devices and application technology has enabled a tech savvy and knowledgeable society. The expectations are high as consumer technology can be even more robust than business technology. They see unprecedented productivity at home and expect the same at work. They experience beautiful and elegant user experience with their consumer solutions and expect the same of their business technology. The productivity they experience with their mobile device leads to a desire to continue that same productivity at work.

The first reaction from IT might be to fight the creep of consumer technologies into the enterprise, driven by security concerns. The reality is that the trend toward consumerization of IT will not go away and will likely increase. This new reality for IT means a change in strategy and approach. The security requirements to protect corporate assets and manage authentication as well as improve worker productivity and improve the bottom line is still there. These accomplishments, however, are now carried out by technologies that were not originally designed for corporate infrastructure, management, and security.

User experience is critical. Gone are the days in which IT can provide great functionality for their employees with user experience as a distant afterthought. The bar is high for IT now where users expect a high-quality, simple user experience. Therefore, IT must build expertise in user experience and interface design.

Consumerization of IT requires forming a partnership between line of business (line of business refers to roles within the organization focused on business related tasks such as marketing, sales, and accounting), IT, and employees. A trust relationship must be formed. IT must understand the passion and interest of end users, whereas employees must understand the importance of security and management. Trade-offs will be needed on both sides. In the end, it will require a thoughtful approach in which risk is managed in context of end user productivity. If IT fails to adapt to consumerization of IT, the implications can be severe. Employees may secretly drift outside of the corporate firewalls to utilize simpler and more powerful applications creating security and management issues. Line of business may bypass IT all together and outsource the mobile solution to a low-cost, alternative out on the web. With a few clicks and a credit card number, a rogue department could easily set up a sophisticated IT solution that might initially meet its needs without consideration for the implications of security, management, and corporate policy. The "act now and ask forgiveness later" mentality can be enticing to line of business if the IT department fails to build the trust and partnership needed. In the end, the mobile application will likely need to come back to IT, and as such, it probably makes most sense to embrace consumerization of IT and form a partnership with employees and line of business to deliver the best solution from the start. Most important, consumerization of IT is an industrywide phenomenon, and if a company cannot figure out how to manage it, its competition will.

BYOD: Bring Your Own Device to Work

Bring your own device (BYOD) is a corporate policy that enables employees to use their personally owned devices for business use. Depending on the policy, the employee may be permitted to access corporate email, corporate applications, and data systems, in addition to personal applications and data. BYOD has become increasingly popular in recent years, particularly with employees, as it enables greater flexibility to get work done from a greater range of devices (for example, smartphone, tablet, and laptop) and not just the device that the company has provided. This is the opposite of a corporate liable model in which the business purchases a mobile device and issues it to an employee. In both models, the enterprise is likely to impose some level of control over the device and data to minimize security exposures.

From a corporate standpoint, allowing employees to use their own device for corporate use saves the cost of purchasing and maintaining a set of mobile devices for its employees. However, this is a small fraction of the overall IT cost, which includes voice, data, middleware, network, and support—just to name a few. The fast pace of the mobile technology space lends itself to frequent updates. Companies have a hard time keeping up with rapid change. Allowing employees to bring their own device may allow companies to have the up to date hardware because employees are more likely to get the latest gadget. In addition, employees may take better care of the mobile device because they own it and would be responsible for maintenance and repair.

From an employee standpoint, BYOD typically provides employees a choice of devices—for example, Apple iPhone, iPad, Google Android, BlackBerry, or Windows® Phone. Because employees use the device all the time, they are most productive with their own device. This in turn can improve morale and give the employee a sense of control. The productivity also extends into personal time. Because the corporate applications and access are on the same device, the employee can break up tasks in which they start to do work activities during nonworking hours and personal tasks during working hours. This further increases productivity and can also help foster better work life balance.

The biggest issue with BYOD is security. Out-of-the-box, most mobile devices don't provide the level of security that enterprises need to safeguard corporate data and to ensure that devices connected to the corporate network are properly managed. Access to corporate data may lead to issues of data leakage in which corporate data may move (or get copied) from the secure back end to the mobile device. As a result, the data may then fall into the wrong hands because mobile devices are more likely to be shared than traditional PCs. If the employee's device is infected with malware, a virus may seep into the corporate network from the employee's device. Lost or stolen devices can lead to loss of data and potentially to unauthorized access. Finally, as corporations allow employees to bring mobile devices into the office, there is no single type of device the corporation will have to manage. There will be a wide variety of devices it will have to contend with, which leads to more complexity.

As a result, the employer might need to add additional technology to the personal device to protect corporate assets. Technology solutions such as application wrappers, containers, and virtualization can help with data leakage protection. Network protection using VPNs can protect access. Antivirus software is important to protect against malware. Other supporting technology solutions are also necessary. Mobile Device Management (MDM) is critical for device management and similarly Mobile Application Management (MAM) for application management.

Employers then need to apply the appropriate policy management to the devices. For corporate issued devices, if the device is lost or stolen, the solution might involve a remote wipe of all corporate data on the device, assuming the device is powered on and connected to the network. This is fine for corporate-issued devices but can become a challenge for a personal device. Employees could become unhappy if their employer performs a remote wipe of their device, deleting all their family photos or other personal data. If the appropriate policies are not agreed upon between employees and employer, this can lead to not only dissatisfied employees, but also potential litigation between employees and the employer. On the other hand, if the employer issues stringent security policies, (such as long passwords) the employee may abandon the BYOD program or worse go around it.

In the end, BYOD offers tremendous opportunity for greater employee productivity and improved morale. It may offer some cost-savings for the employer, but IT costs such as applications, network, and security also need to be taken into account. The employee and employer have to work together to ensure the appropriate security and management structure is in place to drive success.

A Preview of Enterprise Mobility Strategy

As you look at the market dynamics of mobile and its impact on the IT industry, it leads to a set of implications for creating an enterprise mobile strategy for the organization. Developing an enterprise mobile strategy requires input from the line of business within an organization (such as marketing, sales, and accounting), IT (CTO, development manager, IT director), Human Resources, Security, and Legal—just to name a few. What is clear is that mobile is different in many ways and will likely have one of the most profound impacts on your business over the next decade. Speed and agility will be critical in a fledgling market that is constantly changing. This means the entire organization needs to come together to help drive the appropriate strategy, move quickly, learn from your customers as you go, and then adjust. A mobile strategy must be an ongoing process that constantly adjusts and grows over time. But it can't be a free-for-all either. There needs to be a framework that defines an overall strategy structure while enabling underlying elements to adjust as the market changes and matures.

As a result, a mobile strategy framework must be structured in a way that is comprehensive but flexible. A strategy framework should focus on major themes that can help set overall direction, yet at the same time, the framework should be flexible enough to allow for new innovation and technology changes when needed. Issues of consumerization of IT and BYOD, speed of execution, device fragmentation, and user experience are just some of the considerations that a mobile strategy framework should account for. The framework also must be relevant to key enterprise stakeholders: the *IT team* that may build the mobile solutions and connect them to back-end systems, the *line of business* who may have the direct relationship with customers trying to transform their business, and the *operational* organizations that need to manage and secure the mobile solution.

The mobile strategy needs to focus on a set of core goals and aspirations. These include:

- Transform your business by extending traditional systems through mobile context, engagement, and intelligence to deliver new value.
- Develop mobile applications that engage individuals at their moment of need.
- Manage and secure mobile applications, devices, and networks.

These core goals are the guiding principles and structure for an overall mobile strategy. The rest of the book defines key technologies and trends in each of these categories so that you can define a foundational mobile strategy. Then the core strategic consideration is outlined for each of these categories so that you can make decisions on which technology to choose and as such develop a strategy that is unique to your business.

Summary

Mobile is a major milestone in the history of computing on the same order of magnitude as the mainframe, PC, or Internet. Although BlackBerry pioneered the smartphone inside the enterprise, it wasn't until the release of Apple iPhone and Google Android that the smartphone went mainstream in the consumer marketplace. The mobile technology era builds on top of all the previous computing eras and can extend existing back-end systems that were built leveraging mainframes, PCs, and the Internet. It also is the unifying element of other key technology trends around cloud computing, big data, and social computing. In the end, the mobile era is nascent and is in flux. The advantage goes to those companies that can execute on a strategy that takes advantage of the opportunities around mobile while managing the rapid change of the market.

The excitement and energy around mobile has shifted from the consumer market to the enterprise. Also known as the consumerization of IT, the ease of use, simplicity, lower cost and high productivity of mobile technology has raised the bar on IT. Employees want to bring their devices (BYOD) to work to get the same level of productivity at work that they have at home. While businesses should be open to BYOD to reduce costs, they will need to manage the complexity of device management and security.

Many have already dipped their toes into the mobile technology space. They were pressured by the competition to "get an app out." So, they built an app either in-house or contracted a 'boutique' design shop to pull an app together for them. Perhaps it was commissioned by the line of business without IT even being aware of it. Or perhaps it was an IT lead project. After the app got out, everyone was happy and excited that they got their first app in the app store or deployed it across the business.

However, after it got out they noticed that the star rating in the app store was not what was expected—unlike the web where feedback comes back through a feedback link on the home page and all the comments get routed to the web master to address (or choose not to address). In the mobile era, feedback is in real time in the app store, and the comments are available for everyone to see. Quickly, the excitement about their first app turned into horror as they were confident they would have a five-star rating and instead ended up with a one- or two-star rating. The excitement about "extending their brand" to mobile turned into a disaster.

Perhaps there is a different story. You put your first app out and it is an absolute success. People love it, you have a five-star app and your customers (and boss) want more. The press is writing about your app, your competition is scared, and the marketing team wants more versions to reinforce the brand equity you have created. You need to create a new version quickly with more features and function. Also, you need to cover more platforms quickly. Your iOS app is great, but you will also need an Android version. By the way, what about Blackberry, Windows, and being ready for the next OS you never heard of before? Now your head is swimming with the thought of multiple development teams, scarce skills, testing across dozens of devices, and a never-ending set of management and maintenance tasks.

Conversely, your successful app gets downloaded by thousands and exceeds all expectations of adoption. However, you later discover a security flaw in your app. How do you get all those people who downloaded the app to upgrade and have the latest release? Unlike the web, where you can upgrade the web app overnight and everyone has the latest features automatically—after people download an app, they must take an action to upgrade (even if they turned on auto-update features). How do you disable or force an update of an app short of sending a letter to everyone who downloaded the app and begging them to go back to the app store and update?

In the end, you need a comprehensive strategy that addresses the challenges for a mobile enterprise that has its origins in the consumer market. Perhaps it does not completely fit into the way an enterprise develops applications and solutions. There are many unknowns, and perhaps you have made the mistakes already and are ready for a new approach. Perhaps you have been asked to create a mobile strategy and this is your company's chance to do it right. Perhaps you do not know where to start or even the context for how to make decisions. The intent of this book is to help with the process of building a mobile enterprise strategy.

To understand the context for a mobile strategy, the first step is to understand the opportunities and challenges around a mobile enterprise strategy. Chapter 2, "Defining Business Value," and Chapter 3, "Business Challenges," cover these aspects in more detail.

Endnotes

1   Digital Innovation Gazette, "Trends in Device Turnover": http://tinyurl.com/bukmctf

2   Innovation Avenue, *Time* magazine: http://www.innovation-avenue.com/2012/08/time-as-in-the-magazine.html

3   Business Insider, "Chart of the Day: More People Have Mobile Phones Than Electricity Or Drinking Water": http://tinyurl.com/6oj5pym

4   WWL.com, "FCC: Mobile phones fastest growing technology ever": http://www.wwl.com/FCC--Mobile-phones-fastest-growing-technology-ever/13068050

Additional Sources

Forbes.com, "The Mobile Power Shift Will Accelerate in 2013": http://tinyurl.com/ba2oxos

Saylor, Michael. *The Mobile Wave: How Mobile Intelligence Will Change Everything:* Vanguard Press, 2012.

2

Defining Business Value

It seems that mobile is at the center of almost all business conversations today. The entire industry is abuzz about the latest device, technology, and capability associated with mobile devices. Boardrooms have established mobility as a top priority and have rallied their companies around this trend. Much like the early '90s and the start of the Internet, businesses are investing in a mobile technology just so they keep up with the latest trend. Often, the investments in mobile technology are done without an understanding of the strategic value. Companies are invested just so they can stay relevant in the midst of this new technology shift with fear that if they move too slowly the competition will have an advantage. Companies are quickly building apps and bringing devices into the enterprise; however, the rush to "keep up" and stay current or even ahead of the competition can sometimes lead to a failure to capture value.

Business leaders certainly see the potential value in mobility. Executives see the productivity enhancements in their daily lives and want to see the same productivity gains at work. Executives feel engaged and productive using great consumer apps and feel a sense of loyalty to the brand associated with the app. They want to establish the same connection with their customers and employees. The challenge: How do you apply a potential opportunity from the consumer space to the business world? Defining the specific value that mobile technology brings to the enterprise can help form the basis of an overall mobile strategy. By outlining the core business opportunity for a mobile investment, you can then set specific goals. In doing so, you move from reaction to a strategic vision.

In the end, mobile technology can transform businesses in untold ways; however, the potential value can be lost if you do not execute correctly. High expectations for user experience and fast cycle times with unfamiliar technology put pressure on businesses as they try to keep up. As many of the mobile technologies originated in the consumer market, you cannot take the perceived value in the consumer space and apply it directly to businesses. You need to rethink mobile value within the context of business needs and the ability to execute. You need to think in terms of setting goals that deliver value to your customers, value to your business, and at the same time, fit within budget. In other words, making sure you have a positive return on investment (ROI). This paradigm drives focus and clarity around a mobile strategy. It keeps the business from getting buffeted by the latest trend and instead focusing on value.

A Brief History of the Smartphone: The Power of Context, Intelligence, and Engagement

It is clear that the smartphone has had a profound impact on business and society as a whole. If you want to build a mobile strategy that derives value for your business, it is worth taking the time to analyze what gives the smartphone so much impact. Wherever you go, you see people using their smartphone during every free moment they have. They use it throughout their day completing tasks, making phone calls, checking the news, texting friends or colleagues, and posting to their social network. What is it about the smartphone that makes it so integral to our daily lives? If you step back and consider the historical evolution of the smartphone and look at the major products that had a significant impact, you will find three major capabilities that when brought together become transformational:

- **Contextual interacting:** Enabling technologies that allow you to interact with other people, the environment, and behavioral data in a particular moment

- **Mobile intelligence:** Having powerful computational resources when you need them

- **Engagement:** Delivering an easy and helpful user experience that weaves into your daily life

As you look at the evolution of the mobile smartphone, you can see again and again the attempt to bring together these capabilities into a single converged product delivering contextual interaction, mobile intelligence, and user engagement. In many respects, the earliest attempts to bring together contextual interaction (through a mobile phone) and portable intelligence was the IBM Simon. The Simon was released in 1993[1] and brought together the capabilities of a mobile phone with many of the features of a personal digital assistant (PDA), such as address book, calendar, and appointment scheduler. In addition, it also sent and received facsimiles, email, and pages utilizing its touch screen interface. In many respects, the Simon had many of the key attributes of a smartphone, but it was not until 14 years later with the release of the Apple iPhone, that a true breakthrough in personal productivity occurred.

After the Simon, the next major breakthrough was with the PDA. Although in 1996 when the Palm Pilot 1000 was released, it did not include the capability to make phone calls, it truly revolutionized the personal computing market.[2] The Palm Pilot delivered a simple and usable experience that helped people become much more productive by enabling them to bring some of the features they normally had on their PCs with them on the go. At the time, the Pilot delivered a rich set of personal productivity capability for enterprise users that provided applications to help people perform tasks more efficiently when they need to—in other words, mobile intelligence. They could look up a contact, check a calendar appointment, take a note, and synchronize with corporate email and calendar systems. Later, Palm eventually brought together mobile phone functionality and PDA capabilities with the release of the Treo 600 in 2003.[3]

In 2002, Research In Motion (RIM) entered the mobile phone market with the BlackBerry 5810.[4] The 5810 gave business professionals access to emails, schedules, the ability to make phone calls, and surf the web. RIM's focus on security and corporate requirements made it popular in the enterprise, but over time its ease of use made many of its later models such as the BlackBerry 6210 (released in 2004) popular with a broader audience.[5] RIM was successful by bringing together contextual interaction, mobile intelligence, and in many respects user engagement.

The major breakthrough in the evolution of the smartphone occurred in 2007 when Apple released the iPhone. By no means the first smartphone to enter the market, but without a doubt the iPhone has had the most impact on the industry to date. Not only did the iPhone bring together the contextual interaction (phone, GPS, accelerometer, and compass) and the mobile intelligence of several PDA-like utilities (contact lists, voice recorder, calendar, alarm clock, and more)—what set the iPhone apart was that it truly delivered an engaging experience. It revolutionized the entire user interaction from how you bought the device through Apple's retail stores, to how you used the device, to how you obtained apps through the Apple App Store. With an integrated multitouch touch screen, a comprehensive web-browsing experience, and a beautiful design, the iPhone became a revolutionary device. The iPhone was so simple a child could use it. It also masterfully integrated third-party applications and services such as Google's Gmail, Google Maps, and YouTube. Soon after the iPhone, the Apple iPad tablet was introduced, utilizing much of the same compelling capabilities with a larger form factor.

One of the most groundbreaking elements of the iPhone was the mobile app. Productivity applications had been around since the Palm Pilot or even the Simon; however, Apple made the apps engaging by bringing together the latest capabilities of phone and Internet services into an easy-to-use, task-oriented application. It simplified the distribution model through the Apple App Store. Through a link from the home screen of the iPhone, the end user could get an app in just a few clicks for free or for a few dollars. Apple had to approve each app in the Apple App Store, which made people comfortable that the app was safe to use. The built-in ecosystem of third-party developers, enabled with a powerful software development tool (Xcode) and supporting developer program, rapidly increased the number of third-party apps. The app enabled the smartphone to be turned into a tool needed for a particular task. It became the modern day Swiss Army knife, transforming the phone into the appropriate tool at the moment of need. The iPhone brought together contextual information, mobile intelligence, and an engaging experience in an entirely new way that allowed the device and the application to become part of your daily life—filling your spare moments with a productive tool to help you get things done.

Soon after the release of the iPhone in 2008, the first Google Android device was released with similar capabilities as the iPhone. The one major difference was the Google Android operating system was developed as an open source project. Instead of developing their own operating system, device manufacturers could ship the Android operating system at a much lower cost. This further accelerated worldwide distribution and adoption of the smartphone, ushering in a new era of computing.

App Revolution: Bringing Together Context, Intelligence, and Engagement While Driving End User Value

Historically, the evolution of the smartphone has been marked by the convergence of technology that enables individuals to interact with each other and their environment (context), have greater computing power and tools to help them perform their task at hand (intelligence), and have an engaging experience that weaves into their daily lives (engagement). Time and time again, you see that when a product successfully brings these three elements together, they tend to have a significant impact on the market. The mobile app becomes the essential element that brings together the context, intelligence, and engagement into a simple task-oriented application. The mobile app transforms the mobile device into the particular tool individuals need to simplify their lives by reducing the steps in their task or streamlining their task all together. As you build your mobile strategy, you need to consider how you can leverage the attributes of context, intelligence, and engagement to deliver value to your customer or employee.

Contextual Information: Key Ingredient to Improving Outcomes

Mobile puts real-time information in your pocket enabling you to magnify your knowledge in the moment. Executives can make better and smarter decisions with a dashboard on their tablet providing the latest sales stats. Shoppers can make better buying decisions by comparing prices and ratings at the time of purchase. The mobile worker can process an insurance claim in front of the client instead of heading to the office. Customers can self serve themselves instead of calling a call center. Mobile technology, along with contextual information, can help people to organize and become empowered. In many respects, mobility has introduced a new phenomenon—a shift of power to the individual.

You saw this with the Arab Spring in 2011. Despite the best efforts of the governments in Egypt and Libya, individuals shared information, virtually assembled, and organized protests via their mobile devices and social networks. The end result was the overthrow of long-standing governments. Access to information in real time not only empowers individuals, but also can help organize large groups of people.

As a business leader, you need to understand that these forces can be harnessed to help or hurt your company. They can be used to have a deeper relationship with your customer, grow your brand, and deliver better services. Or they can be used to easily find alternatives to your product and switch to a competitor. By engaging your customers through mobile technology, you build a deeper understanding of their needs and can deliver better services.

Retailers are on the frontlines of the shift in power from institutions to individuals. In recent years, a phenomenon known as show rooming has sent shockwaves through traditional retailer stores. *Show rooming* is when consumers use their mobile phones in-store to compare prices with competing retailers. They can look at the product in the store, test it out, and ask advice of the store associates. Then armed with their mobile devices, customers can now scan the bar code on a product, find the best price, and make a purchase at a different retailer. This leaves the brick-and-mortar retailers with the cost of displaying the product and managing the inventory—without the benefit of getting the customer business. It is estimated that 80 percent of retailers will be affected by show rooming—particularly those selling electronics and appliances.[6] Retailers need to rethink their strategy in how to engage with their customers such as price-matching, loyalty programs, improved cross-channel integration, and a compelling in-store experience.

Mobile Intelligence: Ubiquitous Computing and Decision Making

Mobile devices contain the computing power of traditional PCs of a few years ago, yet they are small enough to be carried around wherever you go. This gives you 24/7 access to computing power and software applications in your moment of need. The mobile app specifically delivers an inexpensive and effective way to transform your device into the tool needed to complete a task. In many respects, the app and the smartphone together begin to replace existing applications or even physical products. If you stop and think about it, you will be surprised at how many real-world items have converged into a mobile device as a single all-purpose, universal product—for example, the cell phone, MP3 player, camera, GPS navigation system, and the electronic picture frame. Physical items, such as music, newspapers, magazines, books, television, and movies, are now digitized and delivered through the mobile device. The app can also transform a mobile device into new replicated physical assets. There are apps that can make the phone turn into a flashlight, musical instrument, television remote control, wallet, cash register, and more. The mobile phone can transform into the tool you need to get the job done.

Mobile intelligence also empowers you to analyze situations to determine the best outcome. Computing power at the device, working in conjunction with connected systems (such as the cloud or corporate data centers), can assist in making the right decision at the right time. As you use the mobile app, there is new information about context and past behavior. This information can be analyzed to help you decide the next best action for a particular task. Analytical computing power at your fingertips can deliver real-time insight and advice to help you complete a task.

Engagement: Weaving into Daily Life

Although mobile technology had been available for some time, it was not until the smartphone entered the market (mostly defined by the Apple iPhone) that the contextual information and computing power converged and was delivered with an engaging experience. The multitouch interface, intuitive design, and simplicity made the smartphone accessible to almost anyone and enabled the device to enter into your daily life. From the 3 year old watching a video on Netflix, to the middle school student doing trigonometry homework, to the executive looking at the latest sales figures in a mobile dashboard, to the grandparents watching their grandchild take their first steps through their Skype-enabled tablet—mobile devices are changing the lives of individuals.

As the mobile device enters into your daily life, it can create an opportunity and a challenge for businesses. Companies now have the chance to embed their software or app directly into the daily activities of their customers, consequently providing a much deeper and intimate interaction with customers than was ever conceived with a PC. This insertion of software in the form of a task-oriented app can open a new front in the battle for the attention of your customers. The mobile app can enable you to better serve your customers, gain a much deeper knowledge of their likes, dislikes, and preferences, and as a result serve them better and deliver new services based on their needs. This direct relationship can shorten the cycle time between the creator of the service and the actual delivery to the end user—cutting out the middleman as a result. As you learn about your customer, you can understand which processes are important and which ones are not. As a result, you can make your business processes more efficient, saving cost while learning more about your customers. Companies can gain the upper hand if they deliver the most useful app to the customers. Gaining an app icon on the home screen of your customer's mobile device can be essential for capturing their attention and loyalty.

How the Mobile App Enters into Lives to Add Value

In the past, there was always a separation between your daily life and the actions needed to complete a task. You would go about your life, stop to get to a computer to do some activity, and then go back to the task. For example, walk through the steps of making a TV purchase. In the past, you might do research on a product by surfing the web on your home computer. Perhaps you would print out some information or you might go to a bookstore to purchase a magazine with product reviews. Then you would go to the store and look at the products in the store. You might then go back home and do more research only to make the final purchase at the store. The task (buy a TV) and the steps to complete the task were often disjointed and spread over time. The mobile device enables a much richer and seamless experience that reduces friction between the task steps or even eliminates task steps altogether. In many respects, the mobile app becomes interwoven into your daily life to assist you through the tasks you must complete.

Now look at the same scenario in context of a mobile app. Using a mobile app, you can research TVs with the full function web browser, scan the product UPC code to get the best price, and then make the purchase online immediately (or perhaps negotiate with the retailer for a better price). Figures 2.1 and Figure 2.2 contrast the old versus the new experience of purchasing a TV.

The mobile app can greatly reduce the steps to complete a task at hand. It can do this because multiple tools and capabilities on the device come together to streamline a process. This convergence of tools and capabilities can leverage context, time, and information to help make the steps in the task progress more efficiently or reduce the steps. In the TV purchasing example, you do not need to keep shuttling between the home computer, the bookstore, and the electronics store to gather information for the purchase. All this can be done on the device in the context of the purchase decision.

Purchase a TV tasks (the old way)

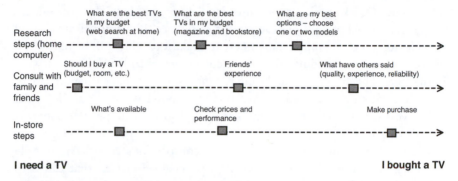

Figure 2.1   Purchasing a TV without mobility

Purchase a TV tasks (the app way)

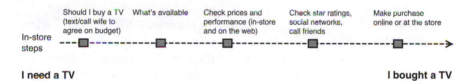

Figure 2.2   Purchasing a TV with mobility

It is clear that the mobile device provides a lot of value to you as a consumer in this scenario. However, what about the electronics store? The mobile device has provided you with a lot of consumer power in the purchase decision based on quick-and-easy availability of function, quality, and price information. In the past, you might have limited information, and given the choices, you might simply buy what was available. While profitable for the retailer, it might not deliver the best price for the customer. The new model provides the customer with instantaneous pricing and quality information and the ability to make a purchase with a single tap on the mobile device. The good news is that the retailer is now also armed with new tools to win customers, increase loyalty, and drive new profits based on the mobile device and app.

The retailer can provide a better customer experience by arming its employees with concierge apps to better assist customers and provide greater service. These apps could offer instant access to product information, locate items in a nearby store, or place orders on the spot, which can help with the sale process. Quick checkout and same day delivery can help close the sale.

Location-based promotions can make a difference. If customers are already in your store, they are much more likely to make a purchase. Why not offer a discount through a push notification to customers when it is known they are in the store? Loyalty points can be offered for those who make the purchase in store. This further keeps people from making a purchase online while in the store. Also, new forms of mobile marketing and advertising provide opportunities to reach customers with offers in context of what they are doing in the moment whether in your store or in the competitor's store. The mobile retailer also may have access to previous purchase decisions that can help drive tailored offers for those who have made purchases in the past. All this can be done in context of the users' daily lives by building a relationship with them while assisting them to accomplish their task.

Augmented reality is another way to engage users during the shopping experience. Here is how it works: Shoppers capture images via the built-in video camera on their smartphone or tablet and use image-processing technologies to quickly and accurately identify a product. After the application recognizes the products, it can display information above the product images in the camera view. Shoppers see a product through their camera and then see additional information placed on top of the image that may rank the products based on attributes such as price or nutritional value. It can also provide shoppers with any loyalty rewards, offers, or discounts that may apply and suggest complementary items based on the shoppers' preference or context.

For example, consider technology developed by IBM Research that can bring some of the benefits of online shopping into traditional brick-and-mortar stores, utilizing augmented reality. Shoppers looking for breakfast cereal could specify they want a brand high in protein (see Figure 2.3). As shoppers pan the mobile device's video camera across a shelf of cereal boxes, the augmented reality app can show which cereals meet the criteria. In addition, the app could provide a same-day coupon to entice shoppers to make a purchase. Although the app can enable shoppers to be more informed about products, it can also help retailers to better connect with their customers. Using the personal information provided by their customers' experience in the store, retailers could gain insight on the preferences of their shoppers, as well as which areas of the store see the most traffic. Using this information, retailers could better organize their store, adjust inventory, and adjust marketing programs.[7]

How the augmented reality mobility shopping app works

Customer creates
his one-time
profile of dietary
and environmental
preferences.

Point mobile phone's video
camera at shelf items.
Products are recognized
when compared to images
in a database.

The application returns
ranking based on
customer's preferences
and also offers promotions
and coupons.

Figure 2.3 Augmented reality in a retail store

Defining Goals Based on Business Value

The previous section established that to be successful, a mobile app must include context, mobile intelligence, and engagement; however, before you can define a successful mobile strategy, you need to define the business goals of your project. These goals must be based on clear value proposition for your customer and your organization. Value-based goals are critical to understanding and measuring the value of a mobile strategy. These goals help to ensure that the mobile project stays focused and delivers on the intended value. Mobile value goals will be rooted in the mobile-solution attributes but will be specific to either a business-to-consumer (B2C) scenario, how the business delivers value to customers, or a business-to-enterprise (B2E) scenario in which the value to the employee is defined. The business-to-business (B2B) scenario or how the business interacts with partners and suppliers can be seen as a special case of the business-to-enterprise (B2E) scenario with some aspects of customer interaction included. The following sections provide a set of example goals based on business value that are summarized in Table 2.1 and then detailed in the remainder of this section. It is important to choose an overarching goal that helps you to define the scope of your project and set measurements for success.

Table 2.1   Value Based Goals for a Mobile Project

Business to Enterprise	Business to Consumer
Increase worker productivity.	Increase quality of service.
Increase revenue.	Improve customer satisfaction.
Extend existing applications.	Deepen customer engagement and loyalty.
Reduce fuel, gas, or fleet maintenance costs.	Drive increased sales through personalized offers.
Increase employee responsiveness and decision making.	Increase competitive differentiation.
Resolve internal IT issues.	Improve brand perception.
Reduce expenses.	Understand customer behavior.
Attract and retain talent.	Reduce cost of delivery.
Improve work life balance.	Use new value-added services.

B2E or B2B Value Goals

Examples of B2E or B2B value-based goals and associated measurements are as follows:

- **Increase worker productivity:** Can be defined in time reduced or number of milestones reached.

- **Increase revenue through sales engagements, improvement in information, and workflow**: Can lead to improved transactions and more customer deals closed. This can be measured in number of deals, pipeline progression, and closed deals.

- **Extend existing applications to mobile workers and customers**: Can be measured by the number of employees who have access to the mobile devices and applications. This may be an indicator of participation and access.

- **Reducing fuel or fleet maintenance costs:** Employees have immediate access to information, improving collaboration and reducing travel and meetings. This can be measured by total fuel and maintenance cost-savings.

- **Increase employee responsiveness and decisions:** Having access to information and improved workflow can make the decision-making process faster and of higher quality. This can be measured by comparing the length of projects and how their cycle time has been reduced.

- **Resolve internal IT issues faster:** Occurs when people have improved access to information in the form of systems alerts and problem tickets. In addition, this improves collaboration and access to information. This can be measured by comparing IT resolution cycle times.

- **Reduce expenses (utilizing personally owned instead of corporate-issued devices):** In the case of bring your own device (BYOD), a business can reduce the cost of issuing mobile devices to employees by allowing them to use their own. The business needs to consider the total cost involved, including enhanced security and data protection that will be required in a BYOD deployment.

- **Attracting and retaining talent:** An effective BYOD program can be critical in helping to retain and attract talent. Employees want to use the mobile technology they are accustomed to.

- **Improved work life balance:** Because individuals have their mobile device with them, they can participate in leisure and travel activities without having to be tied to a laptop or PC. While watching a children's soccer game, an individual can quickly check email and then get back to the game.

B2C Value Goals

Examples of B2C value goals include the following:

- **Quality of service is specific to your particular project:** In the case of a healthcare solution, you might measure the cycle time for lab results and determine how a mobile deployment helps nurses more efficiently administer a test and collect results.

- **Improve customer satisfaction:** Determined by how satisfied your customer is with the service you provide. This can be measured through surveys and feedback forums. In addition, your app can have a star rating that can feed into the measure of overall quality of service.

- **Deeper customer engagement and loyalty:** Can be measured by the growth in the number of customers who download your app, upgrade to the latest release, join your community, or participate in your loyalty program.

- **Drive increased sales through personalized offers**: How does your app's personalized offers compare to a control group? Measurements may include numbered transactions or responses.

- **Competitive differentiator:** May be measured based on comparing downloads and star ratings of your app when compared to the competition.

- **Improve brand perception:** May be measured by press and analyst mentions. Surveys may determine how your app has impacted your brand perception based on customer interviews.

- **Understanding customer buying behavior:** An important measurement to ensure that your mobile marketing system is actually working. A mobile app gathers tremendous information that can give you deep understanding of your customer. This understanding can give you tremendous potential to up sell and cross sell. Is your solution actually taking advantage of the key attributes of mobile?

- **Reduce cost of delivery:** Considers a number of questions. What is the overall cost of the mobile solution and is it sustainable? Is the project within budget? How does it compare with traditional IT projects? Defining a cost metric can ensure that you think holistically about the mobile project and ensure that you make the appropriate technology choices. This might lead to a decision that a mobile platform is required to pull all the aspects together in a cost-effective way.

- **New valuable services:** Essential to keeping your customers happy and preventing them from going to your competitor. Because a mobile application can become an essential part of an individual's life, there is a great deal of information that can be gained as your customer uses your application. This information can be analyzed to deliver new services and capabilities that differentiate you from the competition.

Thinking Through Mobile App Value

As you consider your mobile project, you must root the effort in customer (a customer may be external or a company employee) and business value. Establishing a set of value goals that defines how the end user receives value is critical. This set of goals shapes and defines the project. The previous section outlined a set of example value goals, but all projects have their own set. Value goals may be linked to a particular industry and have their own unique characteristics.

In addition, you want to establish the appropriate measurements to ensure that the desired goal has been achieved. As a result, each value goal should also be linked to a set of measurable performance indicators. This can help answer the following questions:

- Did I achieve the value I want?
- Is the result measurable?
- Does it help me define corrective action such that I can make improvements?

Finally, you want to link the value goal with the type of functions you would want to deliver in the mobile solution. How can you achieve the value goal? What are some of the ways the app can deliver on the value goal?

Building a value table, as outlined in Table 2.2, can help. The table begins to lay out the basis for your mobile strategy by defining an approach that delivers the customer value you have identified. It then ties an approach to specific measurable value indicators. This approach can help avoid getting caught up in chasing the latest device functions or industry fads and instead using the appropriate technology needed to deliver the value goal identified.

In the example in Table 2.2 the healthcare mobile strategy team set their value-based goal to be improving customer satisfaction. They then determined their approach would be to build an electronics patient chart app. From there they outlined a set a value indicators to outline the attributes of success (workflow optimization, quality of care, patient safety, and costs). A set of performance indicators and corresponding measurements were then determined to ensure that they stayed on track to achieve the value they desired. For example, a performance indicator would be to reduce time of patient check-in which would be measured by a percentage reduction in check-in time compared to a base line. Finally a set of key tasks and app functions were determined that would correspond to a specific value-based goal of the project. These functions were based in engagement, context, and mobile intelligence. For example, they could use a tablet-based app to begin checking in the patients at the door or as they drove up instead of having them wait in line.

Table 2.2 Example Relationship Between Value Goals, Performance Indicators, and Approach

Value Goal: Improve Customer Satisfaction
Project Capability: Healthcare—Electronic Patient Chart App

Value Indicators	Performance Indicator	Measurements	Approach
Workflow optimization	Reduce time of check-in.	Percentage of change in check-in time	Staff checks in patients with tablet as they enter the hospital. (engagement)
	Reduce time of diagnosis.	Percentage of change in time to diagnosis	Mobile app contains patient x-rays, latest tests, and recommended diagnosis based on best available information. (intelligence)
Quality of care	Improved communications between doctors.	Survey of employee satisfaction	Sending messages and patient information securely between staff. (engagement)
		Reduced misdiagnosis due to more detailed information	Dictate notes into patients' record or take pictures of injury. (context)
Patient safety	Reduced drug allergies.	Percentage of change in drug allergy-related incidence	Mobile app has access to drug allergies and information about how new drugs conflict with existing patients prescriptions. (intelligence)
Cost	Reduce lab work.	Percentage of decrease in number of duplicate lab tests	Check and track status of lab work to prevent duplicate tests. (intelligence)

Summary

Mobile devices have revolutionized the computing industry and have had a profound impact on personal and professional lives. In many respects, you are just at the beginning of the mobile revolution in which you will continue to see unprecedented new capabilities added to mobile devices to make them even more valuable. Just as with the early days of the Internet, where it seemed everyone wanted to put up a web site just to say they have one, it seems that now everyone is putting up a mobile app just to say they have one. However, people are finding that the cost and complexity of building and managing a mobile app can be high. In the same way people quickly discovered that putting up a web site does not define a web strategy, putting an app in an app store does not define a mobile strategy.

Fundamentally, a mobile strategy needs to be based in the value to the end user and the enterprise. Smart mobile devices have come on the scene with amazing capabilities. However, these capabilities need to be brought together in a solution that delivers the wanted goal based on the value defined by the project. The mobile app needs to be scoped to optimize value. Mobile apps derive the most value as they focus on a specific task the individual needs to perform. Leveraging context and fitting within a discrete moment of time are key characteristics of a mobile app that can derive value. As the app functionality moves from simple information access and capture to engagement and intelligence, the app becomes an integral part of daily life and creates opportunity for the enterprise to have a deeper relationship with the customer or improve productivity of their employee.

You also must ensure that your mobile solution delivers the value that your customer requires in context of your investment. Your return on investment (ROI) must be monitored to ensure that your project delivers on its intended purpose without exceeding your budget. Given the rapidly changing nature of the mobile market, unforeseen costs can crop up sending your project into the red. Having the right tools, technology, and strategy can guide you to increasing value and reducing unforeseen delivery costs.

In the end, the mobile strategy must define a set of measureable value goals. These will help shape the project and align functionality to the proposed outcome. Linking the desired value to a set of task-based functions rooted in the principles of context, engagement and intelligence creates a framework that can define the tools, infrastructure, and technology needed to deliver on a mobile project.

Endnotes

[1] A Brief History of Smartphones: http://www.pcworld.com/
    article/199243/a_brief_history_of_smartphones.html

[2] Ibid

[3] Ibid

[4] Ibid

[5] Ibid

[6] http://consumergoods.edgl.com/trends/80--of-Retailers-to-be-Affected-by-Showrooming83330

[7] http://www.research.ibm.com/articles/augmented-reality.shtml

Additional Sources

Tuesday's Tip: Why Context Matters—Forget Real-Time, Achieve Right-Time : http://www.forbes.com/sites/raywang/2012/07/25/tuesdays-tip-why-context-matters-forget-real-time-achieve-right-time/

How smartphones make us superhuman: http://www.cnn.com/2012/09/10/tech/mobile/our-mobile-society-intro-oms/index.html

3

Mobile Business Challenges

Although tremendous opportunities exist for becoming a mobile business, you must overcome a number of challenges. It is difficult to navigate a fragmented and rapidly changing technology landscape. The expectations for delivering and maintaining high-quality apps that engage users may be outside the scope of your team's skills and expertise.

Building mobile applications requires a unique skill set which is different from those for developing PC applications. Meeting the demand for a highly accelerated development cycle can be daunting. Mobile apps must be enterprise-ready—even though some of the platforms offered by mobile OS and handset providers are not designed to fit within the enterprise development process. Integration into existing enterprise systems is critical, and ensuring that a mobile app can fit within the enterprise architecture and processes instead of being something completely separate is also of paramount importance. The mobile app development process is further complicated by a fragmented market with many different device types and operating platforms. With so many devices to support, this not only makes it difficult to build mobile apps, but also it creates a challenge for testing and maintenance.

Security has been and always will be a concern, because a mobile device is easily lost or stolen, putting data on the device at risk. As mobile devices become more popular, they become a prime target for hackers. Malware and attempts to compromise corporate security is on the rise. Finally, the need to separate work and personal data on personally owned devices presents particular challenges when multiple platforms are involved.

It can be overwhelming to start to develop a mobile strategy that takes into account business-to-consumer, business-to-enterprise, multiple device platforms, different application types (for example, native, web and HTML5, hybrid, and virtual), as well as bring your own device (BYOD).

Developing a mobile strategy starts with answering a few key questions:

- *What business problem am I trying to solve with mobile?*
- *Who is my intended audience?*
- *What mobile platforms do I need to support, and what mobile device features should I leverage?*
- *How can users access my application, and how do I distribute updates?*
- *How do I deliver my mobile solution quickly and with the highest quality possible?*
- *How do I optimize the user experience for my app?*
- *Where do I get the skills to support my mobile strategy?*
- *How do I test across so many devices and environments?*
- *How do I integrate and connect to back end systems easily and quickly?*
- *How do I manage and secure my mobile applications and devices?*
- *How should I gather feedback from my customer to improve the quality of my app?*

Mobile Application Development Challenges

Mobile development is different than traditional application or web development. Unique characteristics about mobile technology can create new challenges for enterprise developers. Perhaps the biggest challenge is developing mobile applications for multiple platforms, including Apple iOS, Google Android, BlackBerry, and Windows Phone (for now). Although each platform has a similar set of capabilities, the operating system and associated programming model is different. In addition, there are multiple ways to develop and deploy mobile applications to consumers and employees. Customers and employees also have expectations that an app is high quality. Developers have more pressure than ever to deliver a "five-star app," yet need the tools, resources, and skills to pull it off. Developers need to extend existing business systems and data to mobile that might not have been originally designed for mobility. Another critical development challenge is the expectation for speed and the constant pressure to deliver more frequent releases. Finally, the mobile development effort must fit within an existing enterprise development effort. It needs to have the tools and capabilities that deliver secure, manageable, and scalable enterprise-ready applications.

Developing for Multiple Mobile Platforms

It is clear that for the foreseeable future there will be a wide variety of mobile devices in the market. Device diversity will increase as more and more vendors enter the market and the cost of hardware and software goes down. You are already seeing this with the open source version of Android enabling a wide variety of inexpensive versions of the Android-based mobile devices. Android has been "forked" (when a developer takes a copy of the source code from one software effort and starts a new and independent software package) and has created even more diversity in the market. Smartphones and tablets are just the beginning. There will be more and more smart devices that will permeate our lives. Sometimes referred to as the 'Internet of things' or Machine to Machine (M2M), these simple devices will be connected, intelligent, and focused on a specific purpose. For example, there are already smart devices with the Nest smart thermostat or the Withings smart scale. There will be more and more of these types of smart devices that will need to be part of an overall mobile strategy, creating implications in application development, management, and security.

One of the critical requirements for enterprises is that the app works across multiple device types. Particularly in the case of a customer or partner facing app, you cannot control which device they will use. This might be less of a concern for an employee-facing app if you issued devices to your employees. However, when a BYOD policy is in place, you might again need to support multiple device types. So it is clear that you must support the latest devices in the market because this is what your customers, partners, or even employees will be demanding.

Developing for multiple platforms is unavoidable in the mobile era. So what are the key requirements for building cross-platform apps? The following list provides a set of expectations that you need to consider:

- **Ability to create the user interface that you need:** Each device has its own set of capabilities that are unique to the device. When you build a mobile application, you want to have the flexibility to leverage any of the unique capabilities of the devices, including any of the sensors, or output functions, such as the camera, GPS, accelerometer, and contact list.

  The user interface must match the mobile device and leverage its unique icons, color scheme, and so on. After all, people often have a "relationship" with the interface of a particular device. They want something that looks, feels, and acts like what they are used to. For example, if you target an iPhone and a BlackBerry 7 device, you want the iPhone app to be touch-friendly and the BlackBerry 7 app to be easy to use with a pointer and keyboard. You might also want the app to self-adjust its user interface based on whether it is on a different form factor (tablet or phone) of a particular operating environment (such as the iOS or Android), taking into account particular screen real estate, resolution, and dimension.

- **Avoiding the lowest-common-denominator approach:** As you consider the complexity of supporting multiple platforms, one approach may be to produce a lowest-common-denominator app where you support the simplest features that are easiest to deliver on every platform. As a result, you sacrifice the unique characteristics of each platform to achieve cross-platform support. This would be a mistake. You want to deliver a rich and engaging experience that exploits the specific features of each device.

- **Learning curve:** Each device has its own native language, operating environment, and platform. Because native apps are not portable across each platform, you need to build distinct apps for each platform. One of the biggest challenges is finding and staffing development resources with the skills on each platform (Google Android, Apple iOS, BlackBerry, etc) or building the skills within your own organization. In the past, the predominant enterprise platforms were Java and .NET. In the mobile era, you need to add the new required skills and techniques. Mobile skills are in short supply and are not easy to obtain. In addition, the development of mobile apps requires some unique experience around the mobile interaction model that exploits the unique characteristics of the devices.

- **Avoiding vendor lock-in or technology that won't keep up:** Unlike the web, which is open standard-based and enables easy switching across platforms, the mobile market is ripe with vendor lock-in. With proprietary technology you can get tied to a particular platform if you do not have the resources to duplicate your application across multiple platforms. Some have attempted to get around this issue with code-generation approaches. However, code generation has its own set of pitfalls and has the potential for lock-in through the use of proprietary code generation languages.

- **Mobile testing:** With so many different mobile operating environments and device types, testing a mobile app can be more challenging than testing an app for the web where there is generally a consistent user interface—the browser. Granted there are many variations of the browser; however, the ability to maintain and test against multiple browsers is within the scope of many enterprises. With mobile, many completely different device environments exist. First, there are multiple operating systems—Apple, Android, Windows Phone, and Blackberry—just for starters. There are also permutations of each operating system in the market, including previous versions. Also, each handset manufacturer might make modifications to the mobile OS environment to meet their particular market needs.

  In addition, there can be multiple types of devices, screen resolution and form factors for each platform. Finally, each carrier network causes the app to behave slightly differently. Add all this together, and you are presented with a complicated test matrix. In order to perform a proper test, you need to have access to the physical devices and the various carrier networks around the world. You need to test against all the possible peripherals and add-on capabilities such as cameras, accelerometers, GPS optional keyboards, or pointing devices. Mobile testing creates a tremendous challenge for the enterprise.

- **Available skills:** When developing a mobile strategy, you must consider available skills. Mobile development often requires unique skills in the particular mobile OS platforms. Deeper skills in user experience design may also be required. When choosing a development platform, ensure it is based on open standard technology in which readily available skills are available in the market. As an alternative, if your organization does not have the required skills, outsourcing may be an option.

- **Avoiding code generation:** Some may consider a development platform that generates code for each mobile device platform. This approach usually entails developing an application once, and then using the development platform to generate code for each mobile device environment. The downside of this approach is that you usually have to write the application in a unique proprietary language and then have it cross compile into each specific mobile OS platform. The challenge is you lose some control of the final output of the cross compiled application. If you make changes to the cross-compiled code, you are now out of sync with the original source code. The end result is that maintenance and management can become a challenge.

Delivering High-Quality Apps That Engage Users and Meet Business Objectives

Meeting high user expectations is a core requirement for mobile. Your end user will expect functional apps geared to a specific task or tasks. They will expect the quality to be as high as what they are experiencing with their personal apps. This creates a challenge for development teams that have not always focused on the aesthetics of their traditional applications. There needs to be a level of understanding of visual design that is not often an available skill within the enterprise.

App performance is also a critical requirement. Users have a much higher expectation for performance. Web users are accustomed to a web site that takes a few moments to load. If there is an issue with the site, they simply press the reload button and continue on their way. Not so with a mobile app. The mobile app is expected to function crisply with fast load and quick transitions between screens.

Connectivity to Back-End Systems and Data

The mobile app must fit in with the existing web and desktop applications infrastructure. The mobile architecture should not be a separate thought but rather integrated into an existing infrastructure. The mobile app infrastructure must be designed with consideration for how it interacts with the existing systems while managing the differences presented by the unique mobile app requirements:

- Mobile development must be able to access existing back-end systems quickly and easily. To execute quickly, you need to avoid complex integration solutions that require a lot of programming and testing.

- The ability to support hundreds of thousands of users all communicating with the back end.

- How will the data be delivered to the mobile app? Will it be binary, Extended Markup Language (XML), or JavaScript® Object Notation (JSON)? How will the format impact the device performance and battery life?

- Ensuring that the app can access data in offline mode when the device is not connected to the network is also important.

- If building multiple apps, it may become necessary to have an intermediate infrastructure or middleware that can mediate with back-end systems and provide app monitoring and management for security and operations.

Another key challenge associated with connecting to back end systems is corporate network connectivity. Smartphones and tablets will connect to corporate networks across a variety of Wi-Fi or cellular networks. Scenarios include the following:

- Connecting employee mobile devices to the corporate Wi-Fi network
- Connecting guest mobile devices to the corporate Wi-Fi network
- Connecting employee mobile devices on a noncorporate network (for example, cellular or home Wi-Fi) to the corporate Wi-Fi network in order to securely access corporate data

Given the variety of network configurations across trusted and nontrusted networks and devices, security and management become important issues. Dedicated connection or encryption of the network via a VPN (Virtual Private Network) becomes important. The VPN may be at the device or the app level.

Meeting Accelerated Time-to-Market Requirements

For developers, one of the stark realities of delivering a mobile app in an era of consumer-driven devices is the acceleration of new platform releases. End users will almost immediately upgrade their operating system after it is released. This means that a development team likely must upgrade your app to a new platform as soon as it comes out. On average, the mobile platform vendors release new operating system updates two to three times a year. This means you may need to release a new version of your app for a particular platform whenever it is updated. Multiply that by the number of platforms you plan to support (which is at least two and possibly three or four) and it is easy to see that you could be releasing 8 to 12 versions of an app each year. Multiply this again by the average number of apps your business may have, which could be four or five apps. You are now looking at between 50–60 mobile app releases a year. Not only that, but the rate and pace of device leadership will change rapidly. Most devices are replaced every 18 to 24 months. As a result, this creates significant volatility in device market share. The leading mobile device platform may drop from leadership to the back of the pack in 3 to 4 years.

A dynamic market that acts with unprecedented speed points to the need for an efficient and agile organization. However, this leads to a challenge in aligning the appropriate teams early in the development process. Getting the right stakeholder involved so that requirements are defined correctly upfront is critical. The development teams need to be efficient and keep the lines of communications open so that the flow of information is nimble and well-defined.

Integration with Existing Development Processes

Companies doing in-house mobile application development have existing software development processes in place. These are not necessarily adapted to mobile app development. Also, not all mobile development tools are designed to be adapted into an existing software development process. For example, iPhone and iPad apps can be compiled only on Macs. The management of support for Macs can be a challenge for some companies. To actually compile and test the app, each Mobile OS platform requires the use of its particular software development kit (SDK), compiler, and simulators. In addition, these SDKs are updated frequently, and integrating these SDKs into an existing development process can be a challenge.

Mobile development is also a multidisciplinary process that involves cooperation and sharing of code across multiple developers who most likely have differing levels of expertise. In addition, when building native code for multiple mobile Operating Systems (OSs) each platform is completely different, requiring a different set of developers. These different developers need to coordinate. In addition, you need to ensure that as teams come together, they have a platform in place that simplifies the interaction between the different developers and simplifies the mutual work done by the different developers across different skill sets.

Quality assurance and beta testing require different processes for mobile development when compared to traditional software development. You need to determine how to test across multiple devices, and in many cases, having the physical device present is a necessity. If your app communicates to back-end services, you may need to have the ability to test against a variety of server environments. One developer may want to work against a production server, whereas another may want to target a test server. In addition, there needs to be a way to distribute the app to your development and test teams. Remember that the app is not available through the public app store yet. So during development, you need a private app store and/or Mobile Device Management (MDM software helps to secure, monitor, and manage mobile devices) solutions to distribute the app.

Another consideration is the scenario in which different parts of the broader organization develop their own mobile apps. Some of these apps may have been developed outside of IT's knowledge and control. Eventually, these apps may need to come under central management of IT for day-to-day operational and security control. Managing and consolidating a variety of app development approaches can become a challenge for organizations. It might make sense to outsource your mobile operations to a qualified partner if there is a lack of resources and skills to execute.

Security and Management

Security is an important consideration for many types of mobile applications. Whether you develop a mobile application for consumers to perform online banking or an internal application to track sales leads, security is a key requirement. As mobile devices become more popular, mobile threats are on the rise. Because these devices are always with them, individuals frequently access unsecured Wi-Fi networks or they lose the device more easily than they would with a PC. With personal devices entering into the enterprise (BYOD) the situation gets even more complicated. In addition, mobile devices are more likely to be shared with others, further putting corporate data at risk.

Following is a key set of security challenges an enterprise faces when developing a mobile strategy:

- **Securing and managing the devices:** With a wide variety of mobile devices in the market today, how does a company manage them all while fitting within an existing infrastructure that manages PCs, desktops, and servers? With a device that is frequently lost, a mechanism needs to be in place to kill and wipe the device remotely to protect corporate data. A roles-based policy can define the content, apps, and level of access appropriate for a particular individual based on membership within a group. A company needs to ensure the integrity of the mobile device by detecting if the device's base operating environment has been compromised by jailbreaking or rooting the device. Jailbreaking (for Apple iOS operating systems) and rooting (for Google Android operating systems) refers to the process of altering the mobile operating system to eliminate restriction or attain privileged control over the device. End users may want to do this to get around the restrictions imposed by the OS manufacturer. For example, users may want to install non-approved apps, change the device clock speed for better performance, or have flexibility in which carrier they want to use. While Jailbreaking or rooting a device may give the end user more flexibility, it also alters the operating environment to open it up to potential threats. As a result, the enterprise will want to detect and block such devices from accessing corporate networks.

- **Mobile threats:** Attacks on mobile devices are on the rise. With mobile devices containing both corporate and personal information, they become compelling targets for hackers. In some cases, the attack vectors will be different than with PCs. A company needs to constantly adapt to new threats and hacking techniques.

- **Network protection:** Mobile network communications need to be secured and protected from eavesdropping or unauthorized access. Encryption from the device or even at the application level back to the enterprise is important.

- **Identity and access management:** The mobile app must integrate with the existing authentication infrastructure. If an app provides access to sensitive corporate data, you must ensure that malicious software that might be running on the device cannot steal user credentials during or after the login process. Multifactor authentication is often a requirement for protecting against unauthorized access.

Single sign-on can also be important so that several enterprise apps can share the same login session, so the user would not have to reenter credentials over and over again.

To speed development and simplify a security infrastructure, you could offload authorization and authentication to an access management infrastructure that is tuned for a mobile environment. A specialized mobile security access management system may include context awareness and strong session management.

- **Data loss prevention:** With personal devices entering the workplace, securing corporate data is a critical challenge to overcome. Encrypting the data on the device is important, particularly when the device is used offline and the corporate data resides on the device. You need to ensure the data on the device is protected from unauthorized users or malicious software. In addition, you must prevent data from "leaking" from a secure corporate space into an unsecure area on the mobile device or to public cloud services where security is suspect. You may want to prevent individuals from cutting and pasting from a corporate document, thus compromising secure data access. In many respects, you need to separate the corporate section of the mobile device from the personal part of the mobile device. This allows for protecting corporate data by managing access and defining a policy-based interaction model, while at the same time, giving free access to the personal side of the device.

- **Application security:** As an application is created, you must understand if the application has been developed in such a way that makes it more vulnerable to attacks. After an application is deployed, it is far more expensive to deal with a security issue than before it is put into production. Providing the appropriate code scans to ensure there are no known security vulnerabilities is a key challenge.

- **People and security:** Even with the best security, management technologies, and strategy, you still need to consider the human part of the equation. People's behavior can counter even the best security deployment. This is why it is important to form a partnership with your employees or customers. Establishing a set of clear and documented policies is critical. Reinforcing policy with comprehensive and thoughtful education can emphasize the importance of policy so that people understand not only what needs to be done, but also why a policy is in place.

Management and Post-Deployment Control of Apps

Another key challenge is what to do after the app has been deployed. As with any software, you can expect that users will experience problems. As such, you need to include a set of server-side logging mechanisms to monitor the application activity and understand what the user's activity may be just prior to having a problem. You may want to include client-side logging so that the app can send diagnostic information back to technical support. This needs to be done even in cases when the user is offline or fails to establish access. Having a feedback loop to constantly improve the customer experience is critical to ensure the highest quality of app.

Sending updates to apps or forcing users to perform an update to the app is another critical challenge for the enterprise. After an app is deployed to a public app store, it is a challenge to keep it updated—unlike a web app, where you can easily update the web site, allowing users to upgrade the next time they access the site. With the public app store, it may take days or weeks to work through a third-party app store approval process. In addition, the users must take an action to upgrade. So building in post-deployment management system where the app can call back to the enterprise to validate its state or currency is important. This allows the enterprise to perform remote disablement or provide new updates.

Summary

Mobile is hot and at the top of the minds of many business leaders. Mobile is clearly the next major IT trend that will be driving growth and opportunity. Business leaders see how mobile technology impacts their personal life and they see the opportunity to apply it to the enterprise. Competitors are using mobile technology to their advantage and putting pressure on business leaders. As a result, the business side of an organization is much more involved in driving decisions around a mobile strategy. This pressure to adopt mobile technology that originated in the consumer market is driving a new wave of *consumerization of IT*. This is raising expectations on IT. Cycle times are shorter, while at the same time there is a higher expectation on user experience. With multiple platforms to support in a fragmented market space, IT is struggling to keep up. In addition, much of the mobile technology lacks the enterprise capabilities for security and management.

To address these challenges and seize on the opportunities around mobile, you must have an overall strategy that addresses the needs across the organization. A strategy needs to address the entire life cycle of a mobile solution. You need to look at the increasing cost of managing multiple platforms, and how to deal with different types of mobile applications (web delivered, hybrid, or native). You want to take advantage of some of the capabilities of new and emerging smartphone technologies and deliver a solution in a consistent way across different channels and markets. As a result, you need to define an end-to-end strategic framework around enterprise mobility. This framework would outline a life cycle for a mobile solution describing how to build and run mobile applications, manage and secure mobile apps and devices, and extend your back-end system and transform your business. The framework for defining a mobile strategy will be discussed in detail in the following chapter.

4

The Mobile Framework

You have looked at the impact mobility has had on businesses and the incredible opportunity it can provide for businesses going forward. It is clear that the smart device can revolutionize the IT industry and enable companies to transform their businesses. Despite the opportunity, there are also challenges in delivering an effective mobile strategy. The mobile market is fast-changing with many new technologies appearing on the scene all the time. There are also the implications of the consumerization of IT—in which many aspects of the technologies have come out of the consumer space and, as such, may not be perfectly suited for the IT environment. You must deploy new enterprise mobile technologies and capabilities within your overall IT environment to enable your business for mobility. New capabilities for building, managing, securing, and delivering a mobile solution require a comprehensive strategy. This strategy must touch major parts of the organization from development to operations to line of business. You need to bring together such capabilities as mobile development, device management, application security, and so on. The market today is very dynamic with technology coming from a variety of sources and providers. Therefore, you need a framework for considering the key technologies and capabilities needed to deliver on your overall mobile strategy.

A Mobile Framework

One of the biggest challenges when considering a mobile strategy is getting a view of an overall context. In one respect, building a mobile app may seem trivial. You just take a mobile SDK, build an app, and put it in an app store. However, building a mobile app that is designed well, managed, secured, and that can transform the relationship with your employee or customer is not a trivial task. You must consider many aspects that can touch almost every part of an organization. In addition, the market is rapidly changing with many new technologies and capabilities appearing on the scene.

Therefore, a strategic framework must start with identifying the business results the business wants to achieve. These business results should be accompanied by specific measurements for success. The business results then point to a specific set of tasks that end users want to achieve. Remember, the mobile app is simple, engaging, and task-oriented. The mobile app should not become a monolithic, complicated application that tries to solve too many things. If you find your app trying to do too much, you should simplify or break it up into multiple apps.

In addition, you must have a framework to set the context of the elements needed to deliver on a mobile strategy. It defines the relationship between the functional elements and the organizational structure that support the delivery of the mobile solution. This gives the organization a means of maintaining a structure and stability needed in a fast-changing market.

The framework helps provide context and a vision for a mobile strategy. It shows a starting point and where you need to get to. It outlines a comprehensive view so that a gap analysis can be performed given where you are. It then provides a construct for a roadmap as you assess your organizational capabilities and what is needed to reach your strategic goals.

Figure 4.1 shows a mobile framework that outlines the major functional elements needed in defining a mobile strategy. This framework starts with a view of the overall business value and the specific tasks a mobile app is trying to address. It defines a set of patterns that are common building blocks for defining the functional elements of the mobile app and points to the core value proposition for your app. The framework then defines how you deliver on the mobile app. What is needed to build and connect the mobile app? How do you manage and secure the mobile app in addition to the network and devices? Then how do you extend your business to deliver a transformative experience with your customer and employee?

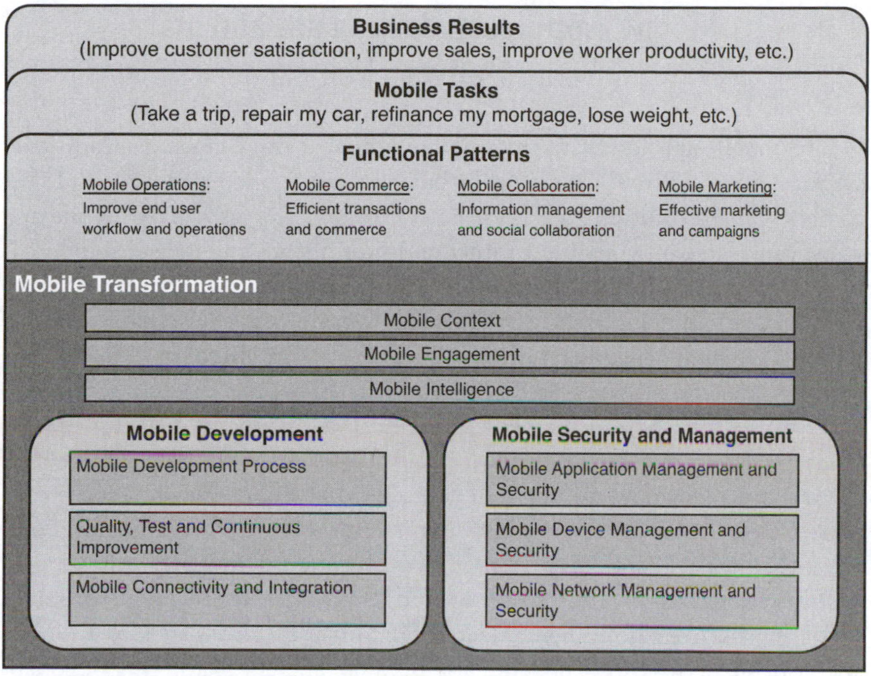

Figure 4.1   A view of an overall mobile framework.

The framework then points to how the organization can align around the mobile project. The mobile development efforts focus more on the IT development teams. The management and security efforts align with the IT and security operations. The overall vision and direction around extending-and-transforming a business are aligned with the focus of the line of business part of the organization.

The remainder of the chapter outlines the details of each element of this framework by walking you through the key imperatives, steps of activities, and functional elements that define the overall framework. The remainder of this book describes the requirements needed to deliver each element of this framework in the context of an overall mobile strategy.

Mobile App Becomes the Fundamental Value Delivery Vehicle

The mobile app can be transformative in that it can connect to traditional systems to extend the value of your business to mobile employees and customers while revolutionizing traditional business processes. The mobile app value can increase by adding context and intelligence to engage individuals in their daily lives to help them perform their tasks more effectively. The app improves individual efficiency by reducing friction between steps in a task or removing steps all together. Ultimately, by adding intelligence to the mobile solution, the app becomes predictive and determines the next best step, further improving the engagement with individuals and delivering greater value.

As you look at how the app will be used, it will likely be within the context of a particular industry, whether it is healthcare, insurance, banking, or any other vertical industry. Although each vertical industry has its own unique characteristics, it uses a set of core functional patterns. For example, a retail app may have commerce-related functional elements such as a mobile wallet or shopping cart. The retail app may also include marketing or collaboration elements to provide a full customer experience. As such, a set of primary functional patterns define core capabilities that inform and direct the overall mobile functional elements you would use to deliver a comprehensive mobile strategy. Table 4.1 outlines the relationship between the type of industry-specific mobile apps and the related functional pattern.

Table 4.1 Example of Mobile Vertical Applications and the Relationship to Common Functional Patterns

Industry	Value of Mobile Solution	Functional Element	Primary Mobile Functional Pattern
Finance and Banking	Enable customers to manage their investment portfolios and accounts from anywhere with access to critical information.	Mobile payments Mobile banking	Transactions and commerce Information management Marketing
Insurance	Enable customers and agents to file claims and document damages, as well as drive claims processes.	Claims processing Taking picture of damage Location of repair shops Insurance document wallet	Workflow and operation Transactions and commerce Information management Marketing
Retail	Engage customers in new ways and intelligently target personalized and location-sensitive marketing offers.	Mobile wallet Augmented reality Smart mobile checkout Mobile commerce	Transactions and commerce Information management Marketing
Travel and Transportation	Provide customers with up-to-date information specific to their itineraries and location and enable customer self-service.	Travel research Reservations Check-in Loyalty point management	Workflow and operation Transactions and commerce Information management Marketing

Table 4.1 Example of Mobile Vertical Applications and the Relationship to Common Functional Patterns (Continued)

Industry	Value of Mobile Solution	Functional Element	Primary Mobile Functional Pattern
Healthcare	Provide patients with improved access to care, improved patient safety, and quality of care while reducing costs and improving efficiency.	Connected home health monitoring	Workflow and operation
		Mobile-enabled Clinicians	Information management
		Hospital productivity apps	
	Use medical equipment tracking.		
Construction and Manufacturing	Equip employees to manage complex projects and operations onsite and streamline survey and work order processes.	Inspections	Workflow and operation
		Contractor management	Transactions and commerce
		Inventory management	Information management
		Logistics	

These functional patterns generally fall into four major categories that are relevant in both B2C and B2E situations as described in the following list. Most apps focus on a combination of these categories. This forms a set of common patterns that works across a variety of apps and prescribes the underlying set of mobile capabilities.

- **Mobile operations—improve workflow and operations:** Improved workflow is about making the task of the employee or customer more efficient. This is foundational to mobility and is at the heart of the value that mobile offers. Having the mobile device with you to supply the contextual information when needed to help you complete a task is a core value proposition.

- **Mobile commerce—efficient transactions and commerce:** At the end of the day, there needs to be a final action. It may be a business decision, a purchase, or a flight check-in. A mobile transaction can be a meaningful exchange of anything of business value (money, information, and so on). The improved access to information and the improved workflow can lead to a final action.

- **Mobile collaboration—information management and social collaboration:** Mobile gives individuals more efficient access to information from enterprise data systems and insight from others at the moment they need it. Social collaboration pulls in insight from peers in social networks or from other employees in an organization (in the form of social business). This enables the individual to make better decisions and take the best next action. Information management is not just digesting and receiving information but also collecting data and information from the environment around the end user. The mobile device enables the individual to take measurements and collect data of assets or the environment, which can then be fed into the existing business processes.

- **Mobile marketing—effective marketing and campaigns:** Marketing capabilities speak to the way you influence customer behavior through communicating a set of messages. Primarily focused on the business-to-consumer situation, effective marketing is primarily focused on communicating a particular message or perception to the end user in the form of campaigns, programs, or advertisements. Delivering, tracking, and managing the marketing efforts for mobile requires a unique set of capabilities. Unlike web marketing, mobile marketing offers functions such as in-app advertisements, QR code campaigns, SMS campaigns, marketing analytics, and so on.

These functional patterns help you think through the aspects of a mobile app that provide value. These patterns do not necessarily operate in a vacuum, but instead, come together to form the basis for the mobile app. For example, improved *collaboration* can lead to improved *operations*, which then manifests in a better *commerce*. Each functional pattern has a set of signature functional elements. As you build your mobile strategy, bringing together these key solution patterns can help to structure the capabilities needed to execute on a mobile strategy. Table 4.2 outlines reusable functional elements that would support the key functional patterns.

Table 4.2 App Capabilities in Context of Key Functional Patterns

Improve Workflow and Operation	Efficient Transaction and Commerce	Information Management and Social Collaboration	Effective Marketing
Device Management	Pricing	Dashboards	Campaigns
Social Networking	Search	Data Lookup	Social Networking
Signature Capture	Purchase	Comparisons	Customer Experience
Check-In	Shipping	Search	Segmentation
Approval Workflow	Quote	Browser	Advertising
Near Field Communications	Contracts	Social Networks	Action Clusters
Tracking	Orders	Analytics	Analytics
Receiving	Workflow	e-meetings	Inference Engine
RFID and Asset Capture	Segments	SMS , Texting, and IM	Augmented Reality
Supply Chain	e-mail Integration	Sensors	Churn Management
Workforce Management	Chat	Asset Tracking	Recommendations
Analytics	Guided Selling	Email	Location-Based Services
Inventory Management	Accounts	Team Rooms	Loyalty
Collaboration	Service	Video Conferencing	Ratings and Reviews
Point of Sale Interaction	Product Catalog	Augmented Reality	Brand Management
	Shopping Cart		Location-Based Services
	Billing		Presence
	Checkout		Products
			Proactive Messaging
			Events

Mobile Development, Security, Management, and Business Transformation

The value of mobility starts with the customer's needs and tasks at hand. The mobile app should enable end users to perform the task efficiently and achieve their goals quickly and with less effort. We walked through the core functional patterns seeing how they relate to the functional elements of a mobile solution and how they support overall value. These functional patterns then come together in the form of solutions that solve specific industry challenges.

However, the next question becomes, "How can you deliver the mobile app?" You need a framework by which the mobile app is developed and defined. As you consider the mobile strategy you have to move from "Why should I build a mobile app?"or "Can I leverage an existing app in the industry instead of building my own?" to "What capabilities should be within the app?" and "How do I build my mobile solution with appropriate security and management?" Ultimately, you must define a strategy that answers the question, "How can the app transform my business by getting closer to my customers, improving employee effectiveness, and growing the bottom line?"

Fundamentally, the mobile strategy requires a framework for thinking through the key capabilities required to deliver on a mobile strategy. Mobile is a fast-changing space with many new technologies and constantly changing market players and functionality. The value of a framework is that it helps to define the major functional elements needed and how the solution can be delivered. Even as specific technologies change, the framework remains consistent as it creates an overall construct for defining a solution. This helps with vendor selection, skills, organization structure, functional definition, and execution—even in a fast-changing market place.

Mobile Development

Unlike the web era when you could build a web site that would run across a ubiquitous web browser with generally standard interfaces, the mobile market space is characterized by lots of fragmentation and incompatibility. There are many devices on the market today with their own unique characteristics; and even within a particular mobile platform, there is variation in platform versions. You need an approach to reduce the cost and complexity of building a mobile app that supports a variety of platforms. Mobile app development should also support the latest device capability while leveraging existing skills such as HTML, CSS, and JavaScript. The mobile development environment must fit within the existing enterprise development process and have the appropriate governance and management. The supporting mobile infrastructure must also connect to existing systems (both on premise and in the cloud) quickly and easily. It must also enable rapid development and continuous customer experience feedback. Continuous feedback is critical because the mobile app, in many respects, may never be complete because user feedback drives new versions and updates. Also, testing becomes a major challenge because your customer and employee will use many types of devices, and you need to test across a wide variety of platforms.

Building and Connecting Imperatives

Building and deploying a mobile app must address a set of key imperatives. These imperatives fall into three major categories:

Mobile development: How do you develop, build, and deploy high-quality mobile apps across a variety of platforms and channels?

- **Cross-platform and multichannel support:** It is clear there will be a diversity of devices and back-end systems that need to be part of a mobile solution. There will be a wide variety of mobile devices in the market that will be unique in functionality and capability. Although standards such as HTML5 are an important part of an overall mobile cross-platform approach, you must address the specific function of a device.

  The mobile strategy must also consider multiple channels as well. As the end user works to complete his task, he will work across multiple channels from web, kiosk, mobile device, and more. There needs to be a way to maintain consistency and state across these different interaction interfaces. Any enterprise will have a wide variety of back-end applications and systems that are cloud, traditional, new, and legacy. In addition, mobile applications must be maintained across all these platforms, and the code must be optimized and reused across all the platforms. The development environment must be open and be flexible utilizing readily available skills in the market.

- **Enterprise agile development and team collaboration:** The mobile project needs to be delivered quickly and with high quality. The development teams must move fast and collaborate effectively. The development teams need the tools and infrastructure to ensure that they can execute effectively and with the highest quality. The mobile project also must be aligned with existing enterprise development and governance process.

Mobile life-cycle management, quality, testing and continuous improvement: How do you manage the life cycle of an app from requirements to test to deployment while delivering continuous improvement?

- **Complete mobile application life cycle development from requirements, design, development, build, quality assurance, test, and deployment:** To achieve the speed and quality you need to deliver a world-class mobile solution, you need integrated application life cycle management. The process, from requirements to deployment, needs to be integrated and delivered so that it becomes part of an overall iterative enterprise development process. The application life cycle management process must consider the diversity in devices and platforms, which must be addressed within an integrated development process.

- **Test automation and planning:** One of the biggest challenges with mobile development is testing. The mobile app likely requires access to multiple physical devices to fully test it. This means that you need to rethink the testing process and ensure that devices are available (possibly virtually through a device cloud) and that much of the testing is automated to streamline the process. You can use emulators and simulators to validate functionality early in the development process. Finally, throughout the process, you should constantly test functionality with end users to ensure you are on the right track.

- **Continuous improvement and quality:** One thing is clear with mobility—user expectations are high. The market expects a five-star app, and employees will not be satisfied with a mediocre app. Building a mobile app requires lots of end user feedback before, during, and after development. In many respects the mobile app is never complete because you must have continuous feedback and input on the mobile app. The app must be instrumented to gather usage data as the end user interacts with the app. You want to do playback of user activity to look for issues or challenges the end user may encounter. You may want to understand what happens when an app crashes and collect information as to the possible root cause. There is also a need to monitor and understand user feedback as it occurs within the app store, or out in social networks such as Twitter.

Mobile connectivity and integration: How does the app integrate into existing systems?

- **Flexible and fast system and data integration:** Because mobile projects move so quickly, you need to quickly integrate and connect to back-end and cloud systems.

- **Manage back-end events:** You need a centralized and common mechanism that enables back-end events that send notifications to the mobile device. Each device has its own notification protocols. Therefore, this mechanism needs to capture back-end events and route them to the appropriate device using the correct protocols and push/SMS service.

- **Service access and integration:** A variety of services are available from within and outside the enterprise. These services must be managed, metered, and monitored for quality of service.

Mobile Development Steps

You must get a sense of the major activities and flow of the activities within the category of building and connecting mobile apps. Although not exhaustive, the following sections provide a step-by-step overview for building and deploying mobile apps as well as incorporating data access and integration.

Building and Deploying Mobile Apps

1. **Plan:** Plan the project scope and goal, and ensure there is a defined return on investment with appropriate success criteria.
2. **Requirements:** Collect user requirements and feedback. Use story boards and wireframes to perfect the user experience early in the development process.
3. **Design:** Define user experience for mobile, and use latest device features and UI to optimize the user experience.
4. **Build:** For cross-platform and manageability, building the setup and configuration for each device environment will be different. As such, a centrally managed build environment can reduce development complexity and cost.
5. **Simulate:** Use of a simulator during the development process can speed up the process. Simulators are often browser based and can be spun up quickly to help developers check how their app looks and functions.

6. **Emulate:** An emulator is designed to provide a software emulation of a mobile device. Often emulating the actual underlying device hardware, the software emulator that is part of the mobile operating system SDK gives the most accurate sense of the application short of actually running on the device. One caveat is that an emulator can be slow when compared with a simulator.

7. **Post for review:** Distribute the app through a private app store to stakeholders. This will not only get needed feedback early in the process, but will also ensure that all stakeholders can provide course correction if needed.

8. **Collaborate**: Coordination of the agile development teams throughout the development process will be critical, especially if you have teams focused on a variety of device operating systems.

9. **Test:** Mobile testing is significantly more challenging than traditional software testing. Unlike traditional PC and web applications, there are many more potentially supported mobile devices and release levels. Testing requires access to physical devices, which can lead to managing hundreds of devices. This can be complex and points to new technologies in automated testing and cloud-based "renting" of physical devices. There also needs to be vulnerability testing to ensure that the coding approach did not introduce security vulnerabilities into the app at development time.

10. **Traceability:** Due to the speed of mobile development, being able to trace a defect to a particular code change and requirement will be critical to quickly resolving bugs.

11. **Deploy:** Publish with either a private or public app store.

12. **Continuous experience**: Gather continuous feedback from users and implement the feedback into the development process to ensure the highest quality. Forensic analysis and playback of user sessions can unveil issues that need to be fixed in the app.

Data Access and Integration

1. **Define endpoints:** Selection of the back-end and cloud application will be important for app functionality.

2. **Connect:** Rapidly connect to the back-end and combine or mash-up data and services. Ensure that the appropriate quality of service and connectivity management is in place.

3. **Convert:** Deliver back-end data in a mobile-friendly format. Sometimes, back-end data needs to be converted to a format such as JavaScript Object Notation (JSON) to avoid draining the battery life of the phone.

4. **Push:** Receive events from the back-end and deliver push notifications to the appropriate device.

5. **Synchronize:** Keep data in sync while the device is offline.

Management and Security

One of the biggest challenges associated with mobility is how to manage and secure mobile technology that was originally designed for the consumer space. The merger of the consumer space and enterprise creates challenges for businesses. As BYOD becomes the norm, how do you secure a mobile device that was not issued by your enterprise? Because the device is always-on-the-go and will be accessed from a variety of networks, network security is also important. After the app has been deployed, you must ensure that it can be managed. It is essential to ensure that the app is secure and that the connection back to the enterprise is not compromised. You must provide security and management at the device, the app, and the network ensuring end-to-end protection. You need to ensure that data access to the enterprise prevents data from "leaking" to the mobile device and becoming compromised as the device is shared or lost or stolen. For example, an enterprise wants to prevent employees from copying a document from a secure corporate repository and then storing it on their mobile device. The simple act of viewing a document may store a copy inadvertently on the device. As a result, the document has leaked from a secure corporate environment to a potentially unsecure mobile device.

Management and Security Imperatives

Key imperatives to consider when developing your management and security strategy include:

Mobile application management and security: How do you secure, control, and service applications?

- **Mobile Application management (MAM):** Mobile application management applies policy and management capabilities to a mobile app instead of the device. If there needs to be a change, the system should remotely disable and update the app. It also needs to monitor and manage security of the app. In this way, when the device is lost or stolen, the individual app and associated data can be wiped or locked down instead of the entire device. An enterprise app store is also part of the overall applications management solution providing a means of distributing the mobile apps to employees.

- **Mobile information protection:** Manage data access and prevent information from falling into the wrong hands. This is particularly relevant for BYOD when personal devices are used for business. The appropriate policies and controls need to be put in place to make sure that data is not unsecure as the mobile device is used for personal use.

- **Secure mobile application development and management:** During development, the app should be scanned for potential vulnerabilities that might be present due to the coding techniques of the developer. Application scanning systems can identify common vulnerabilities such as SQL-injection, Cross-site scripting (XSS), and Cross-site request forgery (CSRF). Application security scanning usually consists of static and dynamic testing.

Mobile device management and security: How do you handle BYOD and ensure compliance for new devices?

- **Mobile Device Management (MDM):** Ensure the devices are managed and protected properly. MDM solutions can manage software distribution and device inventory management along with security, policy, and service management. For example, for a lost or stolen device, the MDM solution can remotely lock or wipe a mobile device. Telecom expense management may also be part of an overall device management policy. This is particularly the case when devices are issued to employees. Telecom expense management can help manage the entire expense and usage of a mobile device from the time it is purchased until it is retired.

- **Mobile threat protection:** Prevent malicious attacks and hacks that can either compromise the device, the app, or the network.

Mobile network management and security: How do you protect and manage network access?

- **Mobile network protection:** The data transmitted needs to be secured and encrypted to prevent unauthorized access.

- **Mobile identity and access management:** Through appropriate policies, it is critical to manage authentication of the user and devices and then authorize them to the appropriate corporate systems.
- **Security intelligence and reporting:** A corporation needs to be adaptive in its approach to security. The mobile space is always changing. New devices and functions appear on the scene all the time with new types of threats. Monitoring the state of mobile threats through comprehensive data analyses and reporting can provide the information needed to adapt to the latest security threats.

Management and Security Steps

The following is a sample of the various steps you would follow to manage and secure a mobile device, network, or app. Although this list is not exhaustive, it gives you a feel for the process associated with management and security:

At the Device

1. **Enroll:** Register owner and services.
2. **Configure:** Set appropriate security policies.
3. **Monitor and manage:** Ensure device compliance and manage telecom expenses.
4. **Reconfigure:** Add new policies over-the-air.
5. **Deprovision:** Remove services and wipe.

On the Network

1. **Authenticate:** Properly identify mobile users.
2. **Encrypt:** Secure network connectivity.
3. **Monitor and manage:** Log network access and events and manage network performance.
4. **Control:** Allow or deny access to apps.
5. **Block:** Identify and stop mobile threats.

For the Mobile App

1. **Develop:** Use secure coding practices.
2. **Test:** Identify application vulnerabilities.
3. **Monitor and manage:** Correlate unauthorized activity and manage app performance.

4. **Protect:** Defend against application attacks.
5. **Update:** Patch old or vulnerable apps.

Mobile Business Transformation

At the end of the day, you want to deliver the mobile solution that has the greatest impact on your business. You want to stay competitive and leverage a mobile solution to transform your business. You want to take your core business processes and capabilities and make them available as a mobile solution that maximizes the impact on your customers, employees, and partners. You want to extend the systems of record (existing back-end systems) to your end users in such a way that they are more engaged and help them complete their tasks more efficiently. You need to understand information, context, and user's behavior in such a way that the app you deliver simplifies your end users tasks.

Mobile Business Transformation Imperatives

In the end, extending your existing systems of record to mobile customers and employees is the way your core business will remain relevant. However, you want to do so by enhancing existing systems to leverage context, user engagement, and ultimately adding intelligence to a mobile solution to differentiate yourself from competitors. In the end, there are three primary directives when considering a mobile strategy to transform your business:

- Leveraging *context*
- Optimizing *user engagement*
- Delivering mobile *intelligence* by collecting insight about the user and situation, and turning it into the next best action for the end user

The following sections examine these three primary directives in greater detail.

Mobile Context: How Do You Deliver Value by Leveraging Context?

- **Environmental context:** There needs to be a constant stream of information about the end user's environment, and often it must be collected in real time so that the contextual information can be used at the moment the end user needs it. A transformative solution needs to know the current location, orientation, and environmental data of the end user and apply it to improving tasks.

- **Individual identity:** To deliver an engaging app, the system needs to understand who end users are and what their preferences are. Insight into their role, past decisions, and current state all provide information about what can be done at this moment to help users as they perform their tasks.

- **Historical behavior:** Where are the people on their task journey? An understanding of the current situation can help determine the next best step for them to take. Taking into consideration their attitude, history, and state can inform a system on how to best help end users complete their tasks more effectively.

Mobile Engagement: How Do You Optimize the Mobile Experience for Customers and Employees and Have It Integrate into Their Daily Lives?

- **Simplified information delivery:** Unlike the web and PC era where people comfortably sat behind a desk and browsed for information, mobile engagement is about delivering the right information at the right time and place to help end users meet their needs and complete a task in the moment. Interaction on the mobile device needs to be radically simplified, exposing just the essential elements end users need in the moment. The experience needs to be useful and delivered with a well-designed user interface.

- **Omnichannel delivery:** Engagement will likely not be limited to just the mobile device. Engagement is about helping end users complete their tasks more efficiently. As a result, the task activity may span across devices and time. Your end users may perform elements of their task at a PC, a mobile device, a smart TV, and an automotive dashboard. Your strategy needs to manage a continuous experience across all these channels.

- **Service composition and application aggregation:** Bringing together the right services to meet end users' tasks must be coordinated, orchestrated, and managed. Rapid assembly of services (or even applications) that are needed to complete tasks need to have simple and open interfacing for easy composition.

Mobile Intelligence: How to Use Mobile to Drive Insight to Action by Extending Systems of Record to Systems of Engagement

- **Analyze:** Information needs to be collected and processed to deliver the insight for end users. Some analyses need to be real time and driven by a scalable infrastructure that can handle the volume, velocity, and variety of big data. Interfacing and understanding social network sentiment will be part of the analysis process. Bringing in feeds of data and injecting them into an overall view of sentiment will be part of the analytics necessary for a transformative app.

- **Adapt:** As you learn about the situation at hand, your mobile solution needs to adapt. Data is coming through sensors, enterprise systems, and user activity. This information needs to drive changes to your system. Perhaps business processes, security posture, or even user interface of the mobile app need to change based on the system's analyses of the situation.

- **Next best action:** The transformative system needs to take in all the information collected and then analyze and deliver the insight to end users to help them take the next best action. Even the user experience of the app might need to be augmented and changed to meet the current state of end user's task.

Mobile Business Transformation Steps

The following are a set of high-level sample steps that you need to consider when developing a transformative mobile strategy:

1. **Gather contextual information:** Gather information from the environment as well as past behavior, role, and situation to understand the tasks in context.
2. **Ensure security and privacy:** Guarantee a trust relationship with the end users to ensure their information is protected and not used inappropriately.
3. **Analyze:** Understand the situation to deliver the insight needed for the next best action.
4. **Insight to action:** Take information from analysis to deliver the information or recommended next step for the end user.
5. **Engage:** Engage the end user with the appropriate service, content, and information to take the next best action. Continually improve the user experience to deliver optimal user experience.

Summary

Mobile technology presents tremendous opportunities for companies to transform their business by extending their core business process, data, and systems to mobile customers and employees. However, the scope of delivering a mobile project can be daunting when you consider all the high-quality expectations, rapidly changing marketplace, and incredibly short delivery cycles. Things become more complex when considering the need to manage a diverse set of devices and apps across multiple networks. As such, there needs to be a structure that helps to define what is needed to execute on a mobile strategy. This chapter outlines a framework to help you understand the core considerations for defining a mobile strategy rooted in business value. This framework can help you to understand potential gaps and point to an overall roadmap for execution. The remainder of the book goes into greater detail of how this framework can be applied to delivering an overall mobile strategy.

5

Mobile Development

The movement toward mobile impacts all aspects of a firm. The epicenter of the change to mobile is with the development teams that build the app and the operations teams that manage and maintain the app.

Mobile is not an evolution of technologies and processes but a revolution that impacts skills, technologies, processes, and engagement models. It completely changes the way you interact with your end customer, employer, or partner. On the surface, a mobile app seems so simple. After all, a mobile app is far less sophisticated than any of the large enterprise apps built in the past. Many development teams enter into the mobile development with this mindset but discover the reality of building, managing, securing, supporting, and maintaining an app across multiple platforms with the speed and quality that end users expect can be daunting. What makes mobile development so challenging? There are three major challenges:

- *User expectation for speed and quality*
- *Unprecedented device diversity*
- *Integrating with existing systems and extending them in transformative ways to engage the end user*

Speed and Quality

From the perspective of the end user, speed and quality go hand in hand. Coming out of the consumer space, the expectation for mobile is high. End users want more capabilities with shorter cycle times. Although the combination of speed and quality was always a core tenet of any good development shop, what becomes radically different with mobile is the significantly higher expectations coupled with many more hurdles from a technology and delivery perspective. There are many more devices that need to be supported than with traditional browser-based PCs. Also, customers are expecting new features and functionality on an almost daily basis. As a result, there is increased pressure to support many devices, with the latest features, as soon as they are available.

Speed

One of the unique aspects of mobile is the speed of delivery. The cycle time for mobile development is weeks compared to months with traditional software development. Users expect new features delivered more often and more quickly. In some respects, the mobile app may be simpler than a large software application, and as such there is an expectation for more capabilities to be delivered in more frequent cycles.

One of the biggest challenges for mobile development teams is keeping up with the rapid changes in the mobile ecosystem. Users upgrade to new devices every 18–24 months—sometimes sooner. In addition, the Mobile OS manufacturers update their operating systems at a much more compressed rate than desktop OS vendors did in the past. Once the new OS is available, end users upgrade almost immediately because the updates are free, and the upgrades can often be done in the background. This means that the development team needs to be prepared with a new version of an app tested on the new OS within days of the new OS release.

Compressed schedules are compounded by businesses' release and delivery constraints. Perhaps you are a retailer and the latest version of your app needs to be out before each major holiday or buying season. Things become more complicated because you likely need to support multiple platforms (each with its own unique OS upgrade schedule) while keeping their functionality relatively synchronized making sure no one platform falls behind. You also must factor in scheduling difficulties that may be imposed on you. For example, you need to factor in the time required for the app store approval process (which may be weeks). All this adds up to compressed and challenging development cycles. This requires you to think through the development process and build in a set of best practices technologies for fast app development.

Quality

A mobile app lives or dies by the star rating it receives in the app store. There is tremendous pressure and expectation to deliver a five-star app. Even internal employees expect a high-quality app. The user experience of the app is critical. The end user purchases a mobile device based on the appeal of the aesthetics and functionality of the particular device platform. Mobile users have developed a personal relationship with the mobile device and feel a strong sense of loyalty and preference for a certain user experience. As such, you cannot let the app experience fail to meet the expectations of end users. End users will not be satisfied with a lowest common denominator approach. As a result, you need a development platform environment that can support the capability to deliver high-quality apps and meet users' experience. It needs to support the UI components and frameworks that deliver the experience needed. You do not get a second chance to make a great first impression. As a result, you also need to think through the development process to ensure the highest quality. Information about the user interaction with your app will be critical in ensuring a quality experience. The mobile app should be designed to capture data about user activity in order to understand if users are achieving their goals.

Diversity of Devices

A wide variety of mobile devices exist in the market today, and this trend toward diversity will continue. The cost of delivering a mobile device to market will continue to decrease. Not only will there be a continued trend toward more and more smartphones and tablets but there will be more smart devices such as TV's, automobiles, watches, glasses, and medical devices. As such, there will be an increase in device diversity for the foreseeable future. This will put pressure on development teams to support a wide variety of device types and formats. With so many device types and technologies that need to be supported, available skills begin to play a significant role in a mobile strategy. Not every organization can afford to have (or even find) skilled resources in each mobile OS. This, in turn, will point to the need for cross-platform technology and capabilities. Currently, open standards such as

HTML5 provide a path forward for cross-platform apps because all major mobile browsers support it. In addition, HTML and web technology skills are more readily available in the market. However, because it takes time for standards such as HTML5 to progress, for the foreseeable future there will be the need for cross-platform technologies made possible by a hybrid approach, such as Apache Cordova. Cordova is an Apache open source project that enables developers to build mobile applications across a variety of platforms while at the same time providing a rich user experience and access to mobile device capabilities. Apache Cordova enables you to write much of your mobile app in web technologies such as HTML5, CSS, and JavaScript while at the same time using features of the mobile device such as the camera, accelerometer, contact lists, and so on.

Integration

Successfully integrating your new mobile app and your existing back-end systems is crucial. Your business processes and data is what separates you from the competition and as a result is what you want to extend to your customers and employees. As you know, speed is essential. You do not want to be bogged down with integration efforts that will slow down the development process. The mobile app must be integrated quickly and have the flexibility to connect to a variety of back-end systems both in the cloud and on-premise.

Back-end systems need to handle hundreds of thousands of users all connecting in short bursts. The data sent to the mobile device must be in the appropriate format. For example, because Simple Object Access Protocol (SOAP) is based on Extensible Markup Language (XML) the data transmitted can be large, and as a result, there could be an impact on the memory and processor—draining the battery. The use of JavaScript Object Notation (JSON) may be more efficient. When you choose a development and connectivity platform, look for the ability to convert existing data interchange to JSON on-the-fly.

In addition to the in-house integration of your mobile app to back-end systems, there also needs to be an integration of services outside your enterprise. Imagine your app requires access to a Customer Relationship Management (CRM) system, cloud storage, or some other third-party capability. You might not want to create these services on your own, but rather connect to an existing third-party service provided by a partner. These services need to be monitored and tracked for quality. You also want to understand the activity on these services to understand which are most valuable.

Rethinking the Development Process for Radical Speed and Quality

Although the development and delivery of a mobile app must be reduced to weeks instead of months, quality and engagement must be top priorities. How do you manage these seemingly contradictory requirements of speed, quality, and engagement? You must rethink your entire development process. Years of development experience have taught the industry best practices and techniques that have served development teams well for traditional software. However, the mobile development process must be different. You need to look at your organization and develop a strategy to extend and transform your existing development process for mobile speed, quality, and engagement.

To deliver a mobile project in just a few weeks, you need to think through the development process, looking for ways to cut all the overhead and execute with speed. Efficiency is critical, and the appropriate tools and infrastructure need to be in place. It can be helpful to look at the key steps in a mobile development process and understand key considerations:

- **Plan for "mobile first":** Mobile is quickly becoming your first point of contact with the customer. Defining the general scope and focus for the mobile app helps set the stage for the entire mobile project. You want to ensure that the app is suited for mobile from the start. Is the app suited for the small screen real estate? An app that requires a lot of data entry might not fit the requirements for mobile, whereas an app that uses a bar code reader may be perfect. Mobile apps are used on the go for short bursts of time. They are more task-focused. So while checking a class schedule might work well, writing a term paper would not.

- **Understand your customer:** Quality is paramount in a mobile project. You need to have a deep understanding of your customers from the start. What role are they playing? What is the journey they are on? What is the task at hand? What can be done based on context and behavior that can help accelerate the process to completing their goal?

- **Deliver omnichannel (multichannel and cross-channel):** When planning your mobile project, think of a particular task or journey the end user must perform. Think how your app can assist the end user complete his task more efficiently. Also consider how the app may transcend the actual mobile device as your end users interact with other channels such as web, kiosks, or point of sale. This is how your systems will be linked into the individual journey and how you can maintain state as they roam from device to device to desktop. Your back-end systems need to be linked as end users move from service to service to complete their task, and as such, the business processes need to be linked and coordinated.

- **Use agile development:** You will not be able to execute with the speed and efficiency a mobile project requires. Without an agile development process in place, you will likely need to augment your process to keep up with the speed and quality expectations of mobile customers. The focus on design needs to be front and center as part of the agile process, and you may need to rethink the requirement process to ensure a deep understanding of the customers' needs and the tasks they plan to perform.

- **Use a phased development approach:** Due to high user expectations and increased pressure to deliver quickly, it is common now for mobile development teams to release a "slim" app with basic functionality and, while working to resolve bugs, work toward an enhanced app with added features and functionality. A single version of the app can be broken into several development runs, but each release lives on in a new version. For example, a bank may develop a mobile app that helps people find an automatic teller machine (ATM). Their initial release may use a simple list of ATM locations based on geolocation. The second release may add a map showing the ATM location. The third release may add augmented reality, so you can point your phone camera down a street and see the location of the ATMs annotated in your camera view. The initial release meets the base function, but subsequent releases build on the first, improving quality and adding capabilities.

- **Develop storyboards:** Understanding the big picture of how end users complete a task is critical. Getting a visual understanding of how they work through their task and achieve their desired end goal is crucial to building the app.

- **Create journey maps:** Journey maps can be another useful way to understand the way end users move along a path to completing their task. The journey map can help illustrate the customers' needs, the steps customers take to accomplish a goal, and their emotional state along the way. The journey map can help show potential steps that could be simplified during the task.

- **Use wireframes:** Once you have a solid understanding of the customers' wants and needs, a sketch of the actual app can help to reinforce and validate requirements, accelerate the project, and improve quality by getting early customer feedback. Getting wireframes in the hand of stakeholders and project sponsors is critical to getting initial feedback and validating the scope of the effort.

- **Design:** Defining a high-quality user experience for mobile and using the latest device features and UI to optimize the user experience is essential. Employing the design skills of the team is an important part of getting the user experience built into the process early. A skilled information architect is key for understanding how the actions flow from screen to screen and managing the limitation of screen size. Some firms do not have this skill in-house and therefore may consider bringing in the skill on a contractual basis. However, having the design skills integrated into the development team throughout the process is critical. As you will see, the app requires continuous updating and maintenance as customer feedback is understood through continued feedback collection. Coordination between design and development is vital. The two skills often come from two different backgrounds and thought processes. A developer rarely has deep design skills and vice versa. However, they need to be brought together to provide the best function and user experience. The design team needs to understand the constraints the developer faces, and the developer must have similar insight into the design process.

- **Use nonfunctional prototypes:** Using a design tool to build screen shots that look and feel like the app with button placement and menus can be helpful to get a sense of the app. Without any coding, nonfunctional prototypes can show screen layout and how functional elements relate to each other. These screen shots can be loaded onto a device and provided to test subjects to get early feedback.

- **Use an integrated development platform with extensible tools:** The development environment must be robust and geared toward rapid development. Simplicity is critical so that teams can execute quickly and be responsive. The tool environment needs to support mobile OS software development kits (SDK) and third-party frameworks. Extensibility of an overall mobile life-cycle platform needs to take into account a diverse development team where each role or project team may have its own preferred tools. Mobile teams are marked by small but focused teams, and with specific skills. There may be a developer skilled on particular OS platforms, a UI designer, a mobile tester, an integration and back-end developer, a product manager and a team lead. The team needs to function at top speed to keep up with the rate and pass of a mobile development project. Collaboration will be critical.

■ **Development tools should be visually oriented:** Allowing the developer to easily see the look and feel of the app as it is developed is critical to ensure a high-quality look and feel. At the same time, the developer needs full control of the underlying code to ensure that the app is optimized from a user experience and performance perspective.

■ **Avoid code generation:** Some in the industry offer code generation to achieve cross-platform development. In other words, they create their app in a design tool or a proprietary language. Then their tool environment generates an app for each mobile platform. This approach should be avoided because it becomes difficult to optimize user experience and performance. In addition, it is difficult to maintain the app because the underlying code is machine-generated, and rapid adjustments and defect correction become a challenge.

■ **Centralized build can reduce cost and complexity:** Build setup and configuration for each device environment will be different, and skills to maintain the infrastructure may be scarce within an organization. As such, a build environment can be centrally managed and provisioned to handle multiple operating systems while reducing the cost of setting up and managing a unique environment.

■ **Use change control:** Mobile projects are marked by frequent changes. As new customer feedback comes in, any needed changes must be rolled into the code. Therefore, having a process to manage changes is more important than ever. The process of making changes or rolling back changes should be simple and fast. This way, the development teams stay efficient.

■ **Incorporate traceability:** As developers work on features, their progress needs to be tracked so that the rest of the team understands the progression. This way the team knows what is being worked on, the progress, and which features are completed. If, during testing, a defect is discovered, it needs to be linked to a particular change or feature. Due to the speed of mobile development, traceability, which shows how defects are linked to particular code change and requirement, is critical. You need to trace back to the original requirements and build; then correlate the defect with a particular code change. You can quickly determine how the defect arose and how it is related to the overall requirements. Full traceability provides an end-to-end view of a project and can help avoid needless effort when tracking where an issue came from and how it relates to the overall project requirements.[1]

- **Collaboration:** Coordination of agile development teams throughout the development process is critical, especially if you have teams focused on a variety of device operating systems.

- **Design for reuse:** Organizations should identify and build components that can be reused across apps so that each new app developed can leverage existing assets, which will accelerate delivery. Reuse can help harden core components while simplifying the development process.

- **Quality Management:** Unlike a traditional PC/Web application where users provide feedback directly to you through a web interface, mobile apps are different. Since the app is running on a mobile device and obtained through an app store, it is a challenge to collect end user feedback. As such, you should consider a set of capabilities such as automatic monitoring of social networks for conversations about your app, automatic collection of app feedback, tracking app store comments, crash detection and logging, and in-app bug reporting.

- **Provide robust management and security:** Building a mobile app is only part of an overall life cycle. After the app is deployed, how is it managed? You need to consider how you can remotely disable or update an app after it is deployed and downloaded from an app store. You need to integrate with existing security and authentication systems. The app should be scanned for potential security vulnerabilities. The issue of app management and security is critical to delivering an overall mobile strategy. More details on this topic are discussed in Chapter 6, "Mobile Security and Management."

In summary, these development process requirements point to the need for a comprehensive mobile application development platform which supports an integrated end-to-end application life cycle. This ensures the various teams, tools, and artifacts are linked and coordinated throughout the mobile development process. To deliver at the speed and quality expected of a mobile project, development teams need to be efficient, staying coordinated and moving quickly on their feet as new insight comes in from customers.

App design and user experience need to be part of the process from the start, ensuring that the entire app development process is customer-driven and focused on the highest quality. This is why testing and continued customer experience management is so critical. Not only is testing one of the most important aspects of the development process, it is also one of the biggest hurdles in the development process due to the fragmentation and diversity of the mobile devices.

Mobile Testing

Testing for mobile devices is significantly more complicated than traditional application testing. It seems that every day a new mobile phone or tablet is announced with an increasing number of players entering the market. This apparent endless supply of mobile devices is great for the consumer because it provides more choices. However, this creates a challenge for a mobile development team that might not have much control over the devices it needs to support for its customer or employees. For the development team, the challenge lies in the diversity of mobile platforms that need to be considered for testing. The development team needs to consider not only the variation of devices, but also the variation in operating systems and device features. Things become complicated when you consider that your app might function differently depending on what network it is running on. Even the carriers can make minor changes to the underlying OS (for example, Android), which can introduce even more variability. You can have a test matrix of hundreds or thousands of permutations. The problem becomes compounded with the seemingly weekly release of new devices in the market, which means new device models need to be incorporated into your test plan on a regular basis. To maintain appropriate test coverage, as much as 20 percent of your devices may need to be replaced with new models introduced into the market each quarter.

In addition, the mobile app may be connected to a broad set of mobile services and back-end systems, which create more challenges with testing. Setting up and maintaining back-end systems for testing can be costly and take time. Setting up and shutting down back-end test environments can add overhead that is not welcomed in a development effort that needs to move quickly.

Manual testing is the first approach that people start with; although, this can become expensive over time. Written test scripts and instructions are distributed to each manual tester to perform the test. However, every test requires a set of instructions for each specific configuration of each device and back-end system. This approach can be an expensive and time-consuming proposition.

Some in the industry are forced to deal with the challenges of mobile testing by simply doing what they can. Some will throw up their hands and decide not to have the required level of device and back-end test coverage. Instead, they test against a few available devices owned by the developers. But this puts the quality of their mobile app at risk. Alternatively, here are practices that can address the challenges of mobile testing, help speed up the test process, and improve the overall speed and quality of the test results:

- **Simulate:** Rapidly checking how the app looks and functions is important during the development process. A simulator that duplicates the behavior of the device can help guide the developers as they create the app and can reduce some of the overhead of testing on an actual physical device.

- **Emulate:** An emulator is software that duplicates the function of the hardware components of the device (such as chipsets and memory). The software emulator that is part of the mobile operating system SDK can give the most accurate sense of how the applications will interact with the device. However, emulators can at times be slow and unresponsive when compared with a simulator. This is where the combination of simulators and emulators can help. Simulators can provide a quick check of the behavior of the app. Then the emulator can be used to get a more accurate idea of how the app will function.

- **Gather feedback with a controlled release through a private app store:** Distributing the app through a private app store to employees outside of the development team allows for critical feedback early in the development process. Using a private app store provides a convenient and familiar (star rating and comments) means of collecting feedback, which can be straightforward and less intimidating on those providing feedback. After the feedback has been gathered and provided to the development teams, the app can be updated and resubmitted to the app store. This iterative process can help improve the app.

- **Device clouds:** Access to a broad set of devices needed to conduct testing can be simplified by using a device cloud where banks of devices are hosted and can be "rented" for virtual use over the cloud. There are several device clouds available in the market today. The advantage is that a device can actually physically reside in various parts of the world allowing for validation against different networks and environments. Reducing the cost of procuring and managing a mobile device can significantly reduce the cost and speed of development. Many device clouds offer the ability to perform playback of test failures by viewing the interaction virtually over the web or through a captured video.

- **Automated testing:** The ability to perform automated testing can significantly reduce the time and effort for testing a mobile app. Automated test scripts generated during the app development process can be used to test the function of the app across various devices.[2] Having automatic playback and validation of test scenarios can greatly reduce the test process.

- **Security vulnerability testing:** There also needs to be vulnerability testing to ensure that the coding techniques used to write the app do not introduce security vulnerabilities into the app during development.

- **Virtual back-end systems:** Setting up a variety of back-end systems only to tear them back down after a test can be costly. Instead of setting up physical back-end systems, a virtual environment can greatly reduce cost and increase execution speed. Virtual back-end environments that simulate traditional back-end systems can be helpful during the early phases of development. As the project progresses, actual back-end systems can be added for further testing.

Continuous Experience Management

One thing is clear with mobility—user expectations are high. Users have little patience for poor mobile experiences and expect the quality of the mobile experience to be better than the web experience. You cannot afford to cut corners in quality in mobile because the impact not only can have a negative impact on your mobile business, but also a poor mobile experience can extend to other parts of your business. Individuals are less likely to do business with a company (in-store or on the web) if they first have a poor mobile experience. In addition, mobile users are more social and likely to spread the word that they have encountered a problem with your app. You can easily see this demonstrated in the public feedback through the mobile app stores.

After an app is published in the public app store, the feedback and star ratings are there for everyone to see. The market expects a five-star app, and even employees will not be satisfied with a mediocre app experience.

The mobile app is a representation of your company's brand. A successful app can have a positive impact on your broader business, whereas a negative experience can have devastating consequences. Compared to a web application, mistakes have an even greater impact on a business and its brand. Building a mobile app requires lots of end-user feedback before, during, and after development. There needs to be an approach that balances speed and quality.

Mobile presents new challenges for developers trying to deliver a top-quality user experience. There is a far greater diversity of devices and platforms that can introduce unintended app behavior and defects not found during testing. The mobile form factor is smaller than the web application, and users expect a simple, responsive, and easy-to-use mobile experience. Given the diversity in device types and form factors, there are few best practices for mobile usability that developers can rely on to help guide them in their app development. There are also new technologies and interaction models such as Near Field Communications (NFC), barcode reading, camera, location-based offers, and "check-ins" that may add value for the end user but may introduce a poor experience if not delivered appropriately. In short, the mobile experience creates new opportunities to engage customers and employees. The stakes are high given the impact mobile has on a company's brand and reputation. As a result, you need to analyze how your customer interacts with your app to determine issues and failures in completing a task. However, it may not be as simple as inserting tags or beacons in the code to validate anticipated behavior. Instead, you need a comprehensive strategy to monitor end-user behavior that collects as much data as possible while maintaining privacy and not interfering with the performance of the app.

Given the nascent nature of the mobile market in general, it is very likely that customers will use mobile apps in ways not anticipated by the developers or testers. Mobile development has been around for only a few years, so best practices are still being defined. For example, one of the most common mistakes companies make is that they design for the PC but expect the mobile user to accept it. However, the PC and mobile experience are different. For example, the notion of touch-click, stretch to refresh, shake to trigger event, rotate to change view, and so on are inherently mobile user experiences that do not exist with a PC. If companies do not introduce mobile-specific behaviors into their apps, they will lose the user.

Also, because distribution through an app store is not real time (often requiring weeks to be approved for release by the app store owners) it can take a long time to get an app updated. As a result, it will be important to instrument an app to gather a complete view of how the end user interacts with the app. In addition, the mobile end user will be interacting across various channels. They may use a mobile device in a store to check a price or call customer service directly from the app to check the status of an order. The interactions across channels can produce unintended behavior and potentially new customer interaction issues. Also, your mobile app should anticipate new behavior and introduce intelligence that might change the behavior of the app to meet the needs of the users trying to complete a task. The intelligent app can introduce behavior that may not have been anticipated and is impossible to test. In the end, you need to deliver a Customer Experience Management (CEM) strategy.

CEM is about developing a deep understanding of how customers interact with a business and removing the obstacles that cause them to struggle. CEM helps determine what works, what does not work, and why. This is achieved by capturing user information both across the network and at the device. This collection of data is then analyzed to discover potential user problems. Because the entire interaction is collected, you can perform deep forensics on the customer interaction and behavior. As potential errors are found, because the complete set of data is collected, you can do interesting analysis such as app playback. App playback allows you to play back the user experience, like watching a video, to see how the customer interacted with the app and then discover if they are struggling to perform a task.

CEM enables you to deliver higher-quality apps faster by enabling you to launch and iterate quickly with less risk of failure. Because you capture all the user interaction, you can have a deeper understanding in near real time without waiting for the customer to provide feedback. You can also pinpoint the actual interaction so that you can link the error to the potential revenue lost. Then you can decide which errors to fix and which to deal with at a later date.

Types of Mobile Apps

In formulating a mobile strategy, you must understand how to consistently build, deploy, manage, and secure the types of applications your customers and employees need. As a result you need to understand the major types of mobile applications and their characteristics: native, web, and hybrid. A native mobile application is built using the mobile device vendors' SDKs and programming model. Mobile web applications are delivered via the mobile device browser. Mobile hybrid applications bring together some of the best features from both web and native applications. Each approach has a set of trade-offs and considerations.

Native Mobile Applications

Native mobile applications are built using mobile device vendor SDKs, such as provided by Apple (for iOS) and Google (for Android). To develop the mobile application, the developer must use the unique language associated with a particular device operating system. This, of course, requires unique skill and expertise for each targeted mobile device. The source code developed with the device SDK is compiled into an executable file for a particular mobile device platform. Native mobile applications are binary executable files that you download and execute directly on the device. As a result, applications written for one device cannot be used for another. An end user would likely obtain the application through an app store or marketplace. App stores might include a public app store, such as Apple's App Store, Google Play, or a private app store provided within an organization. A mobile native application could also be installed by an IT Department on an end user device. When installed, a native mobile application executes directly within the mobile operating system outside the browser.

A native mobile application has direct access to native features of the mobile device. These native features may include such things as the camera, compass, and accelerometer. Because mobile native applications are built using the device SDK, a mobile developer has access to the unique user interface components of the device. As such, the user interface of native mobile applications often have the unique attributes of the mobile device, which may appeal to end user expectations. In other words, a native mobile application does not deliver a lowest common denominator user experience, rather it provides the unique user experience the device has to offer. Figure 5.1 shows the native mobile application running within the mobile OS of the particular device.

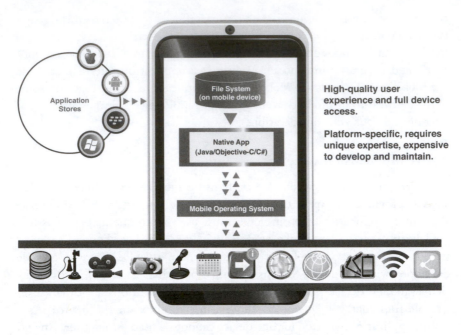

Figure 5.1 Native mobile application.

The native mobile app has a set of advantages that offer attributes that are important in certain situations as outlined in the following list.

- **Native API access:** The user has access to native features of the phone to utilize the features the phone has to offer. Native API access may include:
  - Playing sounds through the speakers or headphones of the device
  - Access to the device camera to take photographs or videos
  - Receive position and orientation information via the accelerometer
  - Read and write data to the device storage
  - Access to calendar, contact list, and so on
  - Well suited for graphically intensive applications such as games
- **User experience:** The user is able to utilize the device supplied UI (User Interface) components such as buttons, input fields, menu items, dialog boxes, and unique gesture interface interaction. This gives the application a look and feel that reflects the experience the user expects from the mobile device.

- **Public app store delivery:** Native mobile applications make it possible to distribute your mobile application through a public app store. If you intend to sell your mobile application or see benefits in obtaining user ratings, delivery of a mobile application through an app store might provide an advantage.

The native mobile app has some disadvantages that need to be considered within your overall mobile strategy as well:

- **Complexity:** Because each mobile device has its own programming model and language, building a mobile application for multiple platforms can be complex and expensive.
- **Unique skills:** Specific skills are needed for each device platform. In many cases, these skills may be difficult to come by and expensive to acquire.
- **Higher management cost:** Because a native application must be written for each platform, maintenance can be high. There is no common code across platforms that can help to reduce maintenance and support costs. In addition, when a native application is deployed to a public app store, users are required to update the applications on their own. This can make upgrades and patch maintenance a challenge.
- **Nonportable:** Because the native mobile app is built using the unique programming model of the mobile device, it is inherently nonportable across device types (Apple iOS, Android, Windows Phone, Blackberry, and such). This is a clear disadvantage when considering a cross-device strategy because you need a specific development team for each platform, adding cost to the overall mobile project.

Mobile Web Applications

Mobile web site technology has evolved from web scraping in the early days of mobile in which companies would simply scrape a few data points from their corporate web site and deliver them as the mobile web site (usually hosted by third-party companies). This typically resulted in poor user experience and often a broken mobile web site that couldn't keep up with the changing corporate site. Today's smartphones and tablets universally have full web browsing support. The web browser capabilities of smartphones support the latest web technologies such as HTML 5, CSS 3, and JavaScript.

It is possible that mobile devices will be the primary way your customers and employees access your web presence. As you develop your mobile strategy, you should ensure that your traditional corporate web site can be easily consumed on mobile devices. Your corporate web site might recognize when a mobile device accesses the web site and then deliver a mobile-friendly version of your web site, or a mobile app designed for mobile device access and navigation.

When developing a mobile presence for your corporate web site, you might also consider a responsive web design. Responsive web design is a web development approach that enables a web site to adjust to the device's interface from which the web site is viewed. In other words, the web site can adjust its presentation based on screen size, platform, and orientation of the viewing device. The web designer would develop the web site using flexible grids and layouts based on the use of CSS3 media queries. The site would automatically respond to how the user views the web site. For example, when the end user views the site from a desktop browser, the menu bar may be at the top of the site. Then, when the site is viewed on a mobile device, the navigation would shrink to a drop-down menu. Responsive design keeps the web app developer from having to build a mobile app for each device screen size, resolution, and orientation.

In addition, you might design a mobile web app that is unrelated to a corporate web site and designed specifically for mobility. A mobile web app has a similar feel to a native application and is built completely with web technologies such as HTML, CSS, and JavaScript. It executes completely within the mobile web browser. To accomplish this mobile application look and feel, the industry has delivered a set of JavaScript toolkits to help developers create a rich user experience. These toolkits include UI components that are comparable in look and feel to native apps, yet they function within the browser.

Mobile Toolkits

JavaScript mobile toolkits such as jQuery mobile and Dojo mobile are optimized for mobile browsers. They're lightweight and avoid dependencies on particular device platforms. They often provide a native look and feel through CSS themes for the particular mobile device platform OS. They provide unique platform controls and widgets. They also give the developer the ability to provide movement through CSS-based animation or JavaScript style animation. This can provide such experiences as flip slide and fade. They also respond to orientation and can change the look and feel of the mobile applications depending on whether the phone is horizontal or vertical.

The mobile web app, as shown in Figure 5.2, gives the broadest reach of all the mobile app types; however, the look and feel is not optimized for the mobile device and it has limited access to device capabilities such as the camera or accelerometer. It is also delivered via a web server and cannot be downloaded from an app store. However, like any web site, it is easily accessed (and bookmarked) from any device.

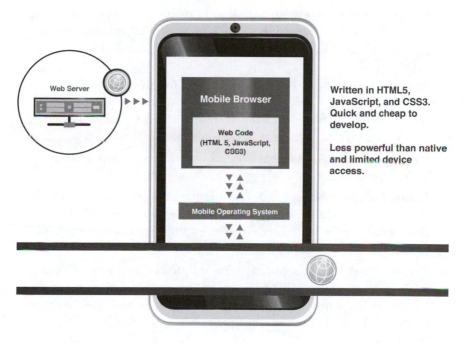

Figure 5.2 Mobile web application.

The core advantages of a mobile web app include the following:

- **Inherently cross-platform:** Almost all mobile phones and tablets include a mobile web browser. As a result, a mobile web app can have the widest reach. Furthermore, because they are accessed via a URL, mobile web applications can be integrated into existing web delivery vehicles such as SMS, QR codes, Twitter, Facebook, and search engines. This means that the app content can be searched by search engines.

■ **Immediate engagement:** Unlike native apps that require the end user to go to an app store to download and install an app, mobile web applications are immediately accessible by your target audience.

■ **Lower development costs:** Because mobile web apps are built using HTML, CSS, or JavaScript, the skills needed to build them are readily available in the market place or within an organization. Furthermore, mobile web applications are developed using classic web development tools, techniques, and testing processes.

■ **Lower cost of management:** Updates to mobile web applications are instantaneous. This makes it easier to keep your application current and provide end users with the latest features and bug fixes.

The disadvantages of a mobile app are as follows:

■ **Access to device features:** There is limited access to unique device capabilities such as the camera, accelerometer, and contact lists.

■ **Network access:** A persistent network connection is needed to run a mobile web application.

■ **Limited native look and feel:** User experience is limited to the capabilities provided by the browser; however, mobile JavaScript toolkits can dramatically improve the user experience and help to close the gap with mobile native applications.

■ **Performance:** Mobile applications must be loaded over a network and run within a browser. When compared to native applications, there can be perceivable performance limitation. However, technologies and techniques can be used to improve the performance of a mobile web application.

■ **App store presence:** In some cases you may want to establish a presence in an app store. If this is the case, you should consider a native or hybrid app since a mobile web app cannot be posted into an app store.

HTML5

HTML 5 is not a single technology, but an umbrella term for many interrelated improvements to HTML. HTML5 includes improvements to such capabilities as multimedia, animation, user interface, and storage. Major mobile operating system vendors have already adopted many of the capabilities of HTML5 before the latest specification has been finalized. HTML5 holds the promise of delivering cross-platform support for mobile applications regardless of the device type. As a result, HTML5 should be a core part of your overall mobile strategy.

Capabilities relevant to mobile devices and widely adopted across mobile device vendors include the following:

- **Gesture recognition:** A mobile application written in HTML5 has the capability to recognize gesture interactions such as swiping and pinching, and provides a touch and feel of a mobile application. HTML5 also enables drag and drop, which is ideal for the small touch interface of mobile devices.

- **Local storage:** HTML5 apps provide local storage within the browser memory. As a result, the mobile app does not need to go back to the server as frequently. This provides a more responsive user experience.

- **Location awareness:** Certainly one of the most significant value propositions a mobile app can provide is to leverage context based on an end user's location. In HTML5, a mobile app can obtain location information from the device, enabling a wide set of mobile-specific applications.

- **Rich visual experience:** With its canvas tag, HTML5 enables dynamic scriptable rendering of two dimensional shapes, which can be useful for graphs and charts. In addition, rich form elements and support for vector graphics can also enhance user experience.

Future of HTML5

The mobile device vendors must see the advantage of adopting HTML5 to expand the number of applications compatible with their platform. Many companies have gone down the path of pure HTML5 apps with great success. *The Financial Times* famously moved from native to HTML5 for a variety of business reasons.[3] However, there will always be some divergence between the state of the HTML5 specification and the actual features adopted by the mobile device vendors. It always takes time for standardization organizations to finalize and publish a web-related specification. In the meantime, mobile browser vendors will anticipate features before they are finalized by a standards organization. This creates some level of inconsistency. In addition, the rapid pace of innovation by mobile device manufacturers means there will always be new features not covered by the HTML5 specification.

From a mobile strategy perspective, HTML5 provides a clear path to protect your mobile application investment. Combining HTML5 with the hybrid mobile application approach can provide some clear advantages. The hybrid mobile application approach provides a native bridge (or container) giving the mobile application access to native features of the phone that HTML5 may not provide. Developers can still build their applications in HTML5 without compromising mobile application function. The hybrid model provides future protection. As the HTML5 specification matures, the hybrid container enables you to start using HTML5 today and to be ready for more extensive use of HTML5.

Hybrid Mobile Applications

Hybrid mobile applications combine capabilities from native and web mobile applications. A hybrid mobile application has two elements:

- Web technology such as HTML, JavaScript, and CSS
- A native bridge that gives your app access to native device features such as the camera, accelerometer, compass, and contacts.

The native bridge or container enables the hybrid mobile application to access the device features such as the camera or accelerometer. Developers can create their own container or use existing solutions such as Apache Cordova (an open source library that enables you to access device capabilities in a consistent way across various device operating systems). From an end user point of view, the app looks and feels just like a native application.

The primary characteristics of a hybrid app are that the core logic can be written in standard web technologies such as HTML, CSS, and JavaScript. The web-based functionality is wrapped as a native container that runs on the device OS. As a result, there is full access to native functionality from JavaScript access calls. Utilizing a true hybrid model, the developer can decide how much of the app will be written in web coding and how much in native code. This provides a great deal of flexibility and control. The hybrid mobile application can be packaged as a native mobile application and downloaded from an App Store. In many respects, the hybrid mobile app can be the best of both worlds. You can utilize existing web skills within an organization while at the same time have access to native functionality of the device. This can lower the cost of development and protect your investment. In addition, if you use HTML5 to build the hybrid application, you will not have to rebuild the application because HTML5 will gain functionality as the standards process progresses. For example, if in the future HTML5 provides access to the device camera, you can extend your existing HTML5 code within the hybrid app and not utilize the container functionality directly.

Figure 5.3 shows that the hybrid app uses web technologies for its core logic while using a native bridge to access the device capabilities. The hybrid app can also be downloaded from an app store, which may have some advantages from a distribution and branding perspective.

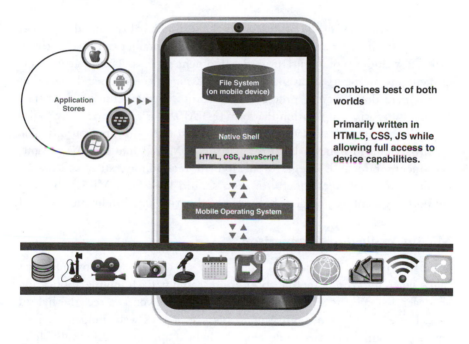

Figure 5.3   Mobile hybrid applications.

The advantages of the hybrid app include the following:

- **Use existing skills:** Because the hybrid mobile application is built using HTML, CSS, and JavaScript, readily available (and lower cost) development skills can be utilized.

■ **High performance:** A hybrid mobile application approaches native application user experience expectations in performance and user interaction.

■ **Access to native functionality:** Because a hybrid mobile application provides a bridge to the native function on the mobile device, it can access features such as the camera, accelerometer, or any future functionality.

■ **App store distribution:** A hybrid mobile app functions within a native container providing a mechanism for distribution through an app store or marketplace.

The disadvantage of the hybrid app is the setup. A hybrid mobile application may require initial setup so that the hybrid container can be effectively utilized within a typical enterprise development process. Third-party development environments are available that can assist in the setup and execution of a hybrid development process. This points to the value of an overall Mobile Enterprise Application Platform (MEAP). It is a comprehensive suite of products and services that enable development of mobile applications. The term was coined by the analyst firm Gartner. A MEAP, like IBM Worklight, can incorporate and integrate the hybrid technology, such as Apache Cordova, into an overall platform. You should look for a MEAP that can support any combination of web, hybrid, and native app development.

Mobile Application Comparison

As you can see in Figure 5.4, there are a set of considerations you must make when selecting a mobile application strategy. Each mobile application approach has specific strengths and weaknesses. As you can see, the hybrid model offers the best of both worlds. Because it uses web standards for its core logic, skills necessary to develop the hybrid app are readily available in the market place. In addition, the hybrid app has similar portability to that of a web app while delivering the performance, functionality, and user experience of a native app.

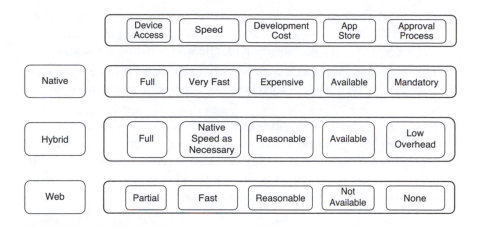

Figure 5.4 Mobile application comparison.

Strategic Decision Making

As you develop your mobile application strategy, you need to think through a set of strategic decisions:

- **Is user experience and performance critical?** The answer may be a function of the expectations of your audience. You might want to invest in higher-performance applications such as a native or hybrid for consumer-facing applications, whereas employee-facing applications may have lower expectations and a web application may be sufficient.

- **Do you have a limited budget and schedule?** Limited budgets and schedules may point you to utilizing existing web skills, and a mobile web app or hybrid application may make the most sense.

- **Do you need to access the device capabilities?** If you need to utilize features such as the compass, camera, and accelerometer for advanced mobile application, you should consider a hybrid or native application.

- **Do you plan to monetize your application?** If you plan to charge money for you application, you may want to distribute through an app store, in which case, you would consider a native or hybrid mobile application.

- **Is management and support critical?** If you anticipate that your application will exist for a long time and will require ongoing maintenance and support, you should consider a mobile web or hybrid application.
- **Do you plan to support a wide variety of devices?** If you plan to support just one type of application, a native application may make sense.

Figure 5.5 shows a set of possible decisions you may make as you work through the choices associated with the type of mobile app. However, a word of caution regarding the mobile app decision process depicted in the diagram. It is not always a linear set of decisions; you need to also consider issues such as budget, available skills, and resource allocation.

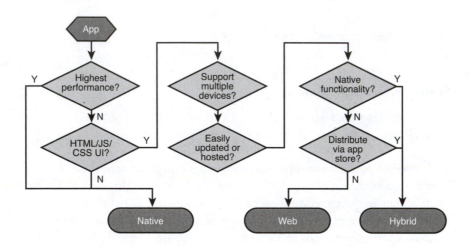

Figure 5.5   Mobile application decision tree.

Determining your mobile application type can be one of the most important first steps in defining your overall mobile strategy. Each mobile application type has its own strengths and weaknesses. Understanding your budget, schedule, target audience, and management requirements can help you to determine the type of application required. For the foreseeable future, you need to support a wide variety of mobile devices with an ever-changing landscape of features and functionality. It is clear that HTML5 will be a critical cross-platform technology that has the promise of enabling cross-device mobile applications. However, adoption of HTML5 features will lag behind the latest device features. Therefore you must understand all the mobile application types and choose the right approach for your particular use case and scenario. You should leverage a Mobile Enterprise Application Platform to help manage the complexity and provide the appropriate level of security, management, integration, and governance for your overall mobile application development strategy.

Mobile Connectivity and Integration

Integration to back-end systems will be critical in that extending your core business processes, systems, and data is what separates you from your competitors. Your systems are what make your business what it is. As such, getting these valuable services and data into the hands of the mobile user is fundamentally the goal of any mobile strategy. As you build your mobile strategy, look for these core requirements.

- **Flexible and fast system and data integration:** As you build your mobile solution, you want to move with speed and agility. You do not want to get bogged down in extended integration projects that are complicated and use valuable time and energy. A mobile platform should have flexible connectivity to back-end systems that enable a wide variety of services and formats. You will likely connect to traditional and cloud services. Visual tools that deliver connectivity with little or no coding are ideal. Look for solutions that have a rich set of predefined integration templates that can help accelerate the integration project. This allows you to move with speed and reduce the overhead of complicated integration coding while maintaining repeatability.

  Your mobile connectivity solution also needs to bring together extended capabilities around your connections to improve the quality of the integration. With your system and data integration, you need to bring together the appropriate security and caching capabilities to ensure that the connection has the highest quality of service and is protected from external threats. You also need to ensure the back-end systems can support the traffic that mobile solutions initiate. Mobile event volume is significantly higher than online event volume. Scalability is a big issue, and if not done right or not tested ahead of time, a mobile project can be derailed. Finally, there needs to be centralized monitoring of your connectivity to ensure that as systems and user interaction evolve, the intended integration is still aligned with business needs. As parameters fall out of specification—these monitoring systems should adjust and provide the appropriate corrective action.

- **Managing back-end events:** Getting a back-end event to the mobile device is not a simple prospect given the variety of devices in the market today. An event can be communicated to a mobile device through a push notification or SMS message. *Push notification* is a means of sending information to your phone or tablet (via a badge, alert, or pop-up message) even when the app isn't in use. Push notifications are sent via a data network and are therefore dependent on an available data plan or Wi-Fi network, while SMS messages are not dependent on a data plan. Each device has its own push notification protocol that is unique and incompatible with each other, whereas SMS is available across devices. As such, getting the notification to the right device in the right format can be a challenge. This is where a mobile middleware platform (MEAP) can provide a great deal of value. Having a common interface for all back-end events so that they can be routed to the right device in the right format regardless of the device type can add a great deal of value.

- **API management:** API and service management need to be an important part of an overall mobile strategy. The proliferation of mobile devices and application increases the need for interaction with back-end and third-party services. As you deliver a comprehensive mobile solution, it comes down to the end user's journey and how he moves toward his goal of completing a task. Often there will be a need for a set of composite services from multiple providers requiring federation and management of the APIs and services. In a multichannel situation, services need to work across a wide variety of mobile device platforms as well as non-mobile platforms. The APIs must be delivered in a format that is friendly to mobile devices such as JSON and REST. You need to ensure end-to-end data privacy and integrity. The API management systems need to analyze the activity across the set of APIs (both internally and partner APIs) to understand usage and activity. Analytics and big data need to be tied in so that you can understand how the services may be augmented to improve the quality or have insight into which new services to deliver.

Summary

Building mobile applications that are compelling, engaging, and that can transform the way your business interacts with your employees and customers is the cornerstone of any mobile strategy. As mobile interaction becomes the primary means by which your customers and employees engage with your company, the app development process becomes critical to your overall business strategy. However, building mobile apps has some unique characteristics that will cause you to rethink your traditional thinking toward development.

The unique characteristics of mobility are marked by high user expectations for quality and speed of delivery. At the same time, the mobile app development team has to contend with diversity on the front end due to a fragmented device marketplace and diversity on the back requiring flexible and adaptive connectivity. These unique characteristics of mobility require you to think differently about your development execution while fitting in with your corporate development overall processes, governance, and life-cycle management. You need to rethink the development process for unprecedented speed and quality. Incorporate new approaches to simplify the testing process, and make continuous experience management a fundamental tenant of the overall development process. Finally, ensure that the process of integrating to back-end systems and managing back-end events and third-party services are flexible, fast, and adaptive to the demands of your customers.

Endnotes

[1] IBM software. "A Mobile Application Development Primer": http://public.dhe.ibm.com/common/ssi/ecm/en/raw14302usen/ RAW14302USEN.PDF

[2] Ibid.

[3] TechCrunch. "FT Bypasses Apple's iTunes, Launches HTML5 Web App (Free Access First Week)": http://techcrunch.com/2011/06/07/ft-bypasses-apples-itunes-launches-html5-web-app-free-access-first-week/

Additional Sources

Example Mobile Enterprise Application Platform (MEAP) that supports hybrid development: IBM Worklight®: http://www-01.ibm.com/software/mobile-solutions/worklight/

Examples of device clouds:

    Device Anywhere: http://www.keynotedeviceanywhere.com/

    Perfecto Mobile: http://www.perfectomobile.com/portal/cms/index.html

Example of a continuous experience management solution: IBM Tealeaf: http://www.tealeaf.com/

Examples of HTML5-based apps: http://www.openappmkt.com/

Status on HTML5 browser support:

    http://mobilehtml5.org/

    http://html5test.com/results/mobile.html

    http://caniuse.com/

6

Mobile Security and Management

In 2000, there were only 720 million mobile subscribers in the world; this was only 12 percent of the world's population.[1] In 2011 there were more than 6 billion mobile subscribers, growing to nearly 87 percent of the world's population.[2] By 2016, more than 350 million people will use their personally owned mobile device for work (Bring Your Own Device [BYOD]). They willl be able to work anywhere, anytime—increasing employee productivity and satisfaction.[3] The key requirement for a successful BYOD program is management and security.

Mobile devices can be twice as appealing to hackers because they contain both business and personal data. Access to mobile devices has never been easier through many new network connections and thousands of mobile apps. In early 2012, there were more than 11 billion Android apps downloaded.[4] With all this activity, mobile devices have grown to become an enticing target for hackers. A recent analysis shows that more than 90 percent of top paid mobile apps have been hacked.[5]

Security is more critical than ever. In order for your business to have an effective mobile strategy, you must pay close attention to security. You need to understand the unique characteristics of mobile and how it is relevant to security. Employees and consumers need to be educated about the importance of security so that they see it as something of value, rather than a burden.

Mobile Has Unique Characteristics That Impact Security

In many ways, securing mobile devices has much in common with securing other endpoints such as PCs and servers. However, mobile smartphones and tablets introduce a number of unique challenges because they were originally designed for the consumer. Although RIM (now BlackBerry) had its roots in the enterprise market with robust security, Apple and Google were developed for the consumer market and have gradually evolved to incorporate enterprise features. That said, unlike RIM, Apple iOS and Android can be made enterprise-ready with software middleware. An additional challenge to security is that consumer games and other highly interactive apps have established a high bar for user experience. As these devices come into the enterprise, the expectations of high user experience can make securing and managing a mobile device a challenge.

Mobile Devices Are Used Differently Than PCs

Mobile devices, like smartphones and tablets, are used differently than PCs. Although the lines between PCs and tablets are beginning to blur, particularly with the introduction of Windows 8, there are still differences that impact security.

- **Mobile devices are shared more often:** Smartphones and tablets are multipurpose personal devices. Therefore, users share them with friends and family more often than traditional computing devices—laptops and desktops.

- **Mobile devices are used in more locations and are always on:** Smartphones and tablets are usually powered on and connected to the network (Wi-Fi and cellular). Unlike laptops and PCs that are often connected to known, trusted networks, mobile devices are frequently used on public wireless networks that are unknown and unsecure. Being able to connect securely to corporate networks is a key requirement.

- **Mobile devices prioritize user experience:** Smartphones and tablets place a premium on user experience, and any security requirement that diminishes the user experience will not be adopted or will be circumvented.

- **Mobile devices have multiple personas:** Smartphones and tablets may have multiple personas—entertainment device, work tool, and so on, and they may even support multiple use accounts. Each persona is used in a different context. Users may want to employ a different security model for each persona. There needs to be a balance between personal ownership of the devices and protection of the business data.

- **Mobile devices are diverse:** The diversity of mobile devices makes it difficult to have a consistent security model, particularly when new devices come on the scene with immature security functions.

- **Mobile devices are easily lost or stolen:** An object that fits in your pocket or purse is easily left in a taxi or restaurant. Mobile devices are prone to loss and theft, thus becoming the weakest link in protecting corporate data.

- **Multiple paths to attacks and data loss exist:** The mobile device has many ways to interact with the world around it, providing a rich set of connectivity. Multi-network and storage access such as Wi-Fi, Bluetooth, telecom networks, memory cards, and cloud storage means more ways are needed to protect the device from unauthorized access or loss of data.

- **Mobile devices are appealing to hackers:** The mobile device has become the center of users' lives in many respects. The mobile device has become indispensable. It is the hub of connectivity, information access, and data and is indispensable. As a result, the mobile device has become a rich target for malicious individuals because once a device is compromised, they have complete access to personal (or corporate) data, contacts, network access, or can even tap into the camera and microphone of the device to spy on an individual. Recently, the usage of mobile devices has surpassed PC usage, making it well worth a hackers time to develop malicious code.

- **Mobile security architecture has some advantages over PCs:** Modern mobile operating systems isolate each app from every other app on the device. Apps aren't allowed to view or modify other data or logic, or even determine if another app is present on the device. In addition, apps cannot gain access to the OS operating system kernel. All third-party apps have the same limited level of device access and are ultimately controlled by the operating system and the user. This is in contrast to PC-based applications that can be easily installed into the operating system kernel and can obtain control of a system.

Enterprise Security Requirements

Enterprises often have strict security requirements for mobile devices, driven in many cases by government regulation. Corporate data stored on a mobile device is particularly vulnerable to loss or theft, data leakage, and malware—just to name a few. In addition, employees may also have personal data on the mobile device (photos, music, games, and so on) and there is a need to separate work and personal data. You must consider all the touch points this new technology has with the enterprise and consider the security implications. Management and security go hand in hand. You have to look beyond just securing the mobile device. You need to take a look at the big picture by securing and managing the device, the network, and the apps.

Mobile Device Management and Security

Mobile Device Management (MDM) and threat management software can help businesses secure and manage their employees' devices.

- **MDM:** It is clear that mobile devices are a critical tool for employees; however, you need to manage and secure these devices. Not every device should be allowed into the enterprise. Although BYOD has become popular, there needs to be a mechanism to allow devices that are secure while blocking those that are not. Some capabilities that come by default with a consumer-based phone may present a security threat to the organization. You need to manage access to corporate data, applications, and networks. Because mobile devices are easily lost or stolen, you must have a mechanism to lock or wipe a device remotely.

- **Mobile threat management:** As mobile devices grow in popularity, the potential for malicious attacks rises. As a result, you need a set of capabilities that protect the enterprise from malicious attacks. Antimalware, firewalls, and filtering software are designed to counter the latest attacks and prevent infiltration from hackers.

Mobile Network Management and Security

Most mobile devices don't have an Ethernet port. Access to the network is typically via Wi-Fi or cellular. The network becomes the critical link in defending against attacks, protecting access to the network and defining who has authorization to perform specific tasks on the corporate network. Network security involves the following aspects:

- **Mobile network protection:** It is critical that you protect the communication channel between your business and the mobile device or app. You must prevent unauthorized individuals from using a mobile device to eavesdrop or infiltrate the network.

- **Mobile identity and access management:** Controlling who (and which device) has access to the enterprise is critical to securing the mobile enterprise. Software and systems that provide identity management in the form of authorization and authentication are fundamental to determining who has access to the enterprise. Authentication asks the question, "How do I know you are who you say you are?" Authorization asks the question, "Okay, you are who you say you are; what are you allowed to do?" These two questions form the backbone to identity management and the associated technologies such as certificate management and multifactor authentication techniques.

Mobile Application Management and Security

Ultimately, the end user is going to be interacting with mobile apps and the associated data. As such, you need to consider how the interaction of people and corporate information is both secure and enables the end users to get their job done in the most-effective way. This can be done during deployment when the app is built. Security and management features can be added as the app is built and managed via a Mobile Enterprise Application Platform (MEAP) administration view. A complementary approach may be to have a separate Mobile Application Management (MAM) system. MAM is software and services that provision and control access to internally developed and commercially available mobile apps for businesses. Unlike MDM, which is focused on managing devices, MAM focuses specifically on application management and stops short of managing the entire device. For example, MAM solutions give administrators the ability to wipe corporate mobile apps and data from an end user's device and prevent future access to corporate applications and data without having to touch other apps or data on the device.

- **Mobile information protection:** A key goal is to protect corporate data. This becomes more challenging in a BYOD environment. Corporate data needs to be appropriately separated from personal data and protected.

- **Secure mobile application development and management:** Much can be done at the time of development to provide security protection for the enterprise. You can perform vulnerability testing to see if there are coding techniques that would introduce vulnerability. You can ensure the identity of the application at deployment so that malicious individuals cannot create a bogus version of your app that looks like your application but is actually a Trojan horse. You should also ensure the identity of your back-end services to prevent man-in-the-middle (MitM) attacks that trick the end user into thinking they can access your systems when actually a hacker is eavesdropping on the entire conversation. Finally, it is important that a mobile platform has the appropriate mechanism in place to remotely disable or update an app.

Mobile Security and Management Consideration

As you take into account all the enterprise requirements needed to provide a secure mobile enterprise, you need to consider an overall framework of key capabilities for mobile security and management. It is critical to have an end-to-end approach that looks at the security and management implications across devices, networks, and apps. Figure 6.1 illustrates the elements of a mobile security and management strategy. The rest of this chapter walks you through the elements of this mobile strategy framework, defining why they are important and how they work.

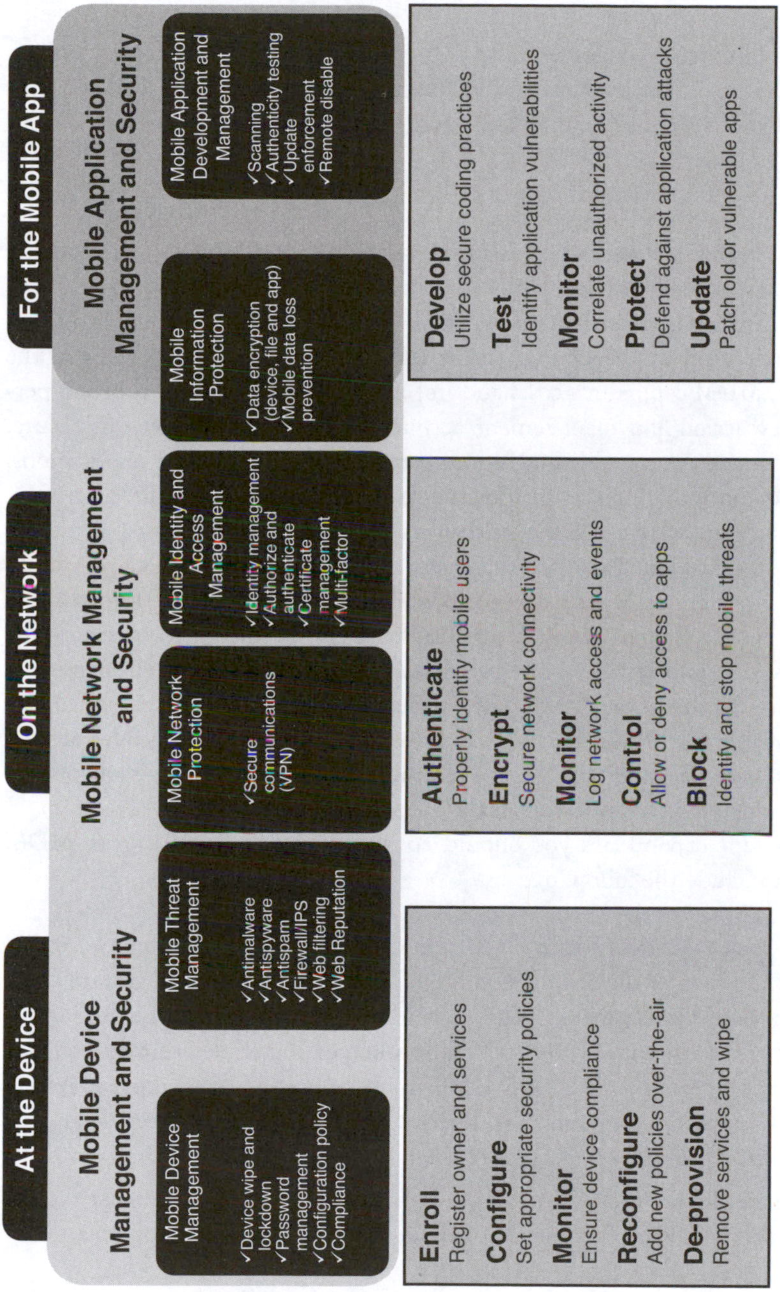

At the Device

On the Network

For the Mobile App

Mobile Device Management and Security

Mobile Network Management and Security

Mobile Application Management and Security

Mobile Device Management

Mobile Threat Management

Mobile Network Protection

Mobile Identity and Access Management

Mobile Information Protection

Mobile Application Development and Management

✓Device wipe and lockdown
✓Password management
✓Configuration policy
✓Compliance

✓Antimalware
✓Antispyware
✓Antispam
✓Firewall/IPS
✓Web filtering
✓Web Reputation

✓Secure communications (VPN)

✓Identity management
✓Authorize and authenticate
✓Certificate management
✓Multi-factor

✓Data encryption (device, file and app)
✓Mobile data loss prevention

✓Scanning
✓Authenticity testing
✓Update enforcement
✓Remote disable

Enroll
Register owner and services

Configure
Set appropriate security policies

Monitor
Ensure device compliance

Reconfigure
Add new policies over-the-air

De-provision
Remove services and wipe

Authenticate
Properly identify mobile users

Encrypt
Secure network connectivity

Monitor
Log network access and events

Control
Allow or deny access to apps

Block
Identify and stop mobile threats

Develop
Utilize secure coding practices

Test
Identify application vulnerabilities

Monitor
Correlate unauthorized activity

Protect
Defend against application attacks

Update
Patch old or vulnerable apps

Figure 6.1 Mobile security framework.

Mobile Device Management and Security

Mobile Device Management and Security is the ability to secure, monitor, manage, protect, and support mobile devices. This is accomplished through Mobile Device Management (MDM) and threat management software.

MDM

MDM is B2E software or cloud-based services that help to secure, monitor, and manage mobile devices deployed across an enterprise. MDM covers both company-owned and employee-owned devices (BYOD). By controlling and protecting the data and configuration settings for all mobile devices in the network, MDM can reduce costs and improve security. A MDM solution performs key action and management activities to ensure the device is secure. Device control is accomplished through remote distribution of applications, data, and configuration settings for the mobile devices within the enterprise. Device lock and wipe can disable a device and remove the data from the device if it is lost or stolen. Password management keeps track of device passwords ensuring they are up to date and periodically refreshed to meet corporate policy. The device content and settings also need to be established to ensure the device is functioning within the corporate guidelines—perhaps ensuring that the device is not allowed to sync up with a cloud service where data could be lost. Finally, only devices that fit within the corporate security guidelines can have access to the enterprise. So the mobile device must meet a set of compliance parameters to become part of the corporate infrastructure.[6]

Important capabilities you should consider when considering an MDM solution include the following:

- **Jailbreak/root detection:** To jailbreak (for Apple) or root (for Android) a device is to alter the operating system in order to get around certain restrictions the OS manufacturer has provided. As a result, the device is also compromised for security. A jailbroken or rooted device may pose a security threat when a BYOD deployment is used at an enterprise. As a result, the MDM system must detect a jailbroken or rooted device and prevent it from gaining access to the corporate systems.

- **Remote device lock/wipe:** The administrators lock or wipe clear the data on the device. This could be done at the device or the app level.

- **Encryption management:** Ensuring that encryption is turned on within the device or is appropriately enabled.

- **PIN/password enforcement:** Ensuring the device can be used only if the ID or password entered has been created according to corporate policy.

- **Location-based security:** Geofencing enables the administrator to define a set of policies and security controls based on your location. Perhaps if a doctor is at a hospital, she has a greater level of security access. Yet when she is in a coffee shop, she may have less access to corporate data since she is no longer located on the hospital campus.

- **Integration with internal systems:** Many corporations already have existing security systems in place for authentication and access. MDM solutions should have the ability to integrate with existing security systems.

- **Device inventory:** The IT administrator should have a view of the state of all the devices under management. This can help the IT team to have a view of the compliance, configuration, and security profile of the devices under management. This view should not just cover mobile but should also span PCs and servers.

- **Device configuration:** The administrator should be able to remotely configure the security and applications settings on the device.

- **Policy management:** Defining who has the right, based on role and directory of groups, to have access to certain apps.

- **Roaming device support:** The MDM system will notify you and the employee, and perhaps restrict the use of the phone, when an employee has begun to incur roaming charges on a corporate issued device.

- **Telecom expense management:** Telecom Expense Management (TEM) is important for managing the life cycle of a device: procurement, billing, provisioning, making payments, managing disputes, maintenance, contracts, and compliance. TEM capabilities can be integrated into MDM solutions as a means of managing compliance, disabling a device if payments are not up to date, and managing data and voice plans.

- **Remote updating:** Ensuring that employees have the appropriate OS version and apps installed on their device.

- **Remote control:** The IT administrator should remotely control the device to help in resolving issues the employees may have with their device.

- **Flexible deployment:** MDM solutions should provide a flexible deployment option such as on-premise or cloud-based deployments. Although most MDM deployments are on-premise, cloud-based deployments may appeal to organizations that might not have the means to set up and maintain an MDM infrastructure. As employees bring their devices into the enterprise, MDM solutions should have broad mobile platform support and stay current with the latest device and OS release versions.

- **Applications' whitelists and blacklists:** Whitelisted apps are apps that have been sanctioned by the employer and can be used on the device. Blacklisted apps, on the other hand, are applications that are not allowed to be downloaded on the device. These apps may have been determined to be a security risk or are outside the scope of the employee's allowed applications.

- **Remediation:** MDM solutions should provide a wide variety of responses to a device out of compliance. You want to have the flexibility to warn an employee or selectively limit corporate access if the employee is out of compliance. The MDMs should have the flexibility to remediate noncompliant situations instead of simply killing and wiping the device.

Mobile Threat Management

Malicious users have typically focused on PCs as their primary target for attack; however, as smartphone and tablet shipments have outpaced PC shipments, the large number of mobile users has created an attractive target for malicious attacks.

As mobile devices become more complex with many more access points (Bluetooth, Wi-Fi, 3G, 4G/LTE, NFC, and so on), the potential opportunity for malicious attacks is increasing. The easy access to apps that can be downloaded and executed on the device opens the opportunities for threats of counterfeit apps, Trojan horses, and other malware. The popularity of these mobile devices makes them a prime target for hackers. The trend is clear, the number of exploits targeting particular vulnerabilities of mobile devices is on the rise.

Securing mobile devices becomes more challenging as BYOD becomes more prevalent in the enterprise, subsequently increasing the opportunity for malware attacks. Businesses are concerned that malicious software could be contained within a personally owned device. This virus could attack the corporate network or could steal corporate data that might reside on the personal mobile device or the back-end corporate infrastructure. In addition, even in the case of corporate-issued devices, there is an issue of end users downloading apps from public app stores. These apps have the potential of introducing a security vulnerability into the organization.

So what is a mobile strategy leader to do? One approach might be to have a complete mobile lockdown. This approach would be to either eliminate mobile devices all together or have strict usage of a few types of mobile devices with limited applications. Although this approach may be the most secure, it is obviously the least effective for employees and customers. A mobile security strategy should be flexible enough to equip employees and customers with the latest mobile applications and device features, while at the same time provide the best security. This approach gives the business a clear competitive advantage and enables businesses to truly harness the power and capabilities of mobile technology. The key to providing both a secure mobile environment while at the same time enabling employees and customers with the latest mobile technology involves visibility. You need to constantly understand and see what devices and applications are used within an enterprise, look for potential threats, and then adjust security appropriately. This might involve grouping people into classes of users and thus providing certain users more trust than others. As such, the following section outlines the key mobile threats in the marketplace today. It also addresses how a business is to defend against mobile threats and provides a recommended mobile security strategy within the context of an overall mobile security framework.

Types of Mobile Threats

A key aspect of an overall mobile strategy is to define an approach to protect your organization against mobile threats. As a result, you must understand the types of mobile threats and the techniques hackers take when trying to attack an organization.

Mobile Malware

Malware, or malicious software, is designed to disrupt mobile devices, gather sensitive information, or gain unauthorized access to computer systems. Essentially, it is a software program or script designed to exploit a mobile device or compromise an enterprise back-end system. Malware has become commonplace as individuals use their PCs on a day-to-day basis. You have been trained, through experience, to have the appropriate antivirus software, firewalls, and latest updates installed on PCs. However, mobile devices are in many ways a new paradigm for individuals. Often, individuals consider mobile devices to be more secure than PCs. Depending on the mobile device, there might be some truth to this assumption; however, the growing popularity and proliferation of mobile devices has made smartphones and tablets attractive targets for malicious individuals who want to gain access to corporate secrets, financial assets, or simply grow their reputation.

Mobile malware comes in several forms: spyware, viruses, Trojan horses, and worms. The goal of the malicious user is to gather sensitive information, steal unauthorized access to bank accounts and other repositories of value, or make the end-user unknowingly get charged for premium services such as SMS, phone service, click through ads, and so on.

Spyware

Spyware is malicious software installed on the mobile device without an end user's knowledge. Spyware is designed to secretly collect end-users' personal information or monitor their activity. The collection of information may take the form of ID and password logins, bank account information, and web surfing activity. Spyware can also change the functionality of the device to improve its capability to monitor and collect information.[7]

Although spyware is generally used to commit fraud or other forms of malicious attacks, commercially available forms of spyware are available, such as FlexiSpy, Mobile Spy, and MobiStealth.[8]

FlexiSpy, for example, works on most major smart phones and has the following capabilities:

- Control cell phone applications.
- Secretly read SMS messages and emails.
- Capture call logs and GPS locations.
- Track individuals location and movements.
- Remotely activate the cellphone's microphone to listen to the surrounding environment, functioning as a bugging device.
- Control a device remotely.

Although software such as FlexiSpy is advertised as a legitimate application to help husbands or wives catch unfaithful partners, it is clear that software such as FlexiSpy demonstrates the possibility of how spyware can be used to capture information without the end users' knowledge. The ability to watch every move and monitor every form of communication through a mobile device certainly demonstrates the magnitude of the threat of spyware. It is certainly conceivable that software developed by malicious characters might have more functionality and capabilities than commercially available software such as FlexiSpy.[9]

Viruses and Worms

The distinguishing characteristic of a mobile virus is that it can replicate itself, moving from one mobile device (or computer system) to another and exploiting security vulnerability (in the case of a worm). If a mobile device has not been jailbroken or rooted, viruses and worms will be constrained to the app that was compromised due to the inherent app isolation provided by the mobile operating system. However, they may spread through various communications channels, such as a network. One way to detect compromised apps is to check that they are not trying to perform unusual actions.

One of the first iPhone worms came on the scene in November 2010 called Net-Worm.IphoneOS.Ike (also known as Ikee). This worm infected iPhones and iPod Touches that had been jailbroken and exploited the fact that many users did not change the factory default root password. Once the device was infected, the worm replicated itself by searching for other iPhones or iPod touches on the network that were also jailbroken. It then started the process all over again spreading throughout the network. The worm then changed the wallpaper image to the 1980s singer Rick Astley. The intent of the worm was to demonstrate the vulnerability of iPhones and did not perform any harmful behavior (unless you consider a picture of Rick Astley as harmful).[10]

Soon after the initial infection, a new version of Ikee came on the scene. This variant was much more malicious because it stole user data and allowed third parties to remotely control the infected devices. In addition, malicious individuals exploited this variant of the Ikee worm to redirect end users to phishing sites, where the end user could be tricked into entering personal data such as banking account information.[11]

Trojan Horses

The unique characteristic of a Trojan horse is that it appears harmless but hides malicious capabilities.

To infect a mobile device with a Trojan horse, a malicious user often produces a counterfeit version of a mobile app. An unsuspecting mobile user will download this counterfeit app believing that it is an authentic mobile app. The download usually occurs from unofficial app stores or web sites. When installed, the app can usually function as if it were the legitimate app. However, the Trojan horse introduces malicious capabilities.

The popular gaming app, *Angry Birds Space*, was the target of a Trojan horse. The Trojan horse was a fully functional version of *Angry Birds Space* that was placed in unofficial Android app stores. This malware would gain root access to the device and install malicious code. The Trojan horse would then download additional malware to further infect the mobile device, giving the malicious user control of the device.

Social Engineering

One of the goals of malicious users is to spread their malware to as many end users as possible. One of the preferred methods of spreading malware is through *social engineering*. Social engineering employs an understanding of the user's social context to add legitimacy to the attack's initial introduction. Social engineering exploits a trust relationship the user may have. Social engineering is part of a trend in attacks that are more targeted at specific individuals, organizations, or demographics. Essentially, end users are tricked into installing mobile malware or giving away sensitive information. Below are several type of attacks that are aided by social engineering:

- **Fake utility:** Often the malicious user advertises mobile applications that provide some form of utility. For example, a malicious user may spread a utility to improve the functionality of a mobile device (such as a utility to improve battery life). After the app is installed, the malware is installed on the mobile device to begin some form of exploit or attack.

- **Illegitimate security:** Multifactor authentication is a common security practice today. Many end users are accustomed to signing up for a service on their PC, and then a numeric code is sent to their mobile device that must then be entered into a PC authentication form. The intent of multi-factor authentication is to ensure that the individuals who fill out the form are who they claim to be and are physical people (not a software program). Malicious individuals exploit the fact that users are accustomed to this secure authentication process. They also exploit the fact that activities centered on security often cause users to let their guard down. To that end, the malicious process starts with an infected PC that asks end users to install a mobile app in order to receive a special authentication code. After the app is installed, the mobile device then becomes infected.

- **Phishing**: A process where end users are tricked into providing personal or sensitive information because they believe they are communicating with a trusted source. In the mobile world, there are variants of phishing where voice, SMS, or text messages can trick end users to visit malicious sites or install malicious code.[12] Social engineering techniques are often used to make it seem that a request received is from someone who is an authority within an organization. Also known as *spear phishing*, the end user then feels the message can be trusted because it came from someone they trust.

Additional Types of Mobile Attacks

In addition to the threats already discussed, there are other threats you need to consider as part of your mobile security and management strategy.

- **SQL injection**: To execute an SQL injection attack, a malicious user would enter data into a form within the mobile app, which is then passed to a database. However, instead of entering regular data, the malicious user would enter a SCRIPT tag that links to a malicious JavaScript to attack the back-end database by deleting, copying files, and so on. After access to the web server is established, the malicious user can then initiate denial-of-service (DoS) attacks or turn a system into a 'zombie' where it sends out spam email. SQL injection can be mitigated by using modern databases and validating input against predetermined values.

- **Session hijacking**: A "session" refers to the state of one's interaction over the Internet. It may mean whether an individual is logged in. It may reflect which items are in a shopping cart. The data that describes the state of a session is passed as a cookie (also known as a token). Malicious individuals can hijack a user's session on the Internet, capture the session cookie, and perform activities on the user's behalf. The malicious individual could capture the session token information. This form of attack is likely to occur in public Wi-Fi hotspots. Malicious individuals can monitor traffic and see unencrypted session token information and then initiate MitM attacks. The best approach to avoiding session hijacking is to ensure that whenever you are in a public Wi-Fi network your address base should show HTTPS:// in front of the URL (or your browser may show an image of a padlock within the browser).

- **Denial-of-service (DoS)**: DoS attacks are when a malicious individual attacks a mobile device with the intent of making it unusable. One possible DoS attack could send hundreds of SMS spam messages to a device, making it useless. Another attack would find weaknesses in the operating systems that could shut down features of the phone.

■ **QR code spoofing:** QR codes seem to be everywhere. They have become the marketing vehicle of choice for many in the industry. It introduces a great opportunity to tie a physical world object to a web site. You simply point your camera at a QR code and are given an opportunity to be sent to a web site. This is all well and good. However, QR codes are illegible, and the destination is not known until after you scan the QR code. As a result, individuals have created QR codes that send people to web sites that can then perform a malicious action—such as signing the individual up for a premium SMS service (see Figure 6.2).

Which QR code is evil?

Figure 6.2   QR Codes can contain URL to download malware or sign up for premium services without end users realizing where they are being directed to.

Behavior That Can Increase Threat Risk

A successful mobile security strategy has both a technical and a human aspect. The following list provides examples of user's behaviors that increase security risks.

■ **Infection from a PC:** Although users may be careful not to download a malicious app from an app store, their device may become infected through the interaction with a standard PC. Mobile devices often sync up with a PC to get new updates or patches. If the PC is infected, this may be a vehicle by which the mobile device becomes infected.

■ **Small Form Factor:** An unsuspecting individual may inadvertently visit a fraudulent site by clicking a bogus URL or using a fraudulent QR code. Given a mobile device's small size, it can be difficult to inspect a web link to ensure it is valid. Unlike a PC, this could lead to individuals visiting a site unintentionally simply because they could not see the URL or they mistakenly clicked a fraudulent link.

- **Jailbroken and rooted devices:** The process of augmenting the mobile device operating system to free it from certain constraints imposed by the device operating system (OS) vendors is referred to as jailbreaking (for Apple iOS) or rooting (for Android). Mobile device OS vendors often impose some limitations on the usage of the device for business or security reasons. Individuals might feel these restrictions are too limiting. As such, they may use specialized web sites or programs to augment the mobile operating system of a mobile device and remove functional constraints.

  For Android devices, rooting is designed to bypass the limitations that carriers and device manufacturers may place on the device. A rooted device enables users to alter or change system applications and settings. A rooted device may run special apps that need administrative-level permission or replace the operating system all together.

  One of the primary reasons users jailbreak their mobile device is to open it to a broad ecosystem of applications and utilities. Apple has made the decision that only apps that come from the Apple App Store can be used on an Apple device. Every application in the Apple App Store is approved by Apple. There is certainly some advantage to this approach from a security standpoint. Apple has provided some review of the application and can verify the source of the application. If there is a security issue with the app, Apple can pull it from the Apple App Store. On the flip side, some may see this restriction as unnecessary. They would prefer more choice in app usage, device functionality, ringtones, and so on. In addition, they would like to augment the base platform capabilities in such a way as to provide new operating system skins, known as *winterboarding* where you can change the device background and user interface to a particular theme.

  One of the most popular alternatives to the Apple App Store is Cydia, which is a software application that enables a user to find software that can be installed on a jailbroken Apple device (iPhone, iPod Touch, or iPad). Cydia hosts applications Apple has declined to host in its Apple App Store, or published by developers who choose to bypass Apples restrictions and fees.

  Jailbreaking or rooting should not be confused with unlocking a mobile device, which gives end users the ability to connect to a mobile carrier of their choice. However, you would likely need to jailbreak or root your mobile device to install the utility that unlocks your phone.

The advantage of a jailbroken or rooted phone is that users can now download any third-party applications or overclock (forcing a processor to run faster than its manufacturer's specifications suggest) their device and get extended performance. However, the device becomes more vulnerable to malware attacks. It may also violate the warranty provided by the device OS vendor. As a result, the device would likely not receive any needed security updates from the OS vendor. After a device is jailbroken or rooted, the device becomes more vulnerable to attacks from hackers and malicious users. As a result, a key part of a mobile security strategy is to detect jailbroken or rooted devices that are accessing a corporate network.

As employees bring their mobile devices to work (BYOD), it is important to detect and block jailbroken or rooted devices. Businesses will need to deploy an MDM system to identify and apply an appropriate policy to any jailbroken or rooted device. They may also choose to prevent the device from accessing the network or restrict it from interacting with corporate data and systems.

What's Next with Mobile Threats?

Because mobile devices are becoming the predominant way by which businesses are reaching their customers and employees, mobile devices are becoming an increasing target for malicious attacks. Currently, Android has gained much of the interest from malicious individuals. This is due to the open nature of Android in which many individuals have access to operating system-level services.

In addition, unlike Apple, where there is a single App Store, the Android ecosystem is open to multiple app stores and download sites where individuals can post malicious apps. Still, even though mobile OS device manufactures make their platforms more secure over time by patching security vulnerability, users will continue to jailbreak or root their devices to make them more flexible and open, while at the same time increasing the opportunity for attacks. Even though apps from legitimate app stores may not be malicious, they may have vulnerabilities allowing them to become compromised and turn rogue. This is why it is critical for organizations to check for vulnerability in the app code that they may develop. In addition, there will be new mobile device platforms that will come on the scene to challenge Apple's and Google's dominance. These new device platforms will have their own security issues and vulnerabilities. Also, new device functions will also be added. Mobile payments will certainly gain traction in the mobile device market. Payments options such as Near-Field Communications (NFC) will offer a new communication channel to the device and thus become another potential avenue for exploit. Finally, security threats will also increase as more and more companies look to leverage a BYOD strategy in which personal devices are brought into the enterprise to reduce cost and give employees more flexibility.

Threat Management Capabilities

From a mobile threat management perspective, there is a set of focus areas and capabilities you should consider when defending against malicious individuals:

- **Antimalware (virus, spyware, and spam):** Perform a system-level scan as well as scanning apps and SD cards for malicious code.

  There is some debate in the industry as to the effectiveness of on-device scanning software to protect against malware. In addition, given Apple's iOS strict isolation model, it is impossible to implement an antivirus scanner across apps within an Apple device. For Android, mobile scanning software is available for the device; however, it is not clear if it provides the same level of protection as desktop antivirus software.

- **Antiphishing/web protection software:** A system that blocks fraudulent (phishing) web sites.

- **Call and text blocker:** Blocks calls and text messages from specific individuals or phone numbers.

- **Web filtering:** Controls what content is permitted to be accessed, and restricts what web material can be delivered to the end user.

- **Web reputation service:** Blocks malicious or abnormal web site source URLs.

- **Firewall:** Provides inbound and outbound traffic monitoring. A mobile firewall can interrogate behavior of traffic and limit access based on network activity. A typical mobile topology is outlined in Figure 6.3 that shows how the firewall is positioned.

  A key part of the firewall consists of a mobile gateway. A mobile gateway functions as a proxy server between the mobile device and the enterprise systems. The proxy breaks up the communication between the mobile device and the server back end, evaluating the communication for malicious activity. Both the mobile device and back-end servers act as though they are communicating to one another; however, they are actually interacting with the proxy. Specifically, a reverse proxy hides the details of the back-end servers from the mobile devices. If malicious activity is detected, it blocks the communication, protecting the enterprise servers.

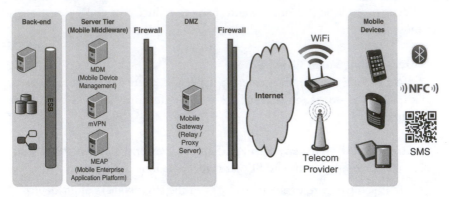

Figure 6.3 Typical mobile topology providing secure access and management.

Mobile Network Management and Security

Just as a PC needs to have a secure connection back to the enterprise, so does the mobile device. However, a mobile device is portable, and it is very likely that the device will be accessing the enterprise through a public Wi-Fi or a variety of communication vehicles, such as Bluetooth, SMS/MMS, Telecom networks, or NFC, as illustrated in Figure 6.4. Therefore, creating a secure communications channel becomes more critical. Any of these vehicles can open the door to attacks, eavesdropping, or data loss, making a secure communications channel more critical.

Figure 6.4 Mobile devices have multiple communications channels that must be secured. Over time, mobile devices will add more and more means of communication that will need to be secured.

Types of Mobile Threats Through an Unsecured Mobile Channel

Ensuring a secure communications channel between the mobile device and the corporate network is critical in protecting against malicious attacks. Examples of such attacks follow:

- **Wi-Fi hacking:** Public Wi-Fi hotspots create an opportunity for malicious users to attack a mobile device. Typically, a hacker would use a software package or utility to find users on a public network, listen in to the traffic across the network, and then steal IDs, passwords, or other credentials. After the credentials are stolen, the malicious individual can then impersonate the mobile user and access personal content, bank accounts, or corporate data and systems.

- **Man-in-the-middle attack:** MitM attack is based on the premise in which a malicious user inserts himself in the stream of communications between two unsuspecting parties. The malicious user is unknown to the other parties initiating or receiving the communications. This form of attack can be performed over an unsecure network. Or in the case of a secure channel, the malicious user would obtain a public encryption key so that he could intercept the messages between the two communications parties. In some cases, public keys are stored on a mobile device in an unsecure manner, thus increasing the potential for an MitM attack.

Mobile Network Protection

The primary protection mechanism for network security will be a mobile virtual private network (mVPN). A mVPN provides secure and private network communications between the mobile device and the corporate network. A mVPN maintains an authenticated, encrypted communications channel (or tunnel) for securely sending private information over a public network.

An mVPN is different when compared to the traditional VPN used with PCs or fixed endpoints. In a mobile environment, the mobile device is moving from network to network. A user may start her day at home with a personal Wi-Fi, go to a coffee shop to access a public Wi-Fi, then use the cellular network, and finally access the corporate network when she arrives at work. A secure channel must be maintained across all the networks and to the mobile application at all times. As the individual moves from network to network, the mVPN manages the appropriate hand-offs of identity, access, and encryption mechanism.

The typical mVPN function would reside between the server tier and the DMZ layer (refer to Figure 6.3).

More advanced capabilities of a mVPN include the capability to optimize the quality of communications based on network performance. Quality of service (QoS) may be adjusted to handle unreliable network connections to optimize network usage and increase battery life. In addition, insight about the device may be used by the mVPN to provide additional security controls or adapt the security posture based on information it receives from the device. The mVPN may detect if the device is compromised or not otherwise secure. As such, the connection back to the enterprise could be denied. There is a growing trend toward app-level VPNs to provide more granular control, better user experience, and better security.

Mobile Identity and Access Management

Mobile identity and access management describes how people are authenticated (who has access) and their level of authorization (what they can do) across a computing system. When defining an overall mobile authentication and authorization strategy, you need to consider how mobile devices fit within existing authentications systems within the enterprise. This means understanding existing authentication systems and how they may need to be adjusted for the unique characteristics of the mobile device.

A continued challenge for businesses is trying to find the balance between user experience and security. For example, users do not want to be encumbered by having to type a lengthy username and password into the mobile device. Having to type into the small form factor of the device can be difficult for users, especially if they have to type usernames and strong passwords that may have mixed numbers and special characters. The user experience can become even more negative by having users type their authentication just to make a phone call or use the device for personal use.

Another key element of mobile access is context. Context enables you to have greater awareness of the situation the end user is in. This contextual information provides for different authentication schemes and allows you to control the use of specific features of the mobile device or app based on risk. For example, if an employee is in his office, the geolocation information can verify he is in a secure environment. As a result, he gets access to more sensitive corporate data than if he were in a public location, such as an airport or taxi. A security access management system may also utilize the time of day or type of device to determine the appropriate level of access based on a predefined policy.

Your end goal is to gather enough information about users that you can give them the appropriate access. You should consider the following techniques that could improve the authentication process:

Identity Management

Employees must be able to access the enterprise from their mobile application. Before employees gain access to the corporate network, you need to verify their identity and determine what information they are allowed to access. You need to authenticate and authorize:

- **Authentication:** Validate that individuals are who they say they are and are thus able to access the enterprise.

- **Authorization:** Determine the user's role or access level to give him access to a specific and appropriate set of corporate data and applications.

Single Sign-on

In order to access corporate systems, mobile users need to prove their authentication credentials (e.g. user id and password) to each and every application. This is an obvious inconvenience to the user. In addition, for the mobile developer, it requires redundant development effort for each application that authenticates users independently. With Single Sign-on (SSO) a mobile user authenticates herself once and gains access to all appropriate back-end services without being prompted to log in again for each app. SSO can improve user productivity by helping eliminate the need to remember and manage user names and passwords, thus improving user experience and security compliance. For example, perhaps a bank provides an app to allow their customers to check their bank balance. They may also provide an app for stock trading. A SSO solution would allow the user to sign into one of the apps and gain access to the other without logging in twice.

Certificate Management

The term Public Key Infrastructure (PKI) is a security method that can provide increased protection of information exchanged over the Internet. PKI cryptography uses a private and a public key to encrypt and decrypt information. Although the public and private keys are mathematically related, one cannot easily be derived from the other. The public key is freely available to others, whereas the private key is secret and not shared.

Although PKI can greatly simplify cryptography by enabling the public key to be used by many people, the challenge is how to distribute, find, validate, and manage the public keys. One approach is to use digital certificates.

A digital certificate is a digital credential that provides proof of identity and supporting information about a digital identity (much like a passport or birth certificate would provide information about a person). For a PKI, a digital certificate is issued by a certificate authority (CA) and guarantees the validity of the public key, provides supporting information, and is valid for only a specific period of time. As a result, a digital certificate solves the issue of finding a public key and guarantees its validity.

The structure of a digital certificate is typically defined by the IETF standard X.509. This standard defines information about the identity of the owner of the corresponding private key, the key length, the algorithm used, the dates of validity, and the actions the key can be used for.[13] The usage by the U.S. government and its contractors and supporting agencies has made X.509 certificates adoption widespread and common throughout the industry.

Many mVPNs and MDM solutions support x.509 digital certificates, which are used to manage a PKI encryption architecture and distribute certificates to mobile devices.

Multifactor Authentication

Multifactor authentication requires users to provide more than one form of verification to prove their identity. A simple ID/password authentication method may not be secure enough for some scenarios. Combining several types of authentication methods can significantly improve security and authentication of an individual. There are three primary forms of verification you can use:

- **Something the user knows:** Password or answer to a question
- **Something the user has:** Smart card, security token (such as a key fob), or a mobile device
- **Something unique to the user:** Biometrics such as a fingerprint

One of the more secure approaches to authentication is combining what you know (User name or password) and have (token or key fob). This two-factor authentication can provide a robust authentication mechanism.

Typically, this approach requires a hardware device users carry with them. This key fob would deliver a new password at a random time period providing a one-time password. The challenge with a key fob is that it can be costly to set up and manage. A system would have to be in place to distribute the key fobs, set up a separate device management system, educate users on how to use the key fob, and deal with loss or stolen hardware.

An alternative approach that has begun to show traction in the industry is the use of the smartphone as a security token in a two-factor authentication process. Also known as a tokenless two-factor authentication (T2FA), this method has some advantages when compared with a key fob approach. The use of an existing smartphone as the security token can reduce yet another mobile device (the key fob) that must be managed and controlled. The device is something the end user is already familiar with and as such does not need additional training or support. In most cases, no additional software needs to be installed or maintained.

The process of using T2FA with a smartphone can be straight forward. After it is determined that users need strong authentication (perhaps based on their role), you determine which communication channel will receive their one-time passcode (OTP). This may be SMS, phone call, or email. For example, end users may want to access a corporate application. They would enter their username and password into the application (what they know). The application would then send a SMS text message of a one-time pass code to the end user's smartphone (what they have). End users would then enter that passcode into the application and complete the authentication process.

There are clear advantages to using a smartphone as a token in a two-factor authentication process; however, there are also some considerations to keep in mind. Sending a passcode to a user at the time of authentication is dependent on network coverage. In those situations in which there is spotty connectivity or the end user is a remote worker, the capability to send a one-time passcode would be limited. There may be ways to work around this by having a set of passcodes stored on the device, and the application would randomly choose one of them during offline use. Or perhaps the passcodes could be generated from an internal mechanism of the phone such as the internal clock. In the end, for end users who access a system relatively infrequently and have reasonable network coverage, the use of a smartphone in a T2FA scheme may prove effective for securing the transaction.

Alternative Authentication Method: Contextual Authentication

Most smartphones and tablets provide information about an individual's location. Proximity-based information can offer new data that could enable the authentication process to be more flexible and adaptive.

For example, after the device is known to be within the corporate campus, the authentication process could be simplified. Perhaps after the user has been authenticated, the device stays unlocked while users are within their corporate office building. Time of day may also be used for contextual authentication. Perhaps the employee has greater access to information during work hours.

Alternative Authentication Method: Biometric Authentication with a Smartphone

Given the small form factor of a mobile device, it can be a challenge to enter passwords and IDs. Individuals might struggle or become frustrated typing lengthy passwords or typing them over and over again. Because mobile devices have a rich set of interfaces (camera, accelerometer, touchpad, and so on), there might be some promise in making it easier for users to authenticate themselves using biometrics:

- **Camera:** Retinal patterns, 3-D facial recognition, blink patterns, hand geometry, finger print recognition, and recognizing photos
- **Touchpad:** Keystroke patterns, finger-tracing patterns, signature recognition, speed and strength of figure tracing, and gesture patterns
- **GPS:** User's location
- **Accelerometer:** Pattern of mobile device motion
- **Voice:** Voice recognition

Although there is some promise for biometric authentication, there are some challenges. Accuracy is always an issue particularly given environmental conditions. Will voice recognition work accurately in a noisy environment? Can the camera perform facial recognition in low light? Accuracy can be improved with dedicated hardware, such as a finger print reader. However, adding a peripheral device to a smartphone or tablet can increase the cost of a security solution and may run counter to the goal of serving the mobile user with simplicity and usability.

Alternative Authentication Method: Image or Pattern-Based Authentication

It can be a challenge for individuals to have to frequently enter a password into a mobile device, especially given their small form factor. The touch pad interface can make it difficult to enter an authentication username and password. An alternative approach is the use of images and the touch screen to authenticate users by having them interact with an image. You could touch a series of points on a picture, draw a particular shape, or single out a set of pictures from their photos, as illustrated in Figure 6.5.

Figure 6.5   Pattern-based authentication (Source: http://www.mobbeel.com/products).

Using image or pattern recognition can be easier and faster for end users. Because end users are not using a keyboard, this approach is less vulnerable to malicious eavesdropping of keystrokes (or keyloggers). Image-based authentication could also be used for marketing or advertising, where images relevant to your brand could be used to reinforce your brand or be a part of an advertising campaign.

There are some challenges to image and pattern-based authentication, for instance, the precision of the user input—making sure you take into account how different individuals may execute a specific gesture. Also, you need to consider that an individual will leave streaks or fingerprints on the screen. If a particular gesture is done over and over again, a malicious individual could figure out the pattern. This can be avoided by changing the image location, which will force the end user to change the pattern of interaction.

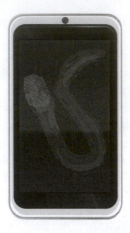

Figure 6.6 Fingerprints give away pattern-based authentication

Mobile Application Management and Security

In the mobile space, it's all about the interaction between the user and the application. Ensuring that the application and the associated data remains secure is critical to providing a secure environment for your customers and employees, and it begins with the development of the app itself. You need to ensure that the way the application is developed does not introduce inherent flaws in coding that may make it more vulnerable to attack.

Scanning the application code against known vulnerabilities, during the development cycle as well as post-production, can help to ensure that the app is not vulnerable to a new threat.

In addition, the application needs to have the appropriate security capabilities built in so that it can protect the user, device, and data associated with the mobile app. When securing mobile applications, it is usually less expensive to address security issues when the app is being developed than after it has been deployed.

Management of the app goes hand in hand with security. If you detect that the app needs to be updated because of a security flaw after a device is deployed, you will need to determine how to get end users to upgrade their application to receive the latest fixes. Unlike web applications in which you can easily fix the security flaw by updating the application on the server, in the case of mobile, the updated mobile application is deployed to an app store, and users must take an active role to update the app. This presents a significant challenge to your security strategy, and you need to assume that end users will not take the time to update the app. In one case, a major company had to write a letter to all its customers asking them to upgrade to the latest version of its mobile app after a security flaw was identified. In the end, it is always better to build security and manageability into the mobile app during the development cycle.

Application Security Scanning

Application scanning represents security technologies that enable developers to build more secure apps by identifying and fixing vulnerabilities early in the development process. Application scanning systems can identify common vulnerabilities such as SQL injection, cross-site scripting, and cross-site request forgery. Application security scanning usually consists of static and dynamic testing:

- **Static app analysis:** Static app analysis (also called code reviews or white-box testing) is designed to identify and remediate mobile application vulnerabilities in source code. This is accomplished through direct observation or scanning of the app code. This static applications testing can analyze the code and provide specific recommendations, which can range from the discovery of keyboard errors to specific vulnerability in the code logic.

- **Dynamic app analysis:** Dynamic app testing (also known as black-box testing) is designed to uncover mobile application vulnerabilities in production and preproduction apps. Dynamic application testing periodically scans the app to understand the security state of an application when compared to a catalog of known vulnerabilities.

App Security Capabilities

Applications should be designed with security in mind. A thoughtfully engineered application can help protect from malicious attacks and prevent data loss, while protecting the integrity of corporate systems. Typically, a development team will choose a Mobile Enterprise Application Platform (MEAP) that provides the tools and middleware to assist in developing the mobile application. The MEAP can also provide key security and management capabilities.

Encrypted On-Device Storage

The platform should enable developers to encrypt any sensitive data that is stored locally for offline availability, thus protecting it from malware attacks and exposure in case of device theft. The mobile app should include support for an encrypted data store for keeping the data protected when stored on the device. The encrypted data store can also enable authentication when in offline mode so that only authorized users access the application and data, even when there is not a connection back to the enterprise.

Offline Authentication

When an app is trying to access corporate data, user authentication is needed. However, when the mobile device does not have connectivity, the enterprise authentication infrastructure cannot be reached by the app, and there is a need to verify user credentials using other secure means. The platform's encrypted cache can be used by mobile apps to authenticate users in such scenarios.

Authenticity Testing

In most situations, downloadable mobile apps run outside the company firewall. Allowing such apps to access company data and even perform transactions requires opening a channel to the outside world. This channel can be exploited by hackers in various ways, including the distribution of modified or re-engineered versions of the company's original app. Hackers are using industrialized practices of obtaining legitimate apps, "unpackaging," and then "repackaging" them with malicious code, and distributing them as the original legitimate app. In the Android world, hackers set up fake app stores to host these tampered apps. They direct unsuspecting users to these stores via in-app advertising messages that are supposedly directing them to the original app. This malicious technique is used by hackers to distribute tampered copies of the original app and presents a significant risk to enterprise data and company brand. A way to counter this type of threat is by using a Mobile Enterprise Application Platform (MEAP) that has linked a server to the app. The app and server can identify each other and can validate each other's legitimacy. When the server recognizes that it is being accessed from a nonauthorized app, it can block access. The MEAP also allows the app to validate that it is connecting to a legitimate back-end system. Sometimes malicious individuals insert themselves between the device and a back-end system. He can then eardrops and steals sensitive information. Utilizing a MEAP to validate the authenticity of both the app and the back-end system can prevent so called MitM attacks.

A mobile platform should provide mechanisms that can prevent the mass distribution of tampered copies of the original app. The server tests the authenticity of apps that contact it and determines if the app is legitimate. When the server identifies that it is accessed by a tampered app, it will prevent it from accessing the enterprise.

Differentiating Between Approved and Unrecognized Mobile Devices

Another means by which you can ensure a device is approved to use an app is to utilize the unique device ID. Organizations can deliver the apps with a custom provisioning process, ensuring that an app (or a group of apps) can be installed only on approved devices. This use of the unique device ID helps organizations support the BYOD trend. It enables employees to use approved personal devices for work purposes but maintains control and enforces security protocols. This helps enterprises ensure that apps with access to sensitive data are not being used on unauthorized devices.

Security Updates Enforcement

In the world of web apps, client-side code is under the direct control of the IT administrator. Distribution of code updates is such a fundamental mechanism of web technology that it has become a nonissue within that context. Downloadable apps present a different situation as mobile operating systems do not force users to update applications to their latest version. If a security flaw is discovered in a deployed mobile app, the author of the application can upload a fixed version to the app store, but users are free to choose whether to download the updated version. Unfortunately, the mobile app store distribution mechanisms, as well as contractual restrictions placed by some mobile OS vendors, make it difficult for administrators to make sure their users are using the correct version of the mobile OS. As a result, administrators cannot leave the responsibility for updating critical security fixes in the hands of the end user.

Remote Updates Enforcement

In the web era, updating a web site with the latest code and security fixes was straightforward. Updating the back-end app server would automatically update the web site. This approach is not necessarily possible with mobile apps, however. Once the mobile app is distributed (in a B2C application) through an app store, it is up to the end user to take the action and make the appropriate updates. A security issue within the app will lead to vulnerable apps in the field.

A mobile platform should provide a means to ensure an app is updated, even after it is deployed. This is possible by ensuring that the app is connected to a mobile platform (MEAP) central server. With either a native or hybrid app, the mobile administrator can remotely disable and force the user to get a new version of the app. This ensures that the app is the most current or prevents unauthorized use of an app if the user or device does not comply with a specific authorization profile. In the case of a hybrid app, the administrator should also be able to update the core web logic of the app. The above consideration points to an advantage of the hybrid app in which the core logic is developed in web technologies (HTML, JavaScript, and CSS). With the hybrid app, an update can be done automatically and still be compliant with the public app store restrictions.

Enterprise App Store

Businesses are finding that managing apps within the enterprise is just as important as managing devices. Apps need to be distributed to employees in a way that is consistent with enterprise governance and management. This is particularly important for BYOD deployments in which there is an increasing need to manage at the app level instead of at the device. In the case of a security breach, employees with personal information on their BYOD device would prefer that the corporate data and apps be targeted and deleted rather than an indiscriminate wiping of their entire device.

Current consumer app stores do not meet enterprise security requirements for app deployment and management. In addition, they do not provide a process to track license and expense reports associated with individual apps downloaded by employees. Yet the employee needs access to do his job. This is where an enterprise app store comes in. It is an internal app store that manages pre-approved consumer apps and apps developed by the enterprise.

Using a consumer app store for enterprise deployment of apps can be problematic. Consumer app stores offer free versions and push for premium upgrades. The corporate employee is looking for the functionality needed to do his job, not to be upsold. There needs to be a process to track license and expense reports associated with individual apps downloaded by employees from a public app store. This creates an important compliance issue in which the solution is generally not offered by consumer app stores. Security is a big concern for businesses. There needs to be certainty that an app does not contain malware.

An enterprise app store should include the following requirements:

- **Support for multiple platforms:** The enterprise app store should support a comprehensive set of device OS platforms, such as the top market leaders Apple iOS and Android. However, there may also be a need to support legacy platforms (J2ME, Windows Mobile 6.5, Blackberry 6).

- **Full spectrum of app types:** The enterprise app store should support web, hybrid, and native apps. The app store should also support apps that have been built within the enterprise in addition to apps developed by third parties.

- **Security:** Full identity management and an authentication system should be part of an enterprise app store. There may also be a need to tie into a MDM solution to provide device-level authentication and policy management. Download of the apps should be provided over a secure channel.

- **Access control:** Only users who are authorized to download a particular app are given that right to do so. The access should be managed against an access control list (ACL) to ensure the employee has the appropriate role and responsibility to download a particular app.

- **Push notification:** The app store admin should send a message to individual users or group of users to inform them of apps that need to be upgraded or key maintenance tasks.

- **Over The Air (OTA) updates:** In order to ensure that the mobile app is up to date, OTA updates should be used instead of relying on the end user to take the action to upgrade.

- **Inventory:** There should be a database that tracks apps, users, and devices to ensure there is control of which app is available and who has the right to use it. This becomes particularly important when devices are shared across individuals.

- **Code of conduct:** There needs to be a clearly documented policy and management criteria for uploading, deploying, and using the mobile apps.

- **Policy enforcement:** Having all corporate apps come from a single source gives the enterprise a means of controlling its mobile environment. Defining which apps are approved in the enterprise ensures that rogue apps with malicious code do not enter the enterprise.

- **Star rating/social feedback:** The enterprise apps store should have the same experience as its consumer counterpart. Collecting user feedback and ratings can help IT operations to get a sense of which apps are providing value to employees.

- **License management:** The enterprise app store should manage usage, licensing requirements, and entitlement rights so that the enterprise ensures that they are compliant. It will also want to ensure that the enterprise does not issue licenses that it does not have or that licenses are not issued in violation of a specific agreement.

Mobile Information Protection

Today, companies face the enormous task of protecting their businesses from all sorts of threats. Protecting their networks and mobile devices from hackers and malicious individuals requires a well thought-out strategy. What about an equally important issue of data loss from the inside? Many organizations have not thought through the likelihood of data loss associated with the use of mobile devices within the enterprise. Mobile devices are by nature always on the move, easily lost, or stolen. The propensity to use mobile devices for social interaction provides a rich opportunity to share and transfer information between individuals that could lead to sensitive information falling into the wrong hands. In addition, as organizations move forward with their BYOD strategy, the chances of data "leaking" from the corporate section of the phone into the unsecured personal section of the phone can open an organization up to the loss of data.

Should data loss occur, it can create havoc for an organization. The financial implications through fines, legal actions, loss of competitive advantage, regulatory actions, bad publicity, and loss of customers can be enormous. According to the Ponemon/Symantec 2011 Annual Study: U.S. Cost of a Data Breach, the average cost of a data breach is on the rise. The average organizational cost of a data breach in the United States is at $5.8 million with a cost per compromised record at $194. Obviously, the cost to the enterprise for lost or stolen data is extremely high. According to the Ponemon research, 24 percent of the data loss was due to system errors. There was a rise in malicious attacks when compared to a year earlier resulting in 37 percent of the breaches due to malicious attacks. Malicious attacks account for the most expensive remediation costs at $222 due primarily to the cost of dealing with third parties. However, the most likely cause of a data breach is from negligence or human error due to an employee mistake. In fact, 39 percent of organizations in the study had a data breach as a result of individual negligence, such as their device was lost or stolen.[14]

Given the intense competitive nature of today's marketplace and strict regulatory environment, data loss prevention (also known as Data Leakage Prevention [DLP]) is one of the most critical issues facing enterprises today. Historically, enterprises have protected their corporate data by building walls around their business. Businesses have sought to prevent data loss by keeping data within the walls of the physical buildings or guarded by software firewalls. As mobility becomes the norm, and more and more employees use mobile devices for their business activities, there is a need to rethink some of the strategy and technology around securing corporate data. New approaches and technologies such as data encryption and data isolation in the form of containers, wrappers, and virtualization can be a critical part of an overall mobile strategy.

Mobile Data Loss Defined

The scope of data loss can range from confidential customer data, corporate secrets, employee data, to even source code files for a future product. Unfortunately, with all the different ways data could be lost, the implications for an organization can be much greater than typical malware attacks.

When considering DLP, there are several key locations of data that need to be protected:

- **Data at the enterprise:** This is the data that resides within the corporate infrastructure servers and databases. This data will likely be protected using traditional methods of data loss protection and does not necessarily have any unique characteristics for mobile.

- **Data in motion:** This is data that is transported between the enterprise and the mobile device. Securing and encrypting the transmission of this data will be important to ensure appropriate software is on the device and the back end to guarantee a secure channel of communication.

- **Data at the mobile device:** The portability of mobile devices and the propensity to share and distribute information make securing the data on a mobile device a significant challenge.

When considering what type of data is most important with regard to data loss, it falls into two primary categories:

- **Intellectual property**: Competition is more intense now than in any time in history; as a result, intellectual property protection is a top priority for businesses. Hackers, industrial espionage, or even employees moving to a competitor all play into the concerns for data loss. In the end, a company's intellectual property and trade secrets can be its most valuable asset.

- **Regulatory compliance**: Nearly all businesses must comply with some sort of state, federal, or international regulation. Businesses are required to comply with such regulations as the Health Insurance Portability and Accountability Act (HIPAA), Sarbanes-Oxley (SOX), or Payment Card Industry Data Security (PCI DSS). Unfortunately, compliance can be complicated with transmission and storage of mobile data. Compliance can be a challenge, with mobile devices adding complexity and raising the chances for a regulatory violation.

How Does Mobile Data Loss Occur?

As discussed, data loss (or data leakage) can have a significant impact on an enterprise. The cost of data loss can be high. To understand how to prevent data loss, you need to consider the causes. As you can see, mobile offers some unique characteristics that can lead to increased probability of data loss:

- **Data communication interception**: Mobile devices are more likely to access public Wi-Fi networks; as a result there is an increased risk of interception by malicious individuals.

- **PC synchronization**: Mobile devices are often synchronized with other computers to download music, store photos, or update contacts. Although convenient, this synchronization can open the door for corporate data to move to unsecured computing devices.

- **Cloud storage**: Many mobile devices will not only sync with PCs, but also sync with cloud storage offered by the mobile device manufacturer or by a third party. Popular cloud-based storage offerings provide an easy way to store documents. This ease of document movement off the device to a potentially unsecure environment can create a significant security concern for businesses. This type of synchronization often occurs in the background, and the user may not be aware that a sync is happening. As result, corporate data and information may be transferred off the device to an unsecure location.

- **File attachments and viewers:** Documents opened from a corporate email or web site might need to be opened within a viewer on the phone. This viewer may come from a third party, and the integrity of the viewer may raise concerns over data loss. In addition, opening a file within a viewer often creates another copy of the file on another area of the mobile device, which might not be protected.

- **Cut and paste from documents:** Businesses would like to control the use of documents that are opened on a device. As a result, they want to prevent individuals from cutting and pasting content from the document and then storing or sending it in an unsecured manner.

- **External memory:** After a document is opened, it can easily be stored on an external memory card within the mobile device. This can create a concern with enterprises wanting to control access of documents.

Protecting Against Data Loss

To protect against corporate data loss, users need to secure the data (with device, network, and data encryption) and manage access to the data (through data separation).

Encryption

Encryption is the process of applying an algorithm to manipulate the data into a "scrambled" set of characters and symbols. Only those individuals with a "key" can unscramble (or decrypt) the data so that it can be readable again. From a user standpoint, this activity happens behind the scene when users enter their username and password to access the encrypted mobile data.

There are a number of approaches to encryption available, and fortunately the mobile device manufactures offer a variety of encryption capabilities. Unfortunately, each vendor can approach encryption slightly differently, which requires special attention from an enterprise mobile strategy perspective. In addition, several MDM vendors and MEAP vendors can add additional security features to provide easier and more consistent security management capabilities. IT generally has two approaches to handling data encryption that should be used together: on-device encryption and encryption of data transmitted to and from the device.

On-Device Data Encryption

Most of today's modern smartphones and tablets offer some type of encryption for the mobile device whether it is at an application level (Apple) or full-disk encryption (Android, BlackBerry, and Windows Phone). A MEAP can also provide a means to have an encrypted data store within an app for off-line use.

Network Data Encryption

A complete data protection strategy not only covers the device encryption, but also the network encryption. Corporate data transmitted between the mobile device and the enterprise must also be protected from malicious users attempting to intercept network communications. At one time, when the BlackBerry device was the only device used by an enterprise, the BlackBerry Enterprise Server provided end-to-end secure communication between the device and the back-end systems. However, with a much broader set of devices entering the enterprise, encrypting and securing data transmission has become a much bigger challenge.

There are a variety of approaches you can take. Some vendors offer cross-device MDM software that includes encrypted communications. Exchange ActiveSync® or Lotus® Traveler provides email management capabilities that enable encrypted communications. Third-party encryption software is also available that can encrypt messages between the device and the enterprise. In addition, you could include a secure mobile gateway within your network topology or VPN.

Encryption Versus Data Separation

Although encryption is a critical part of an overall data protection strategy you must consider the end user's impact on security. Every time users attempt to access encrypted data on their device, they must enter an ID and password (PW). This can create a usability issue if users must frequently access the data or the ID/PW is too complex. In addition, if BYOD is part of your overall strategy, the on-device encryption may cover the end users entire device. They may have to enter an ID or a PW to access their own personal information and apps or simply to make a phone call. This can cause users to either abandon your mobile strategy or, worse, bypass it in some way.

Approaches to Data Separation

There are several technology approaches to data separation and data leakage protection. Each has its own advantages and disadvantages.

Mobile Containerization

Containerization enables a single or multiple apps to reside within a container to secure the application. As a result, you protect the app from potential threats, prevent data leakage, and allow for the apps to apply centralized management capabilities and policies. The mobile container is a level above securing at the application level. The mobile container secures the mobile content at the document and workspace level. There are two major forms of approaches around containers:

- **Document container:** Enterprises are concerned with losing control of documents that are utilized within a mobile device. Many mobile services make it easy to distribute documents between mobile devices and PCs. A mobile container can manage the redistribution of documents or prevent cutting and pasting specific content within a document.

- **Workspace container:** Enterprises look for a way to control, secure, and manage all their corporate mobile applications and content. A mobile workspace container could contain a centralized email, browser, calendar utility, and contacts—personal information management (PIM). These applications could be provided by the container vendor or could be developed by the enterprise. This provides one central place on the mobile device to manage, secure, and control all the data and content. If the device is lost or stolen, the enterprise could wipe just the container, thus preserving the rest of the phone's content. This is particularly valuable for BYOD strategies.

An advantage of containerization is the ability to enforce a password for just the "work" container and not enforce a device password, which would make it more cumbersome to access the "personal" area of the device. Although the mobile container approach is often well received by the IT organization and enables a straightforward approach to managing mobile applications and content, there is sometimes push back from the enterprise user community. Because the mobile application within the container is unique and separate from the rest of the device, users may not feel the application meets expectations. For example, most container solutions have their own email, contacts, and calendar applications, which are different from the default out-of-the-box experience that comes with the mobile device. In addition, because the applications are customized for the container, existing mobile applications that are preferred or used by employees may not be available within the container. Essentially, the container vendor or internal mobile development teams are forced to duplicate existing applications that may already exist in the market place. The challenge is always trying to maintain the same level of quality and user experience.

Data Separation with SDK Development

When building a mobile application, a developer can incorporate security and data protection functionality within the mobile app using a software development kit (SDK) provided by a mobile device/app management vendor. Utilizing the SDK, the developer can incorporate the interfaces of their chosen device/app management vendor. In that way, the app management software can control and secure the app that was developed by providing direct support for authentication, authorization, monitoring, security, and enforcement. This approach works well for in-house development where you can incorporate app level security features (enabled by the SDK) at development time.

Mobile Application Wrapper

A mobile wrapper enables you to "wrap" an existing mobile app to apply security policy and management capabilities to the app. In most cases, this is done without recompiling or updating the app, which can be time-consuming and cumbersome.

The mobile app wrapper approach gives the enterprise more control over securing and managing at the application level instead of at the device level. An enterprise concerned with data loss is faced with the option of complete lockdown in which personal devices are banned from the enterprise, or perhaps have a container approach in which the enterprise apps may not have the look and feel that users expect. In addition, the enterprise may have to build custom apps within the container to provide the functionality needed. The mobile wrapper approach wraps existing mobile apps that you would get in the market place, thus preserving the look and feel while applying the appropriate management and security capabilities.

After an application is wrapped, the enterprise can define several control and management tasks around the application:

- **Access:** Based on user roles and defined usage, lists define who has access to a particular mobile app.
- **Threat management:** Defines appropriate encryption, authentication, and secure access via a 'mini' VPN associated with the app.
- **Data protection:** Manages attachments and prevents copying or data leakage from the app.

- **Audit:** Records log activity of the app for audit and compliance.

- **Management:** Detect policy violations through continuous monitoring usage and application activity.

- **Remediation:** Take corrective action at the application level by disabling, wiping, blocking, or removing users from an access group.

The key advantage to the app wrapper approach is that it provides app level security and management and can be applied to existing mobile apps. This eliminates the need to redevelop/recompile an existing app. However, one should understand the terms and conditions of the 3rd party apps that you want to wrap. It is difficult to bypass the app stores to obtain the app code (iOS IPA or Android APK files for example) directly from app vendors. In addition, each OS vendor has specific terms and conditions for how apps can be distributed. Finally, you will need to receive updates directly from the app vendor instead of getting the updates directly from a public app store.

Mobile Virtualization

Virtualization on mobile devices can take multiple forms—separations through multiple operating systems or virtual applications. Running multiple operating systems can be done either via hardware or software (for example, hypervisor). Each operating system appears to have the base operating system resources (processor, memory, and so on). The hypervisor controls the allocation of the base system resources to each guest operating system (or virtual machine). This way the different guest operating systems do not conflict with each other.[15]

Virtualization has long been a standard technology in mainframes and more recently cloud computing. Given the robust computing power of mobile smartphones and tablets, mobile virtualization has become a promising technology that the mobile industry can use to tackle some specific technical challenges around data and application management.

Handset manufacturers see the value of mobile virtualization in helping to consolidate hardware and chipsets within a mobile device. This can help reduce the overall bill of material of the device, which can reduce cost, simplify manufacturing, improve portability, and increase performance. However, the real focus for mobile virtualizations is security.

As you consider the use of virtualization technology, the conversation generally focuses on the Android operating system. Apple's terms and conditions would not allow a virtual machine to be added on its device. However, with

Android (and potentially future mobile operating systems) mobile virtualization can provide significant security advantages, particularly for a BYOD strategy.

As a growing number of enterprises consider a BYOD strategy, virtualization may provide a means for needed application isolation. A hypervisor enables individual-liable devices to isolate data and applications on one OS from the other OS, separating corporate from personal apps and content. Because the hypervisor enables a complete operating environment, the user experience of the device is preserved. Users can use their device as they would any other personal device; however, once they have entered into the corporate virtual environment, they are in a secure environment with the appropriate authentication, encryption, and management already in place.

Mobile Data Protection Strategy

When planning a mobile data protection strategy, consider the following:

- **Ensure it is part of an overall company focus by assembling the right leadership:** You need to make sure that a mobile data protection strategy is a cross-organizational effort. You should identify leaders in IT, development, operations, and line of business that will take ownership in delivering on an overall data protection strategy. A cross-organizational team is important because data protection involves not only managing the technology but also people's behaviors. Corporate policies will be important in addition to the technology implementation. You also need to identify key executives (CIO, CTO, CISO, and so on) who can provide the appropriate support and leadership to help you execute your strategy.

- **Define your data loss protection scope:** Initially, you need to understand the scope of the data protection effort and an inventory of the types of data to be protected. You need to understand the impact that regulatory compliance and intellectual property have on your organization.

- **Determine existing gaps:** Perform an inventory of existing systems and policies and determine if there are any gaps. What worked in the past and what has not? Understand if any new requirements do not have a supporting infrastructure.

- **Prioritize on the types of data:** After the scope of data has been determined, you need to prioritize the effort. It is likely that you need to implement your strategy in stages. As a result, you need to prioritize which data sets should be tackled first. Determine if it is email, web-based applications, or internal mobile applications. Consider if it is employee-to-employee (E2E) or employee-to-business partner (E2BP) communications of data that is most important. Determine what would be the most critical data loss prevention method for your strategy (data on the mobile device, data that is in transit between the back end and the device, or data at rest on the back end).

- **Define user groups:** Not all users should have the same access and usage requirements for sensitive data. Determine which user groups have access to which data, and establish a policy for access enforcement and management. Have a set of requirements for memberships in the group. As users change roles, their access requirements and group memberships will change. Or if they violate group membership requirements, they should be removed from an access group. Creating data access groups can reduce the complexity of managing data access.

- **Determine the appropriate device:** Not only are there many types of devices available today in the marketplace, but the security capabilities of each device vary widely. You must determine which devices you will allow within your enterprise and which controls are needed to satisfy your data protection strategy.

  Will you require that the company issues phones that may be expensive or will you allow BYOD? This may tie into your definition of user groups. Those individuals who must access the most-sensitive data may require corporate-issued phones with custom security features. At the same time, those individuals who have less access to sensitive information may have sufficient coverage with a BYOD approach. One of the fundamental aspects that needs to be understood is the state of the encryption capabilities of the device. (Does it support 256-bit AES encryption, for example?) Also, does the encryption cover the entire device and peripherals such as SD cards? Does the device provide encryption at the application level or just the entire device? Is there an appropriate key management policy in place to ensure that encryption keys do not fall into the wrong hands.

- **Minimize risk by reducing sensitive data on mobile devices:** Given that mobile devices are easily lost or stolen, minimize the amount of sensitive data on the mobile device. Although it is unrealistic to eliminate all data from mobile devices, keeping as much sensitive data stored on corporate back-end systems or on a cloud-based environment can reduce risk.[16]

- **Partner with end users when defining a data loss policy:** In the end, the user of the mobile device will be the first line of defense. End users can open their devices to data loss through user error, or letting their guard down and increasing the probability of a malicious attack. The end user needs to comply with policies, while at the same time trying to do their job. It is critical to have end users participate in defining your mobile data loss strategy to gain buy-in and compliance.

- **Ensure that any solution is easy and user-friendly:** Employees are busy and have a specific job to accomplish. Security policies and technologies should not inhibit end user productivity. In addition, one of the unique aspects of mobile is the high-quality end user expectations. Your end users will be accustomed to a high-quality user experience through the use of their personal mobile apps.

   Also, end user behavior is hard to change. The more you have to adjust users' behavior and give them new security 'tasks' to perform, the more likely they will skip steps or figure out a way around your mobile security policy. This may mean separating corporate data and applications from the personal aspects of the device. Wrappers, containers, or virtualization can ensure that corporate applications and data include the appropriate encryption. This way the personal user experience is unencumbered by security challenges and passwords.[17]

- **Educate employees, and then hold them accountable:** When end users have been part of defining the data protection policy and you have done your best to make any solution as unobtrusive as possible, it is now the employees' responsibility to do their part. Employees need to understand the implications and cost of data loss and be part of the solution. Employees should be careful how they carry and store their mobile device to reduce the chances of loss or theft. Travel is an especially vulnerable time as employees are out of their normal routine and can easily leave a device in a hotel room or taxi. Employees should know precisely what to do when they lose their device and report the loss to IT quickly. Employees should know and understand the implications of a remote wipe and lock particularly for a personally owned device.[18]

- **Manual versus automated enforcement:** Where appropriate, remove the end user from the day-to-day decision-making process by making as much of the data protection as automated as possible. This prevents user error and removes the burden from the end user; however, you must keep the employee informed of what is happening in the background. You want to ensure that there is a trust relationship established between the employee and the security team.

■ **Use multifactor authentication for the sensitive data:** Ensuring the appropriate person has access to the appropriate information is critical to an overall mobile data loss strategy. For the sensitive data you might want to consider a multifactor authentication scheme. This is accomplished by using several input methods of the mobile device. In addition to a typical ID/PW challenge, you might send a special code via SMS that can be entered through a mobile app. This gives an additional means of verifying the identity of an individual. You could also utilize other aspects of the phone such as the camera, contact list, device ID, or bar code reader to provide an additional layer of authentication.

■ **Establish an adaptive authentication policy:** One of the biggest challenges in delivering a data loss protection strategy is to find a balance between security and usability. If you make your security policy and user interaction too difficult or complex, users will either abandon your mobile strategy or bypass your security policies. This is further emphasized by the fact that user expectations for mobile devices and applications are greater than with PCs. The authentication process can be one of the biggest challenges for finding a balance between security and usability. One approach may be to use the unique aspects of the mobile device to make an adaptive authentication strategy. For example, you could leverage the device location information to adjust the security profile of an individual. For example, if the individual is in the office, you could assume she is an employee of the company and not a hacker who has stolen the device. As such, the authentication policy could be adjusted. On the other hand, if the user is in a coffee shop, the authentication challenge could be more complex to ensure validation of the individual's identity. An adaptive authentication policy can help find the right balance between security controls and user experience.

■ **Ensure device security is available even when outside of a network connection:** On-device encryption and security can ensure protection even when a network connection is not available.

■ **Have a plan for a data breach:** Assume the worst. If a data loss happens, speed of execution can significantly reduce the cost and impact. Have an outline of specific steps, actions, and protocols defined. Be ready to bring in the right expert to help mitigate and manage the incident. Having a prepared list of authorities, communications agencies, and government official contacts who are ready to spring into action will be critical in mitigating the impact of a data loss.

- **Implemented and integrated solutions:** Implementing an integrated security solution is critical. All aspects of your technical solution need to work together. Leveraging open standards so that your systems work together improving efficiencies, reducing complexity, and allowing for the architecture to adapt to changing requirements is important. Your threat protection, firewall, network security, intrusion prevention, gateway, device security, and management need to work together in a cohesive way.

Data loss is a serious issue. Of all the security issues facing an enterprise, data loss has the potential to have the most significant cost, especially if there is a loss of sensitive information. Data loss can occur as a result of systems' failure, a malicious attack, or human error. You need to protect not only intellectual property, but also comply with regulatory requirements. Building a successful mobile data loss strategy depends on how you establish the right partnership with leaders in the organization and your user community. An end-to-end approach is needed to manage data on the device, data in transit, and data at rest at the back end of the enterprise. Encrypting the data is critical to preventing unauthorized access. Several techniques are available to separate corporate data from personal data on the device. Containers, wrappers, virtualization, and SDK security measures can provide a means to not only protect data on the device, but also to minimize the impact on user experience, particularly in a BYOD environment.

The Adaptive Mobile Security Approach

The mobile industry is constantly changing. New devices and technologies are entering the market at a rapid pace. In addition, the threats to security continue to increase as malicious individuals create more sophisticated attacks. Over time, new threats will outpace your best security practices and policies.

This rapidly changing market will require that you adapt quickly, remaining alert to potential security risks and initiating changes to your strategy when necessary. To do this you must equip your enterprise with advanced analytics that assist you in detecting threats, prioritizing risks and automating compliance activities. In other words, you need to adopt a mobile strategy that can quickly adapt to the rapidly changing industry while maintaining your IT security. As you develop your mobile security strategy, consider the following recommendations:

- Be alert and invest in automation and constant monitoring.
- Be proactive and don't wait until an attack occurs.
- Look for IT anomalies, assuming you have already been attacked.
- Look for signs of unexpected events.
- In addition, to defend against external threats, watch what is going out of your network and where it is going.
- Education is important. Explain the threat in business language so employees (and customers) understand the importance of security and work with you instead of against you.

Summary

This chapter defines the key trends for a mobile security and management strategy. It presents characteristics unique to mobile security and highlights the importance of securing corporate data at the level of the enterprise network, the mobile device, and finally, the mobile app itself. The chapter proceeds by identifying a mobile security framework that outlines various capabilities for securing the device, the network, and the mobile app. These key capabilities include Mobile Device Management (MDM), mobile threat management, mobile information management, mobile network protection, mobile identity and access management, and mobile application security. Along the way, you learned why these capabilities are important, how they work, and key decision areas to consider for each one.

Mobile offers unique opportunities and challenges for security. With an ever-changing landscape of technologies, fast turnarounds, and high user expectations, a mobile security strategy can be a challenge. In some respects, mobile devices create a bigger security risk than traditional PCs but have a higher impact on employee productivity and customer satisfaction. In addition, mobile devices provide more information about context that can enable you to analyze a situation and deliver a more adaptive security posture.

Endnotes

1   International Telecommunications Union

2   Ibid.

3   Juniper Research. "Mobile Security Strategies": http://www.
juniperresearch.com/reports/mobile_security_strategies

4   TechCrunch. "250 Million Android Devices Activated, 11 Billion Apps
Downloaded": http://techcrunch.com/2012/01/19/250-million-android-
devices-activated-11-billion-apps-downloaded/

5   Arxan. "App Protection Resources": http://www.arxan.com/resources/
state-of-security-in-the-app-economy/

6   Gartner. "Mobile Device Management (MDM)": http://www.gartner.
com/it-glossary/mobile-device-management-mdm/

7   Republic of Turkey Ministry of Justice. "Spyware": http://www.
justice.gov.tr/e-journal/pdf/cybercrime_essay.pdf

8   Howzz it? "Latest Mobile Spying Apps for Android Phone":
http://www.howzzit.com/2012/06/14/latest-mobile-spying-apps-for-
android-phone/

9   United States Computer Emergency Readiness Team. "Technical
Information Paper-TIP-10-105-01 Cyber Threats to Mobile Devices":
http://www.flexispy.com/ , www.us-cert.gov/reading_room/
TIP10-105-01.pdf

10 Naked Security. "First iPhone Worm Discovered - Ikee Changes
Wallpaper to Rick Astley Photo": http://nakedsecurity.sophos.com/
2009/11/08/iphone-worm-discovered-wallpaper-rick-astley-photo/

11 TechChunks. "How to Remove (Fix) iPhone Worm – 'iKee'"
http://techchunks.com/technology/apple-technology/how-to-remove-
fix-iphone-worm-virus-ikee/

12 CSO. "Social engineering: 3 Mobile Malware Techniques":
http://www.csoonline.com/article/print/686655

13 SearchServerVisualization. "Hypervisor": http://searchserver
virtualization.techtarget.com/definition/hypervisor

14 Network World. "Mobile Data: Are You Carrying a Suitcase or a Safe?":
http://www.networkworld.com/news/tech/2012/012312-mobile-
encryption-255209.html

15 Ibid.

16 Ibid.

17   ftp://public.dhe.ibm.com/software/tivoli/analystreports/IDC_
Identity_and_Access_Management_report.pdf

[18] Cloud Security Alliance. "OAuth – Authentication and Authorization for Mobile Applications": https://blog.cloudsecurityalliance.org/2011/05/06/oauth-authentication-authorization-for-mobile-applications/

[19] Ibid.

[20] Artic Soft. "An Introduction to PKI (Public Key Infrastructure)": http://www.articsoft.com/public_key_infrastructure.htm

Additional Sources

http://www.tomsitpro.com/articles/mobile_security-mobile_management,2-64-5.html

Cydia: http://cydia.saurik.com/

IBM X-Force Threat Reports: http://www-935.ibm.com/services/us/iss/xforce/trendreports/

7

Mobile Business Transformation

The mobile app changes the way people interact with information, data, and technology in general. The mobile app empowers individuals with information in context of their tasks. Never before in human history have individuals had access to so much computing power and information at the tips of their fingers. The mobile app is more than just a view into existing systems and web content. The mobile app takes information and existing systems and brings them together in context to offer end users the ability to perform a task with much more efficiency and clarity than ever before.

The mobile app can provide information to assist individuals in their moment of need. The mobile app has access to unprecedented information and data with just a touch of a button or a voice command. This information can be in the form of corporate data or information from peers or colleagues. Connectivity to the Internet, social networks, and relevant data at the precise instance the end user needs it can deliver tremendous value.

Mobile devices provide access to unprecedented computing power. The mobile device today has as much computing resources as a PC of a few years ago. As such, the mobile app can perform sophisticated computational processes with ease. Even the graphics horsepower is impressive, offering the end user rich user interaction. In addition, given the always-on access to the web, the mobile app can also leverage the computing power of the cloud.

The mobile device can sense the environment and provide contextual information. The mobile app has access to sensors and input capabilities. This enables the app to pull an interface and interact with the environment around end users. This contextual information enables the app to provide information pertinent to the individual at the precise moment of interaction. It enables the end user to make the best possible choice to help complete tasks.

So how do you apply these new capabilities enabled by the mobile device to transform your business? The key is to apply these capabilities to an overall mobile strategy that focuses on bringing together context, intelligence, and engagement to help your customers perform their tasks more efficiently and provide them the next best action. As you deliver value to your customers, they will allow for a deeper relationship. This relationship will then allow you to deliver better and more compelling service to you customer, driving more business.

Mobile Business Transformation

As discussed in Chapter 2, "Defining Business Value," your life is full of a series of tasks. These tasks may be as simple as making breakfast or going to work. They may be more involved, such as taking a trip or buying a TV. In the end, you perform a set of tasks throughout your personal and work life. Each task is also broken down into a set of task steps. Each task step then takes place in a particular moment of your life. These task steps can take place in sequence or can happen over the course of the day when you have time or when it is most convenient. The real power of the smartphone or tablet is that at the particular moment you perform a particular task step, you have a power computing device at your fingertips that can assist you with that particular task step. Now look at a road trip to the beach as an example. Before you leave you decide to grab lunch at a nearby restaurant. You may try to find something interesting using the Yelp app (a service to help you find local establishments based on your current location). You decide to make a reservation ahead of time using OpenTable (an app that enables you to make reservations). You then may want to check to see if your car is ready for a long trip, so you check your repair history by looking at your auto repair app. You then start your vacation using your GPS navigation app. When you arrive, you download your favorite book to your tablet or e-reader. You may also want to make one last check of your business email and your Facebook page just before taking a dip in the ocean. What becomes interesting is that every moment that you perform your daily activities, a mobile smart device is with you all the time. The computing power and access opens the door for untold efficiency and productivity improvement. Mobile devices that tie together past behavior, information, environmental data and information from systems of records can significantly reduce the complexity involved in each task you need to perform.

You have a device that is always on and connected to supply you with the latest information. The smart device can sense the environment to assist you with information about the context you are in to provide additional information at your particular moment of need. The delivery of this intelligence and contextual information is provided in the form of a mobile app. The mobile app offers a discrete application designed specifically for your task and assists you with the latest information and insight to help you take the next best action in your task journey. In the end, the mobile device has the capability to simplify the task by either reducing friction between task steps (by providing information that makes it easier to perform the task) or removing steps.

The linkage between the mobile device, and your daily lives is revolutionary and has far-reaching consequences. The mobile app opens the door for efficiency and productivity improvements in the lives of your end users. This leads to a transformative experience between your company and your employee or customer which will change the way business is done today and going forward. The transformational experience occurs when you have a deep understanding of your end users and engage them in their task by extending your existing business systems and leveraging intelligence to further deepen the engagement. A transformative mobile app can deliver value in several critical ways:

- **Deeper relationship with your customers:** As you engage with your customers by helping them make their lives easier, they will have a greater affinity, trust, and loyalty with your company. You mobile app is used in their daily lives, making your end user more efficient, giving them more free time, performing their task more efficiently. In response to you providing value for them through engaging at the right moment, you can gain a deeper relationship with customers who in turn give you more business, providing deeper information about who they are and what they need. This in turn gives you the opportunity to offer more valuable services that help you have an even deeper engagement.

The deeper relationship with the customer does not necessarily need to happen in a self-service model of an individual interacting with your company via a mobile app. The improved interaction can take place face-to-face with a mobile app assisting your salesperson, insurance agent, or bank employee. The mobile app helps provide your employee with the latest status of information such as store inventory, claims processes, or loan status. The mobile app in the hands of a sales associate can deliver information and resources to truly engage the customer and take the relationship to the next level.

- **Improves business processes:** As the transformative mobile app helps to make the life of the individual more efficient, it can also make the business process more efficient for your company. For example, as end users perform their task, they can become more self-sufficient requiring less assistance, and they begin to answer their own questions instead of contacting a call-center.

  In addition, as steps are removed from customers' overall tasks, the supporting business process becomes simpler. As the business process "listens" to end users and adapts, the business process will become more efficient while reducing costs.

- **More productive employees:** There are many ways that a transformative app can improve employee efficiency. As steps are taken out of a set of tasks, the employee can get more done faster. Collaboration is streamlined as employees can interact with each other on the go and at any time. Rich interactive dashboards help employees gain access and analyze data quickly for better decision making.

- **New business solutions:** As you engage your customers in their task, there will be new opportunities to develop new services and offerings that were never previously conceived. The combination of smart devices, environmental sensors, contextual information, and an array of third-party services can be brought together into new solutions that can transform the way you interact with your customer.

Delivering a Mobile Transformation: Extending Existing Systems to Mobile Employees and Customers Through Context, Engagement, and Intelligence

To deliver a mobile transformation for your business, you need to consider "mobile first" from a design, development, business, and interaction point of view. More and more consumers/employees are shifting from PCs to mobile devices as their primary means to interact with a company or each other. New systems need to be put in place that are more focused on engaging people instead of managing the process around a transaction. As the market shifts from a PC-specific interaction model to a mobile/smart device model and mobile becomes the primary interface, you need to build systems of engagement.

The notion of *systems of engagement* was termed by Geoffrey Moore as a means of describing a new system focused on delivering value to individuals at the moment it is needed. Systems of engagement are different than *systems of record*. While a system of record (or traditional back-end systems) focuses on a company's business process, transactions, and financial systems, a system of engagement is focused on people. A system of engagement is *empowering customers, employees, and partners with context-rich apps and smart products to help them decide and act immediately in their moment of need.*[1]

Not every app is automatically going to transform your business. What makes an app transformative and as a result will have the biggest impact on your business? Thinking in terms of *mobile first* and extending systems of record to systems of engagement leads to a mobile transformation. In other words, it is not enough to simply put a mobile interface on a preexisting application. You must redo the application so that it takes advantage of mobile technology. This transformation is about rethinking your business in context of constantly connected employees and customers. It means empowering your end users with contextual information that helps them make decisions on how best to complete their task. As discussed in Chapter 4, "The Mobile Framework," to deliver a true mobile transformation, you need to focus on mobile engagement and mobile intelligence. *Mobile engagement* is having a deep understanding of the task your end users are trying to perform and, as a result, making the task steps easier or removing steps all together. *Mobile intelligence* is about understanding the context of the task and determining the end user's next best action. Finally, a transformative app ties back to existing systems linking in business processes, past customer behavior, and transactions. Entering into the daily lives of your customer or employee and bringing together engagement, intelligence, and existing back-end systems into a cohesive solution are the ingredients of a truly transformative mobile solution. Figure 7.1 shows how putting a mobile face on traditional back-end systems can deliver a simple mobile app. It is not until you extend your traditional systems with mobile engagement and mobile intelligence with context that you can deliver on a transformative mobile app.

System of engagement leads to a mobile transformative

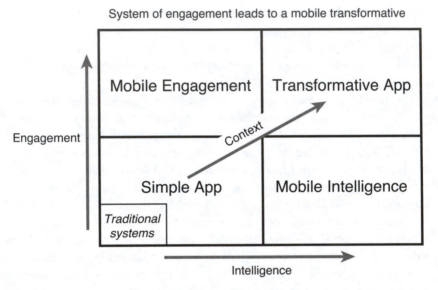

Figure 7.1 Delivering a transformative app is about extending your traditional business systems with engagement and intelligence to help your customer or employee complete their tasks.

Mobile Context

A mobile transformative app is fundamentally contextual in nature. For a mobile solution to simplify an individual's task, the experience must take in to account a complete view of what is known about the individual in addition to what he is experiencing at a particular moment. Mobile context pulls together information about the *environment* (what is happening to the individual), the user *sentiment* (his role, attitude, perception, and social network sentiment), and *historical behavior* (what is known about the individual's past activities). The contextual information about an individual is always in motion; it is constantly changing, revealing new understanding.

Environmental Context

Location, time, and environmental inputs give richer information about the context of the moment. The end user may directly engage with the physical environment—scanning QR codes, price checking by scanning bar codes, and gathering insight through augmented reality. A transformative solution needs to know the current location, orientation, and environmental data of the end user and apply it to improving the task at hand.

Has the end user just entered a museum for the first time and likely needs a map to become oriented? Is she about to enter a meeting and needs all the pertinent data available for that meeting in a handy dashboard?

Individual Identity

To deliver an engaging app, the system needs to understand who the end user is and his preferences. Insight into his role, current state, situation, and attitude all provide information about what can be done at this moment to help the user as he performs his task.

Historical Behavior

Historical behavior is important since it gathers the information about past interactions, transactions, and decisions the end user has made with you. This information can be used to help provide a better service or predict what the end user needs next. This information is usually pulled from traditional systems.

For example, do your customers have a propensity for purchasing apparel? Do they prefer aisle seats or window seats when they travel?

Mobile Engagement

How do you interact and engage your end users in the new era of mobility? A focus on engagement means empowering your end users with contextual information that helps them more efficiently complete their task. For example, take the task of requesting a taxi. The process involves standing on the corner of the street (inevitably in the rain) and waiting for a taxi to arrive. Or perhaps you look up a phone number for a taxi service and call to make an appointment (hoping the particular service you call has a taxi available when you need it). A transformative approach is to have an app that with a click of a button notifies all available taxi drivers that there is a person in need of a ride. Based on the location and proximity, a particular taxi driver then accepts the request and proceeds to pick up the person. The end user can see the taxi driver approaching on his GPS-enabled map. The user then completes the transaction on the app. This approach radically simplifies the taxi process and provides a high-level of engagement for the end user.

Simplified Information Delivery

Unlike the web/PC era in which people comfortably sat behind a desk and browse for information, mobile engagement is about delivering the right information at the right time and place to help end users meet their needs and complete tasks in the moment. Information delivery needs to be radically simplified, exposing just what users need at the right moment. Mobile interaction happens in short bursts. The average app usage may be just a few seconds or a minute at most. So how can you, in a short amount of time, present information that is relevant and consumable in context of what the end user is trying to accomplish? Content delivery systems need to be related to context where information delivery is provided based on geolocation, role, time, and end user intent. Information may need to be converted into mobile-friendly formats to be consumable; perhaps images need to be compressed, or XML may need to be converted to JSON on-the-fly. User interaction and interface is significantly simplified where just the essential navigation and user experience is exposed at a particular relevant moment. Interactions between the mobile user and the environment are radically simplified. Think about how a check can be cashed simply by taking a picture of it, or contact information can be transferred simply by "bumping" two devices together. Extreme personalization can occur when the app learns from the interaction based on your past activities and updates its user interface and functionality. Adoption of the app is also simplified through almost zero barriers to entry. Complicated logins and forms, or even paying for the app, goes against mobile user expectations. A freemium pricing model is now the norm where users get immediate value from the free app and then may pay for enhanced features later as they progress.

Omnichannel Is Both Cross-Channel and Multichannel

Omnichannel provides a seamless, consistent experience across all channels of interaction. The user may not use a mobile device to perform an entire task. The expectation is that the transformative experience transcends time and place. As users perform their task, they may have a variety of interactions with the overall system. There can be single-channel interaction in which end users interact through a single app. However, more likely, a transformative system is *multichannel* in which end users interact with your business through a variety of touch points that may include physical interaction (such as a bank teller or sales associate), mobile, social, video, and web channels. These interaction vehicles must come together to enable a seamless experience that is responsive to a customer's constantly shifting context. A transformative system is also *cross-channel*; as end users try to perform a task, they interact with a variety of systems such as customer service, fulfillment, order management, and so on. The state, data, and experience must be managed as end users move across the systems to complete their task. Cloud-based storage and synchronization become critical to the overall omnichannel approach. As users move from interaction to interaction, their data can move with them. In the end, your mobile strategy must ensure that as end users interact with your system across multiple device types and systems (see Figure 7.2), there is a means of keeping the systems coordinated and orchestrated so that end users can efficiently complete their task.

To illustrate an omnichannel experience, consider a business trip. There is one large task (get to a destination and back), but there are a set of smaller subtasks that span time and channel. Before the flight, a customer may use a PC to make a reservation and select seat assignments where it is easy to see which flights work best. As he gets closer to the flight, he might switch to his mobile device to check in and get an e-ticket on his phone. At the airport, the customer goes to a kiosk to check a bag. The kiosk data is tied into any changes the app may have made. The customer may use his phone to check departure time or see if he can get access to an airport lounge. During flight, the app may then provide status on arrival time, GPS coordinates of the plane, weather, or entertainment. After the customer lands, the app can provide baggage carousel location information. If there is a lost bag, the customer can make a claim from the mobile device. After the trip, the customer may switch to a PC and may check award mileage status, get receipts for expense claims, and so on. So a system of engagement ties together multiple channels, interfaces, and systems to bring together a complete solution that helps the end user perform his tasks.

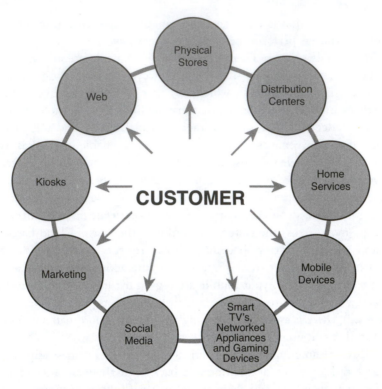

Figure 7.2   A transformative mobile solution puts the customer or employee at the center of an omnichannel interaction model that will span a variety of input mechanism and business systems.

Service Composition and Application Linking

A transformative solution will focus on streamlining the end user's task at hand. It integrates into the life of end users making a difference in the way they conduct their lives. However, there may not be a way to have a single app meet all the needs of the end users. It may need to bring together capabilities from across a variety of apps and services to complete the task. Some of these services and apps may have been developed by third parties or partners. To provide the best experience for end users, you may need to bring in a variety of capabilities you may not own or have the expertise in delivering. As such, you will likely need to bring together services and apps in new ways to provide a complete experience for end users. To accomplish this, a transformative solution must have the means to enable both *service composition* and *app linking*.

Service Composition

Service composition is about bringing together services the end users must have to solve their task. These services need to be delivered, managed, and orchestrated cohesively in order to accomplish the desired task. Think about a photo sharing app; end users need to take a photo, perhaps tie into a photo storage service in the cloud, and then link into their favorite social networking service. The app needs to link capabilities on the mobile device with other services that may be available in the cloud or traditional back-end systems. Together, these individual services are then used to compose new applications.

In some cases you want to expose your business services to others so that they can build apps that leverage the services that your company offers. For example, perhaps you are a marketing company and you want to offer campaign management services that others can easily include in their app. The following considerations will help you deliver your services to the market so that they are consumable. Each service has access to federated-identity in order to manage consistent and seamless access based on role and identity. Usually these services will be cloud-based for ubiquitous access. These services may need to have access to native capabilities of the device. Service management also needs to be in place, providing the appropriate management, monitoring, orchestration, and analytics of the services. This way you can govern how the services are used and delivered so that you (or your partners who provide the services) understand how the services are used and if they need to be improved or adjusted. There also needs to be a developer program associated with the delivery of the services to ensure that the services are easily consumed by developers and to provide them with supporting tools, education, and sample code.

Application Linking

Perhaps there will be a need to link a variety of apps together. Actually, many of the present-day mobile tasks are composed of sequences of apps, manually "integrated" by users. What if this integration was enabled by you through appropriate partnerships and technologies to deliver a complete experience?

Think about the scenario of a stock trader. She might constantly jump from a market news app, to her brokerage account app, to a trading community app, to her futures market app, and back again. It would be valuable for these apps to be linked or chained together in a way that makes it easier for her to bring all the essential capabilities into a more powerful tool to solve her task. Or perhaps consider a health management app designed to help people lose weight. There are other complementary apps that may be needed to provide the end user with a complete experience. Linking a weight management app with an exercise app, a health monitoring capabilities (perhaps blood glucose monitoring in the case of diabetes) app, and a diet app would give the end user a complete 360-degree experience that could drive greater value, loyalty, and more business.

Mobile Intelligence

Mobile intelligence is about having a complete view of the mobile end users' situation and how to provide the best service, experience, and insight to complete their goal. It means *analyzing* the situation by tying into past behavior, current context, and events. Based on this analysis, mobile intelligence is about providing a mechanism to *adapt* given the situation. Adaptation is often done in real time where user interface menus or security posture may change based on the best available information. Mobile intelligence is also about offering the *next best action* to the user: suggesting the step they need to complete their task.

Analyze

In order to obtain a full picture of how best to engage the end user and provide the greatest value, you must collect and analyze data about the user's context, events, past behavior, and current intent. Data may be collected over a period of time to analyze users' behavior to better understand how best to serve them or do business with them. Consider how mobile technologies in automobiles can feed driver-behavior information directly to the insurance company, which in turn would use that data to adjust the premiums it charges. Data can be used to understand usability and feed into a continuous development process that can further improve the users' experience. For example, perhaps the data feeds into a playback mechanism to study how users perform a particular task. Data may be collected as part of a marketing campaign to better understand usage and engagement trends, in-app ad response, searches and purchases, or perhaps session duration, frequency, and conversion history. Perhaps data is collected as part of an ongoing under-standing of your system security posture. Data needs to be collected to understand new threats and their nature of attack. Information needs to be collected and processed to deliver the insight into the end users' needs at a particular moment. Some analyses need to be real time and driven by scalable infrastructure that can handle the volume, velocity, and variety of big data. Interfacing and understanding social network sentiment will be part of the analysis process. Bringing in feeds of data and injecting them into an overall view of sentiment will be part of the analytics necessary for a transformative app. The data may also reside in traditional systems that may show past pur-chase behavior. Finally, with all this data being collected, there needs to be a process for handling sensitive data. You need to ensure that trust is estab-lished with end users and the data is used for its intended purpose to deliver value to end users.

Adapt

New events may occur from back-end systems or external sensors that require your system to react. Some of the data may be collected and stored for later analyses (such as usability) whereas some of the data needs to be moni-tored in real time (such as security threats). Adaptability is a hallmark of a transformative mobile solution. As data comes in, and is analyzed, you need to adapt given the best available information. This data may require you to update the app with new navigation and provide an update to the end user.

Next Best Action

Has something new happened that requires the app to adjust? Perhaps the end user has entered a new step in the process and as such, the app menu should change so that the most pertinent tasks are most visible. For example, if you are about to check into your flight, the check-in button is highlighted instead of the baggage claim menu.

In-the-Moment Offers

The in-the-moment offer matches past behavior with current context to deliver an offer at the moment of transaction. This scenario provides an ideal situation for the retail industry in which the customers' location, context, and past behavior come together to help with the next best action in their retail process.

First, customers would opt into the program. Customers would under-stand and sign any privacy and terms and conditions information. Customers would grant access to location and past purchase history and location information. At the same time, customers would understand the value of the program and recognize that it is greater than the price of sharing personal information.

As customers shop, they swipe their credit card at a particular retailer. The system then looks up their preferences based on past credit card purchase decisions. The system will know they purchase a new pair of shoes every 8 months and are due for a new purchase. The system would then check the location of end users and determine that there is a shoe store nearby that they purchased from in the past. A text message or email would be sent to end users with an offer for a discount at the shoe store.

By bringing together past buying behavior from traditional systems of records, along with context through location, you can make compelling offers that can drive more transactions.

Building Trust Through Independent Information

At the moment of decision, you need all the appropriate information. Sometimes the best information is from others who have had to make a similar decision in the past. This is where tying social insights into a task becomes valuable. Consider the following scenario at an auto repair shop.

You own an auto repair shop. A customer comes in for an oil change. During the course of performing the oil change, you discover that the customer needs a new water pump that will soon fail. As you present your finding to the customer, he immediately becomes suspicious. He came to your store to perform a particular task (change oil for $29.99) and instead you are changing his task to a water pump repair for $150.00. The customer might feel as though you are trying to take advantage of the situation by selling something that is not needed.

What if you were to introduce a third party as an arbitrator into the situation? This is where mobile intelligence can provide value by leveraging social sentiment. Assume the same situation, but on a previous visit, your auto repair shop had offered the customer a mobile app that provided a mechanism to deliver a deeper relationship with the customer. The intent of the app was to arm the customer with the latest information and tools to provide the best maintenance for his car. For example, the app provided the customer with his past repair history and latest information about recommended repairs from independent parties. Repair manuals and other industry documentation were also available at the customer's fingertips. The app might also provide a tool to help save for future repairs. Perhaps the app would even provide access to diagnostics data from the car. And finally, it would provide access to opinions from individuals posting on social networks and discussion forums. In this way, the customer could validate any car repair with input from others who had the same experience.

In the particular scenario in which the customer is armed with a mobile repair app, he realizes that others with the same make of car, with the same model, and same number of mileage, also needed a water pump repair. In the end, the mobile app provides a means to build relationship and trust by providing independent information at the moment of decision. This empowers the individual to make the right decision and keeps him coming back to you as a trusted partner.

SoCloDaMo: Coherent Integration Between Social Networks, Cloud, Big Data Analytics, and Mobile

In order to maximize the reach of your business, your app must be available worldwide and around the clock, and you must have access to an almost unlimited supply of user data. You can achieve this through the integration between several key technologies: cloud, social, data analytics (big data), and mobile (also known as SoCloDaMo). These technologies are critical for delivering a transformative mobile solution. Linking in data from *social* networks provides a source of sentiment information that can be analyzed to help end users with their tasks. *Cloud* provides a ubiquitous platform that delivers computing power to help analyze all the incoming data and information from the mobile devices. Then, of course, *mobile* devices and technologies provide the interface and means of interacting with end users in their time of need. More is discussed about SoCloDaMo in Chapter 9, "SoCloDaMo (Social + Cloud + Big Data + Mobile)."

Security, Privacy, and Trust Become Paramount

A fundamental tenant of a system of engagement is that you will be collecting, analyzing, and linking all sorts of information. Historical data, data from sensors, and social data all come together to deliver context. This data then provides greater value to end users and helps them to deliver on their task. This improves the interaction with your business and can help drive more business and a deeper relationship with your customers. However, great care must be taken as you enter into the daily lives of your customers or employees. It goes without saying that the data you collect must be protected from unauthorized access. However, data must be used only to provide value for the end users and the end users must understand the intent and use of the data. There should be clear opt-in and opt-out mechanisms so that people can have an easy and straightforward way to enter or exit your program. Making it easy for the end user to start and stop sharing information will ensure that you are not seen as violating privacy and trust with individuals. There needs to be clear understanding of the exchange of value; for example, your customer will provide you their location information in exchange for notification of local discounts. As you construct your mobile program, remember that the deeper the trust relationship with end users, the richer information they will provide, which in turn allows you to provide greater value, which will lead to more business.

Strategy for Delivering a Mobile Transformation

A mobile transformation brings together key technologies and capabilities that separate it from a traditional simple app. To build a mobile transformation, you should start with a solid foundation of capabilities and then grow over time. You need to start by defining a strategy to build your mobile app and connect it to your business processes, logic, and data.

The mobile development strategy is based on bringing together the right tools, technologies, and capabilities to enable an application development process that is fast and provides the highest user quality. To accomplish this, you need to have a means of providing a comprehensive mobile life-cycle management system that provides the appropriate testing and continuous improvement, while at the same time provides quick-and-easy integration to traditional back-end systems.

The management and security strategy needs to provide mobile application management to ensure that the entire life cycle of the app is governed. In this way, the app can be updated if a new version is needed or disabled if there is a flaw with the app and a new one needs to be downloaded. In a bring-your-own-device (BYOD) scenario in which employees bring their devices to work, there can be an advantage to managing corporate data and assets at the app level instead of the device level—so that personal information is not touched. The mobile device must be managed and secured to prevent malicious attacks and unauthorized usage. Finally, the mobile network needs to be managed and secured by ensuring that the access to corporate information is controlled and appropriate encryption of data is performed.

These foundational capabilities of build and connect and manage and secure, as shown in Figure 7.3, form the foundation for a transformative mobile solution. Bringing together the mobile context, engagement, and intelligence then allows you to deliver a compelling mobile solution for any industry.

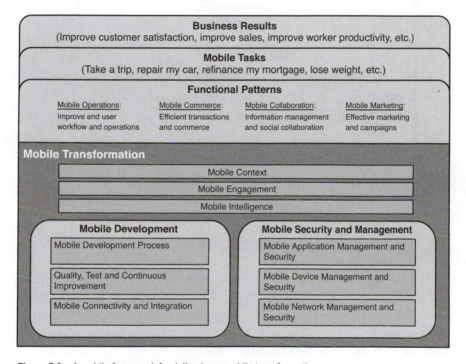

Figure 7.3 A mobile framework for delivering a mobile transformation.

After you have the mobile foundational capabilities, how do you move toward transformative mobile solutions? This does not have to happen all at once. You can start small and grow as you engage your customer. Begin by adding contextual features to the app while extending your systems of record. You then ensure that your mobile app is omnichannel by engaging the end user across devices and processes. Finally, utilize past behavior and social sentiment to help predict the next best action the users should take.

As shown in Figure 7.4, a transformative app is delivered by bringing all these aspects together into a cohesive system that builds on each other and can transform your business.

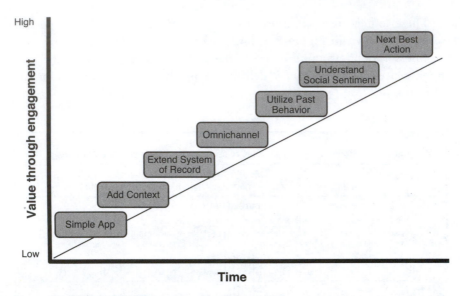

Figure 7.4 Steps to building a transformative mobile solution.

Summary

Delivering a transformative mobile solution is based on extending existing traditional back-end data and services with systems of engagement marked by intelligence, context, and engagement. As you deliver a transformative solution, you need to consider the key attributes and how they come together in context of an overall framework.

Systems of record have information that is critical to a system of engagement solution. Historical information such as buying behavior, inventory status, and order status are all key elements that play a critical role in defining a contextual interaction. Your core business logic is what makes your company different and unique. Taking your core business processes and delivering them as valuable services within a mobile context across multiple channels can separate you from your competitors. The end result can empower customers, employees, and partners to more effectively decide and act in the moment.

Systems of record were never designed for mobility; therefore, a new set of capabilities is needed to extend systems of record to systems of engagement. Systems of record were designed for a particular business process and workflow. They were not designed for a particular task—or how the task breaks down into atomic steps that can be dynamically rearranged and updated based on the particular user's context. Systems of record were more focused on transaction and less on user engagement and experience. Your existing systems of record did not consider a user interface since business processes worked against other business processes. Systems of record were never designed to incorporate the contextual information available from mobile devices.

As you look to extend existing systems of record, you will need to consider all of the following: First, there is a need for a set of foundational technology to deliver the mobile app—you need to build and connect the mobile app, and manage and secure the app, network, and device. Next, you need to extend your traditional systems with mobile context, engagement, and intelligence to help your users to solve their tasks. The delivery of these capabilities requires a comprehensive mobile strategy. A mobile strategy that delivers on the promise of a mobile transformation enables a deeper relationship with your customers because you engage them in their daily lives. It can improve business processes by cutting steps that are no longer needed, therefore reducing the cost of your existing business processes. Your employees can be more productive as they become more efficient. Finally, the transformative mobile solution can enable new business solutions that were never conceived of before.

Endnotes

[1] Blogs.Forrester.Com, "A Billion Smartphones Require New Systems of Engagement," Ted Schadler: http://blogs.forrester.com/ted_schadler/ 12-02-14-a_billion_smartphones_require_new_systems_of_ engagement

8

Planning a Mobile Project

As discussed throughout the book, mobility has become front and center in the way enterprises conduct business today. There is tremendous opportunity to reach new customers and help employees become more productive; however, challenges remain with a dynamic ecosystem of constantly changing technologies. Mobile devices have come out of the consumer market and do not always have enterprise-ready capabilities. Customers and employees expect extremely high-quality applications, yet also expect new features and evolving releases with unreasonable speed. Organizationally, mobility creates a challenge because it can span the entire company, which can have implications across functional boundaries. Teams need to come together in ways that they may not have in the past.

What is the best way to navigate all the challenges and capture the value that mobile has to offer? Use a comprehensive mobile strategy. Yet many struggle with how to deliver on a strategy on a topic that is difficult to get their head around. There are so many new technologies that appear on the scene every day. You need an approach and methodology that is future-proof and relevant regardless of which new technology is introduced.

You must create a comprehensive strategy and a framework to define and execute on the strategy. It needs to start with the organization and leadership. As you begin to build a comprehensive mobile strategy, you need to consider the following steps:

1. *Define mobile team structure and leadership.*
2. *Define value goals. What will drive value?*
3. *Define value indicators and value measurements. What does the customer want to accomplish?*
4. *Choose an approach: Define functional patterns and capabilities.*
5. *Assess gaps: Use mobile framework to assess gaps.*
6. *Define an overall roadmap and plans based on a mobile framework.*
7. *Assess against measurements then adjust approach and improve functional capabilities.*

These steps outline a basic methodology for creating a successful mobile strategy. The mobile framework starts with establishing the appropriate cross-functional teams and leadership to make the critical decisions with speed and insight. Today, many organizations are floundering with a lack of team structure to make decisions across functional teams. Next, the methodology focuses on goals and value creation for the organization and the customer. The methodology sets a direction for the effort by choosing an approach based on functional patterns and capabilities. This must be driven by an overall approach of helping customers achieve their goals based on completing their tasks. Next, you determine the technical and functional gaps in your approach based on an overall mobile capability framework. The structure of build, connect, manage, secure, extend, and transform can guide you in defining an overall gap analysis and a definition of a roadmap for execution. Finally, you need to measure the success of the project. Mobile technology is constantly changing, and the speed of execution is critical. As such, you must constantly measure and assess the success of your mobile project and then put in corrective actions to improve your strategy. Figure 8.1 shows the major steps in a mobile strategy methodology.

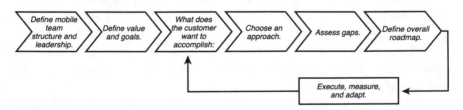

Figure 8.1 Mobile strategy methodology.

Define Mobile Team Structure and Leadership

Defining the mobile leadership is vital for a successful mobile project. The mobile space is fast-changing, and as a result, you must have the appropriate leadership in place to drive project success. Many organizations are not prepared for the intense focus on speed and quality needed for a mobile project to be successful. The mobile leadership likely must coordinate teams from across the organization. Mobile is not just an IT initiative, but it also draws on expertise from across the organization. Mobile is inherently cross-organization. The mobile leadership needs to coordinate across all the major disciplines within the organization: sales, marketing, legal, IT, HR, procurement, call support, partners, and so on.

There needs to be a mobile champion or czar that leads the mobile effort and aligns the cross-organization team. This can be an existing business or technical leader, or in some instances, a new position may need to be formed. (Some have started to use the term CMO, or chief mobile officer.) The mobile leader needs to have deep technical knowledge of the mobile market and stay on top of major changes. The mobile champion needs to think strategically and holistically. Think in terms of a mobile project as not just a B2C or B2E effort, but as a single effort that draws on the entire organization. This helps to avoid duplicate efforts but also uses the precious skills that are in short supply. The mobile champion needs to stay on top of the mobile effort across all the various projects and keep a keen focus on the broader mobile vision for the company.

The mobile champion needs to set the vision and focus for mobility in the company and set the expectation that mobile is different and will be the cornerstone of the company's success. Given mobility's strategic nature, the mobile champion needs to reign in and coordinate all the different efforts that may have already started. Some in the organization may have ramped up a rogue effort that needs to be "brought into the fold." Other projects may need more emphasis on mobile and given direction to become "mobile first." In the end, establishing the mobile leadership and cross-functional team is critical to the success of a mobile project. Under the mobile champion's leadership, the appropriate goals can be established and linked to value for the customer and employees.

Define Value Goals

When the leadership and cross-function organization has been established, you must establish the overall goal for the mobile effort. There may be multiple projects that occur over the life of a mobile strategy, but there needs to be an overarching goal for the organization's mobile effort. These higher-level goals help to set overall direction and keep the teams focused in the midst of rapid change while keeping the end state in mind. These overall business goals can likely be geared to either B2C or B2E. These business drivers can include increasing worker productivity, improving customer service, improving customer satisfaction, and so on. Table 8.1 outlines an example of high-level mobile goals.

Table 8.1 Examples of High-Level Mobile Goals

Business-to-Enterprise	Business-to-Consumer
Increase worker productivity.	Improve customer satisfaction.
Improved claims processing.	Deepen customer engagement and loyalty.
Increase revenue through sales engagements.	Drive increased sales through personalized offers.
Extend existing applications to mobile workers and customers.	Improve customer service.
Reducing fuel, gas, or fleet maintenance costs relevant in particular industries.	Use a competitive differentiator.
Increase employee responsiveness and decision-making speed.	Improve brand perception.
Resolve internal IT issues faster.	Deepen insight into customer buying behavior for up sell and cross sell.
Reduce personnel cost (utilizing personal-owned instead of corporate-issued devices).	Improve in-store experience with mobile concierge services.

These high-level goals may be too high level for the purposes of execution by the IT teams. As such, you need to take it to a more specific level with more detail about the specific feature goals and how it can relate to the tasks.

The team needs specific measureable goals with a definition of how they explicitly apply to mobile. You need to set the direction of what specifically a customer wants to accomplish.

Define Value Indicators and Value Measurements (What Does the Customer Want to Accomplish?)

Building a mobile app is different than a traditional app. A mobile app is about immediacy, context, and engagement. A successful app involves having a deep understanding of a task and what the user needs to do to accomplish the task. There needs to be a deep understanding of the flow of tasks today and the desired state going forward. You must be creative because you are not bound by a single location or single time. Think creatively about how you can remove steps and streamline the process for the end user. A mobile solution also touches multiple business processes and potentially partner services.

Setting goals and tying these goals to the overall organization goals is a key first step. You then must tie to core business drivers at the appropriate level to drive-specific function and capability development. You must link the high-level goals with key performance indicators (KPI). Getting to the level of KPI involves interviewing key stakeholders, end users, and customers to get the true indicators of value. Interviews, research, and brainstorming sessions can also help break down the higher-level goal into actionable focus areas that can be measured. You should also consider the future state and how the future applications may be created. You may also want to benchmark what the competition is doing or compare to industry leading apps.

As we saw in Chapter 2, "Defining Business Value," Table 8.2 shows an example of how the core goal (improve patient satisfaction) of the overall mobile strategy is linked to a particular mobile initiative (electronics patient chart app). The mobile initiative is then linked to value indicators (quality of care and patient safety) and KPIs (improving communications between doctors and reducing drug allergy interactions). Then, you must link to proposed measurements and a possible approach to execution. These items certainly evolve as the strategy is iterated and more understanding of the customer is gained through more interviews, prototypes, and so on.

Table 8.2   Linking Mobile Goals with Value Indicators, Performance Indicators, Measurements, and Possible Approach

Value Goal: Improve Customer Satisfaction
*Project Capability: **Healthcare**—Electronic Patient Chart App*

Value Indicator	Performance Indicator	Measurement	Approach
Workflow optimization	Reduce time of check-in.	Percentage of change in check-in time	Staff checks in patients with tablet as they enter the hospital.
	Reduce time of diagnosis.	Percentage of change in time to diagnosis	Mobile app contains patient records latest tests, and recommended diagnosis based on best available information.
Quality of care	Improve communications between doctors.	Survey of employee satisfaction	Send messages and patient information securely between staff.
		Reduced misdiagnosis due to more detailed information	Dictate notes into patient's record or take pictures of injury.
Patient safety	Reduce drug allergies.	Percentage of change in drug allergy-related incidence	Mobile app has access to drug allergies and information about how new drug will conflict with existing patient's prescriptions.
Cost	Reduce lab work.	Percentage of decrease in number of duplicate lab tests	Check and track status of lab work to prevent duplicate tests.

Choose an Approach: Define Functional Patterns and Capabilities

When there is a clearly defined goal for the overall project and a set of core value propositions, you have established the direction for the overall project. By defining a set of measurements, you have guideposts that define the overall direction for the initiative and ensure that you stay on the right path going forward. You should then define a high-level approach for accomplishing the goals and capturing value.

Next, you need to think through some core functional patterns that can help to determine the functional scope of your project. What is the flavor of your project? Is it focused on improving workflow, commerce, information management, or marketing? Perhaps it may be a combination of several of these areas. Choosing a set of functional patterns can help to define a set of capabilities that likely are needed in a mobile project.

A functional pattern (originally introduced in Chapter 4, "The Mobile Framework") falls into four categories relevant to both employee-based and consumer-based apps:

- **Mobile operations:** Improved workflow and operations
- **Mobile commerce:** Efficient transactions and commerce
- **Mobile collaboration:** Information management and social collaboration
- **Mobile marketing:** Effective marketing

These categories help to scope the overall project by defining a set of common patterns that work across a variety of apps. The focus on these functional patterns can help refine skills and technology that can be repeatedly used across a variety of projects. This helps to streamline execution and build deeper skills and expertise.

After you have the scope of how you plan to execute, you need to assess the approach to execution and make some initial technology decisions. Do you need a web, hybrid, or native app? Which business processes are impacted? Do you need to support multiple device platforms? If so, which ones will you target first, and which ones do you anticipate you will support in the future? What other channels are needed—kiosk, desktop, and so on?

Assess Gaps: Use Mobile Framework to Assess Gaps

Now that there is a sense of what needs to be done, the next step is to see if you have what it takes to execute. A gap analysis (determining the difference between your current state of capabilities and the desired state outlined by your strategy) is needed both technically and organizationally. Overall, the mobile framework outlined in this book can help to provide a checklist against the major functional elements that are core to a mobile strategy. This framework defines the core capabilities needed to build and connect mobile applications, manage and secure applications and devices, and finally extend and transform a business. By assessing current capabilities within the context of a comprehensive framework, you can build a plan to fill the gaps or scale your project for success.

The mobile framework can also help to set expectations for a realistic mobile solution. If budgets are not available to fill all the gaps, you need to reassess the overall goals for the project and set expectations. Too many projects jump into mobile without taking into account what it actually takes to be successful. Organizations get stuck in a situation in which they enter a mobile relationship with an end user but fail to have the resources, skills, and capabilities to fully develop the relationship. Then they cannot set or meet expectations.

The output of the gap analysis provides input into an overall architecture and solution strategy along with a roadmap and timeline to visually see the gaps in your strategy. Originally introduced in Chapter 4, Figure 8.2 illustrates an overall strategic framework that can help you visually see the key consideration for an overall mobile strategy.

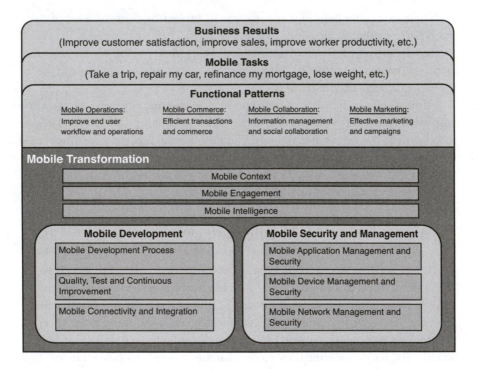

Figure 8.2 The mobile framework for assessing gaps and defining an overall roadmap.

Define Overall Roadmap and Plans Based on a Mobile Framework

After you define the gaps within the context of organization capabilities, the next step is to define a blueprint for technical capabilities. A complete set of recommendations within the context of a strategy roadmap can be completed only after the architecture is defined. The roadmap and architecture will be rooted in the overall organization development and deployment process. The level and details of the architecture will vary by organization. Some need great details, whereas others require high-level direction that allows for implementation teams to define details on their own. The mobile framework defined in this book can provide a high-level view of the major capabilities needed in the architecture. The overall solution architecture will likely span several dimensions:

- **Physical architecture:** Defines the overall topology of the systems and assets needed to deliver the mobile solutions.
- **Logical architecture:** Defines the systems, interfaces, and data flow.
- **Usage architecture:** Defines the behavior and activity of the individual and how they will interact with the system and business processes. For B2C, the usage architecture defines the engagement with the end user and may define marketing and promotional campaigns. From a B2E perspective, the usage architecture may help derive a set of corporate policies and organizational structure in order to deliver on the mobile solution.

The mobile architecture then defines an action plan for delivering the mobile implementation within the context of overall mobile goals and a value proposition. The mobile architecture can lead to a specific set of action items. It may indicate needed additional gaps, refinement of performance indicators, or a definition of new business processes. Each action item should be tracked along with associated risk, benefits, and corrective next steps. Action plans should also point to skills needed, organizational changes, budgets, and technology adoption plans.

The next step is to use the mobile architecture as a basis for an overall mobile roadmap. A mobile strategy does not need to address every aspect of a mobile agenda at once. You can stage mobile execution to align with organizational capabilities. Executing on what is possible today sets the stage for the future. You can then iterate based on customer feedback.

Assess Against Measurements and Improve

After the mobile solution has been deployed, it is now time to assess the project against performance indicators. Did you achieve your goal? Did you meet you measurement targets? You may find that some of your goals were not as easy to measure and may require new means of determining if the solution is achieving the desired results. In the end, a mobile solution must be customer-driven. Getting feedback and adjusting is critical and vital to a successful mobile solution.

Summary

Mobility will be one of the most transformative technologies in your lifetime. The potential exists to completely revolutionize the way you do business and transform your company. Mobility will impact every aspect of your organization from internal operations, to employee productivity, to the relationship with your customer. Mobility is in constant flux with new technologies appearing on the scene every day. As such, it is critical to have a comprehensive strategy that brings together an end-to-end view of the best way to execute for success.

A method for defining the strategy is critical to help navigate the dynamics of the mobile market. You need to define a process to move from setting goals to executing a plan with a long-term roadmap. The methodology outlined can help you set the organizational structure, goals, performance indicators, architecture, and overall roadmap. The mobile strategy is rooted in an overall capability framework that can help you to execute on your strategy.

9

SoCloDaMo (Social + Cloud + Big Data + Mobile)

SoCloDaMo is the evolution of four key technology trends—social, cloud, big data, and mobile—that has begun to converge into a new IT delivery platform. It is driven by consumer behavior, smaller IT budgets, and unending supply of connected smart devices. Most people see these forces working in their personal and business lives; however, there are profound implications to IT leaders.

There is a growing interdependence and convergence between social networking behavior and mobile interactions, enabled by "around the clock" availability through cloud and big data. Social, cloud, big data, and mobile come together to reinforce each other, and when combined deliver greater value than they do individually. Mobile brings location, context, always-on capability, and convenience. Mobile reinforces—and is a vehicle for—social networks and collaboration. Social networks link people to each other to work in new and interesting ways. The cloud offers a utility that provides an always-on platform for mobile and social interaction. The multitenant nature of the cloud enables everyone to interact with the same application at the same time, thus reinforcing social interaction. The cloud also delivers a platform for collecting and analyzing information. The mobile device is generating information that gives the context for behavior. Sensors are collecting information as a result of GPS coordinates, social interaction, and past buying behavior. This information is then generated as a result of the tasks people perform on their device. The resulting data then gives the enterprise new insight about behavior that can provide new value to customers and employees in the form of new features, new offers, improved processes, and customer retention. The reality is that a SoCloDaMo platform is here to stay and will grow in prominence in any mobile solution. You must consider the key ways that SoCloDaMo can contribute to an overall mobile strategy and use it appropriately.

This chapter outlines the key capabilities and trends around cloud, social, and big data as it relates to mobile. The chapter then covers how these four major trends come together to offer a set of new capabilities for businesses that compliments an overall mobile strategy.

Cloud and Mobile

Mobile and cloud computing are often talked about together as two major computing trends that reinforce each other to create new value. Mobile applications can utilize the cloud for storage and computing power. Cloud computing can provide a set of services and capabilities that can complement the mobile applications on the device. Even with the first release of the Apple iPhone, cloud-based applications such as Gmail and Google Maps were part of the mobile story. Over time, the cloud and mobile story has evolved, and new capabilities such as Apple's iCloud for offline backup have provided more convenience and value for end users. Cloud-based storage complements mobile devices by reducing the need for local storage on the device. This frees the device to devote more of the hardware footprint to other capabilities. Cloud computing can also reduce the complexity of setting up and managing a mobile infrastructure. Mobile Enterprise Applications Platforms (MEAP) and Mobile Device Management (MDM) systems can be deployed as virtual images, saving time and effort in deploying a mobile infrastructure solution. In addition, mobile specific cloud services—such as notifications, location services, advertising, and social integration—can assist developers as they build their mobile applications.

Defining Cloud Computing

To understand how mobile and cloud computing come together to provide new value, you need to first understand what cloud computing is and how it is defined.

Cloud computing enables an on-demand network access to a shared pool of computing resources (for example, networks, servers, storage, applications, and services) that can be rapidly provisioned and released.[1]

Cloud computing is attractive to businesses as an additional computing deployment model for computing resources. For those situations in which the complexity of setting up and managing a computing environment might be prohibitive, cloud computing can provide an alternative. It can be particularly attractive for small companies and startups that do not have the skill and capital to set up and manage a full-blown computing environment. Cloud computing can also be valuable in situations in which there are temporary or seasonal spikes in computing resource. In this case, a cloud environment could be used to handle the extra computing demands.

Cloud Characteristics

There are several key distinguishing characteristics of cloud computing. In the same way an electric utility company provides power, cloud computing relies on the sharing of computing resources to achieve economies of scale. The cloud provider's computing resources are pooled to serve multiple end users (multitenant). Resources are provisioned and deprovisioned based on end user demand. To the end user, the cloud computing resources appear to be unlimited and can be accessed through any device.[2]

Service Models:

There are a variety of types of clouds that vary by the level of abstraction to the end user or developer. There are three primary service delivery models for the cloud:

- **Software as a Service (SaaS):** A software delivery model in which applications are hosted by the service provider. The end user does not manage or control the underlying infrastructure (storage, network, and operating systems). Examples include Gmail, Google Docs, Netflix, Google Apps, Box.net, Dropbox, and Apple iCloud.
- **Platform as a Service (PaaS):** Provides a computing platform or operating environment over the Internet. The end user creates software applications using a PaaS development environment from the provider. The end user does not manage or control the underlying infrastructure (storage, network, servers, and so on); however, the end user may set deployment

and configuration settings. Examples include Windows Azure, Google
App Engine, and IBM SmartCloud Application Services.

- **Infrastructure as a Service (IaaS):** Delivers underlying computing and
  processing resources such as storage, network, hardware, servers, and so
  on. Examples include Amazon.com Web Services, IBM SmartCloud
  Enteprise, and Rackspace Cloud.

The industry has also coined derivative terminology for particular niche
cloud capabilities such as Monitoring as a Service (MaaS), Network as a
Service (NaaS), and Communications as a Service (CaaS). In addition, as you
will see, there is an emerging new cloud approach for mobile development
called Mobile Back End as a Service (BaaS).

Deployment Models:

The following are several ways that a cloud infrastructure can be deployed:

- **Private cloud:** The cloud infrastructure is managed and provisioned for
  use by a single organization. Some choose the private cloud approach
  when more control of the cloud infrastructure is needed. This is the case
  when security or control of corporate data may be a concern.
- **Public cloud:** The cloud infrastructure is provisioned for use by the general public. This approach may have the lowest upfront cost.
- **Hybrid cloud:** The cloud infrastructure is a combination of attributes of
  both the private and public cloud approaches. In this case, an organization can take advantage of the particular attributes of the private or public cloud to meet its particular needs.

You need to consider all the ramifications of cloud computing before
adopting it as a solution. In the case of a public cloud, you need to understand the total cost of cloud deployment. You might find that over the life-
time of a computing solution, the pay-as-you-go approach might end up
being more expensive than an in-house deployment. You also need to understand the security implications of cloud computing. Particularly with a public cloud, you need to consider where the data is located and who has access to
it. Sensitive corporate and government data might not be appropriate for a
public cloud deployment. Also, many of the cloud computing environments
are proprietary in nature, in which solutions developed for one cloud cannot

be moved to another. Although standard efforts work to provide more freedom and choice for cloud users such as the Open Cloud Manifesto (which initiated the cloud standards movement) and the Cloud Standards Customer Council (defining the cloud standards requirements for the industry), continuous work is needed. As a result, you must consider the implications of vendor lock-in and freedom of choice.

Why Mobile and Cloud

As you consider a mobile strategy, you must understand the unique aspects that drive the use of cloud computing in a mobile solution. These are described in following sections.

Device Limitation on Computing Resources

Even though mobile devices today, such as smartphones and tablets, offer unprecedented computing power in the palm of your hands, it is not unlimited. Relying on cloud computing to provide additional storage and computing power can give the end user a complete experience. Cloud-based storage can offer value to a mobile solution. With technologies such as Apple's iCloud, the ability to back-up data, pictures, videos, and applications to cloud storage not only provides a needed storage solution but also protects the information if the device is lost or stolen. Storage of large documents with solutions such as Dropbox or box.net can help overcome the limitations of on-device storage and make it easy to share the files with others. Applications such as Gmail or Google Maps can give the end user a comprehensive application on the cloud outside of the mobile device. However, the use of third-party cloud-based solutions should only be considered in context of an overall security strategy and policy.

Short Cycles

A consistent characteristic in any mobile project is the short development cycles. The expectations for shortened timelines makes any mobile project a challenge. There was a time when software projects took years; then with the web the expectation was "web years," which were actually months. Now you have a new era of ridiculous expectations in which the inception to deployment of an app should be done in a "mobile minute."

Development teams cannot afford to spend weeks trying to debug and set up back-end systems. When time is short and the pressure is on, developers turn to cloud-based solutions. Computing resources that are already set up and easily accessed on demand can radically accelerate development processes. Instead of reinventing a storage, security, or network solution for each app, it makes sense to rely on an available cloud infrastructure with all the required capabilities already available.[3] This is where the emerging cloud capability BaaS comes in. A BaaS is a cloud-based set of services specifically tailored to mobile developers that can significantly reduce the cost and complexity of a mobile project while speeding up delivery.[4]

BaaS providers deliver key mobile services such as storage, push notification, messaging, analytics, user management, and other essential services for mobile developers, using a pay-as-you-go pricing model.

Small Budgets Create Cloud Interest

Budget constraints have always been an issue in the IT industry. "More with less" seems to be the norm. With the speed and frequency of mobile development projects, however, budget constraints are more important now than ever. Small companies and startups most likely do not have the initial capital needed to set up a sophisticated IT infrastructure. Even for large companies where experimentation in mobile solutions is common, the mobile project return on investment (ROI) might not be clear or perhaps the project is short lived. Setting up a cloud infrastructure quickly and with low upfront costs can make a lot of sense. With cloud computing, you can pay as you go, start quickly, and add more resources over time. After the Mobile project proves its value, you can move more of the infrastructure to a traditional infrastructure if needed.

Emerging Markets

Not every part of the world has the same infrastructure in place for a complete mobile development and delivery process. Remotely accessing a mobile infrastructure for development and deployment can be critical in emerging markets in which there may be limited availability of the necessary hardware, network, and software infrastructure.[5] In this case, a mobile cloud infrastructure delivered as a complete service can be indispensable for emerging markets.[6]

Mobile Cloud Development Considerations

Mobile Cloud Services

You can build and deliver a mobile application in a variety of ways. You can use the software development kits (SDK) provided by the handset mobile OS manufacturers, such as Apple iOS or Google Android. This approach is fine for a single and simple app targeting a particular mobile OS. However, if you need to build for a variety of mobile devices and connect to a heterogeneous enterprise infrastructure, you will need a more comprehensive mobile application platform. You can use an installed software approach such as a MEAP.

Generally, a MEAP is a middleware platform installed within the enterprise. It has a cross-platform mobile application development environment that supports connectivity to back-end enterprise applications and databases. A MEAP also provides a centralized management component that enables administration, management, and enterprise security of the applications. In addition to an on-premise deployment, the MEAP itself could be deployed as a virtual image within a cloud environment. This can help save IT teams the steps to set up and manage the MEAP environment and may offer a rental pricing model which may be attractive to some development teams. Additionally, some companies (also known as Mobile Back end as a Service or BaaS) have begun to offer specific cloud based mobile services, such as storage, user management, analytics, advertising, payments, push notifications, and integration with social networking services. These mobile specific services can be complimentary to your MEAP deployment by incorporating these mobile specific cloud services into your mobile development process.

Centralized Build Environment in the Cloud

When building for multiple device platforms, each build environment has its own compiler. As such, each development team (Android, Apple, Microsoft, and so on) needs its own build environment. Maintaining multiple build environments can be a challenge for some operation teams. For example, with the popularity of the Apple products, you might think that an iOS platform would be a mainstay in today's enterprises; in reality, many businesses do not support the deployment of Apple products. This is due to a variety of reasons including skills, security concerns, or just capacity. In the end, this can create a challenge for those trying to define a mobile development strategy. Developers need access to the Mac operating system to compile the source code into an executable mobile app. Without access to Macs, the ability to develop a cross-platform mobile app strategy is not viable.

One approach to solving the challenge of building mobile applications when supporting multiple device platforms is to outsource the development or consider a centralized build in the cloud. You can access the build environments through a centrally managed cloud remote desktop. In addition to solving the issue of accessing Macs, the cloud approach can also provide a centrally managed build environment, significantly reducing the cost of managing the app build process for a variety of platforms.

Testing Mobile Apps: How the Cloud Can Make Mobile Testing Simpler

It is clear that users have many choices for device types, sizes, and platforms. It is even common for users to have more than one device. As a result the mobile device landscape is fragmented—forcing businesses to support many different types of devices. The interfaces are nonstandard with a variety of screen sizes and resolutions. Each device type has its own operating system with unique characteristics and user experience. There are many variations of mobile operating systems. This is most prominent with the Android platform. There are many different permutations and versions of the operating system and even forked versions of the Android open source project. Each carrier may tweak the mobile OS to optimize for a particular hardware platform or a particular network. As a result, the test matrix for a mobile app can be huge with many, many permutations. Unlike the web, where the test target was essentially the web browser, with mobile development you need to have access to the mobile device to understand it. You also need to simulate the back-end systems, network, and environment. Development teams located across multiple locations need to collaborate and share access to the mobile devices. A typical mobile development project needs 30–40 devices that are currently in the market, and 30 percent will need to be replaced each quarter.[7] Add to this the dynamic nature of the mobile market and short development cycles, and the cost in logistics, procurement, and management of these devices can be cost-prohibitive. In the end, complexity of mobile testing can be a significant challenge for any IT department.

A cloud-based mobile test environment can significantly simplify the testing process. There are vendors in the market, such as Perfecto Mobile and Device Anywhere, which offer web-based access to a large pool of physical mobile devices, connected to live networks worldwide. Developers and testers can access these devices through a cloud interface. This gives developers access to a wide variety of mobile devices during the testing phase for both manual and automated testing. The development team is essentially renting the latest collection of mobile devices it needs to meet its test plan. The mobile devices can be set up in a variety of locations around the world to validate the experience on a specific carrier network. Because these devices are centrally managed, the testing can be automated to ensure that specific test cases are validated with all the interaction recorded on video. The cloud-based test facility then provides the developer with a complete view of all the test results. After the test phase is complete, the mobile devices are returned to the centralized pool of devices. In this way, each developer feels they have unlimited access to mobile device whenever they are needed. This saves the enterprise from having to maintain and manage all these devices and gives them a true on-demand test environment. Because all the devices are available in the cloud, there is no need to procure and manage the devices. Devices can be added or replaced immediately, and development teams can access the same device to replicate bugs and resolve test issues.

Not only can the device test experience be delivered through a cloud, but you can also simulate a back-end system through a cloud-based environment. Solutions such as IBM's Rational Test Virtualization Server help you in modeling and simulating real system behavior to eliminate application test dependencies and reduce infrastructure costs. This helps improve the quality of software applications by enabling developers to use cloud computing technologies to conduct testing of software applications, including mobile applications, without having to set up the actual infrastructure.

Social and Mobile

Social networking has become a prominent way by which people interact, share information, and collaborate. Because smartphones leverage GPS and the camera, they enable much more interaction and contextual engagement. As a result, social applications are among the most popular for mobile devices. Applying the social networking philosophy and capabilities to the enterprise can certainly add to the bottom line. McKinsey and Company report that the revenue growth of social businesses is 24 percent higher than businesses that do not apply social capabilities.[8] Enabling the workforce to share information and collaborate can make the organization more effective. Applying social technologies such as blogs, wikis, social bookmarking, instant messaging, e-meetings, and document sharing can help a workforce to collaborate, uncover innovation, and improve competitive posture.

In the consumer space, mobile devices have become the main way that people interact with social networks. For example, 60 percent of Facebook updates are from mobile devices.[9] In the enterprise, when combining social capabilities with mobile devices, you are now adding context (location through GPS, environment through sensors, orientation through compass, and so on) to an overall social strategy while enabling employees to collaborate anytime and anyplace. Mobile adds a new level of insight into enterprise information sharing and collaboration. This can tremendously increase the value of a social business strategy and improve the bottom line. Your enterprise social strategy, both internally and externally to the enterprise, should have a mobile component and be tightly aligned with your overall mobile strategy.

Mobile Social Discovery: Attracting and Retaining Customers

Social discovery is a way to use mobile phones and tablets to find nearby people, events, and places that are relevant at a particular moment. This information helps customers gain insight and information that can drive purchases, create loyalty, and create community. They may also be swept up in the activity of the crowd and make a transaction based on the activity of other people.

To drive social discovery, a system is needed that understands a user's past buying habits, behavior, and activities. End users would opt in to get value from the interaction at the same time the system is learning about the customers' behavior, matching tailored offerings that would have the greatest likelihood of closing. All this information must be collected, analyzed, and sorted for value.

A great example of this is the Foursquare app. When you start the Foursquare app it offers you the choice to 'check-in' to the establishment where you are currently. For example, if you are at a coffee shop, the Foursquare app would determine your location based on your GPS coordinates. You can then check-in to the coffee shop. You are then given the option to type a few words describing what you are doing, which can be shared through your Twitter or Facebook. Once you check-in, you may be presented with a badge that you earn based on certain achievements (first time check-in, most check-ins, and so on). You may also receive coupons or other offers from the coffee shop or tips from other visitors. This process helps the coffee shop get free advertising based on Twitter and Facebook posts. The customer can gain offers, the enjoyment of reaching various levels of achievement, and tips from others.

What Is Unique About Social and Mobile?

When mobile and social are brought together, there are some unique considerations:

- **Mobile devices can sense the world around you providing context and driving innovation and business value:** Mobile devices have a rich set of new sensors such as compass, GPS, accelerometers, gyroscopes, and NFC. This can enable many new business scenarios such as identifying colleagues based on GPS coordinates, e-meetings on the go, mobile device transcription of conference calls, and many other new innovations.

- **Mobile and social can increase information and data:** As social tools and mobile apps take advantage of new devices sensors, they can provide more consumer data and more contextual insight. This massive amount of available data will create new opportunities to better serve your customers and employees. Data analytics and Big Data (likely related to cloud computing) can play a major role in understanding the data that can drive innovation. Organizations must become better at collecting, protecting, managing, interpreting, and acting on the data collected via social interaction through mobile devices.[10]

It is clear that mobile amplifies social networking, giving interaction a context. This context provides a much richer level of interaction and insight—in the moment. The contextual information, in the form of sensor and location data, generates a tremendous amount of data that must be sorted and analyzed in order to have any value to a business process. Social information can be combined with analytics to help users gain insight to perform the next best action. Consider how the GPS traffic app called Waze uses social information from app users along with analytics to determine traffic patterns, speed traps, and car crashes in real time. This is where big data and the cloud come in to the mobile story.

Big Data

Big data analytics is defined as data sets that go beyond the capacity of conventional databases. Big data usually relates to collecting massive information about the world. Data collected can be too big, streams too fast, or arrive in a structure that cannot be easily analyzed. The idea around big data is that new techniques and approaches are needed to deal with these new types of information. If analyzed correctly, this massive amount of data can give new insight that can help differentiate your business. The sort of technology needed to analyze and process large data sets has been around for some time but only available to a few companies with deep pockets. New technologies leveraging commodity hardware and scale via cloud computing have made big data analysis available to smaller companies, startups, departments, and individuals.[11]

What Is Unique about Mobile and Data?

Cloud-enabled data analysis gives mobile the information context that can enhance the social and mobile experience. Advanced analytics, stream processing, Hadoop, and other technologies have given businesses unprecedented power to analyze complex behavior within manageable costs.

People are sharing information through their social interactions—information about the latest project, best practices, and latest data. Customers provide information about their preferences through buying and searching behavior. Harnessing this information gives businesses unprecedented insight into the behavior of their customers and how to empower their employees to be more efficient. Mobile increases the volume, velocity, and variety of data and gives it greater context and relevance.

Summary

There was a time when an individual's technology experience was much more sophisticated at work than at home. This has changed. The consumer-based services that you use daily in your personal life are so compelling because they effectively bring together social, cloud, data and mobile. It is as though the computing platforms of your personal life have set high expectations for the IT departments at work. As a result, IT is catching up. Companies see the consumerization of IT as both a challenge and an opportunity to differentiate. Bringing together social, cloud, data, and mobile in the right way can create a platform for IT that can form the basis of a "system of engagement," as shown in Figure 9.1. The SoCloDaMo platform can deliver a system that empowers customers, employees, and partners through mobile apps that address their specific task in context of their immediate need. It brings together the behavior and preferences of their peers (social) with access and context (mobile) to give them insight (data analytics) when they need it (cloud).[12]

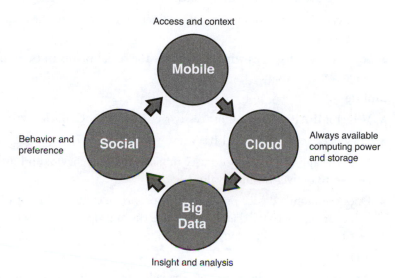

Figure 9.1   Four elements of a SoCloDaMo platform.

Mobile Strategy Decisions

The following are many strategic considerations that can help to guide your strategy:

- Cloud
  - What service model is needed (IaaS, PaaS, or SaaS)?
  - Considering security and access, which deployment model is needed (private, public, or hybrid)?
  - Are there specific needs that can drive the cloud adoption—speed of development, reducing cost, test, deployment, and so on?

- Have all the security, vendor lock-in management issues been considered?
- How can your cloud strategy link to your existing IT and security infrastructure?
- Social
  - Will the app inherently drive social interaction, or is social training and education needed?
  - Does the social behavior drive value linked to your business goals?
  - How can the data from the social interaction get fed into the data analysis systems?
  - Social insight happens with scale. Does the social platform tie into a cloud-based system?
- Mobile
  - Which MEAP platform most easily ties into the SoCloDaMo vision?
  - How does your MEAP and BaaS systems tie together?
  - Does the app engage the end user to generate the behavior and insight needed to deliver business value?
  - Does the mobile device provide the appropriate context of location, behavior, and activity that can generate the appropriate data while protecting privacy and personal information?
- Big Data
  - Are systems available to manage the velocity, variety, and volume of data based on the mobile and social data streams?
  - Are the tools in place to analyze the data that may be structured and nonstructured?
  - Are the analysis systems tied into the business processes so that insight can drive new value for customers and employees?

Endnotes

[1] NIST. "Final Version of NIST Cloud Computing Definition Published": http://www.nist.gov/itl/csd/cloud-102511.cfm

[2] Wikipedia. "Cloud Computing": http://en.wikipedia.org/wiki/Cloud_computing

[3]   The Server Side. "Why Mobile Developers Embrace the Cloud. Why Others PaaS on It": http://www.theserverside.com/feature/Mobile-Developers-Embrace-Cloud-Computing-Platforms

[4]   Forrester. Mobile Backend-As-A-Service: The New Lightweight Middleware? http://blogs.forrester.com/michael_facemire/12-04-25-mobile_backend_as_a_service_the_new_lightweight_middleware

[5]   How Cloud Computing Transforms Emerging Markets: http://asmarterplanet.com/blog/2011/03/how-cloud-computing-could-transform-emerging-markets.html

[6]   Ibid.

[7]   Mobile Application Testing. "Three Key Recommendations/Considerations for Choosing a Mobile Testing": http://www.mobileappstesting.com/category/cloud-mobile-testing/

[8]   ZD Net. "Social tech in biz more than collaboration": http://www.zdnet.com/social-tech-in-biz-more-than-collaboration-2062302300/

[9]   http://blog.pontiflex.com/2012/01/03/70-of-mobile-users-access-facebook-via-mobile-apps/

[10] ZD Net. "The convergence of mobile and social: The next IT battleground": http://www.zdnet.com/the-convergence-of-mobile-and-social-the-next-it-battleground-7000003015/

[11] Strata. "What is big data?": http://strata.oreilly.com/2012/01/what-is-big-data.html

[12] http://www.gartner.com/DisplayDocument?doc_cd=234840&ref=g_noreg

Additional Sources

Gartner: "Every budget is an IT budget":

http://www.zdnet.com/gartner-every-budget-is-an-it-budget-7000006151/

Rational Test Virtualization Server

http://www-01.ibm.com/software/rational/products/rtvs/

10

International
Considerations

It is clear that the market is shifting toward smartphones and tablets as a dominant computing model. Since 2007 and the initial release of the iPhone, the adoption of mobile smartphones and tablets has outpaced the adoption of any other technology adoption in history. However, not every part of the world is adopting smartphones and tablets at the same rate. Some parts of the world are still primarily using feature and basic phones—wireless phones that can make phone calls, some text messaging, and perhaps some web browsing but do not provide a mechanism for a mobile app. Over time, you will see a worldwide shift from feature and basic phones to smartphones and tablets. However, as you build your mobile strategy, you need to consider that some parts of your worldwide audience will not use a smartphone or tablet. As such, you need to think through how you can reach an audience who does not have the ability to utilize a mobile app. You may consider alternative means of reaching your audience if you determine that there is a limited access to smartphones and tablets. Short Messaging Service (SMS)-based applications may provide viable alternatives for regions of the world that may not have the infrastructure in place to enable smartphones and tablet-based apps.

A variety of issues determine the rate and pass of adoption of smartphones and tablets. They include the cost of the device, network connectivity, and end user willingness to accept the smartphone and tablet technology paradigm. In the end, you must segment your audience and determine the state of technology adoption.

It may also be the case that in some parts of the world the technology adoption of certain mobile technologies may be at a different pace. For example, in some areas of the world, the adoption of mobile payments and mobile money may be further along than, say, in North America and Europe.

In the end, you need to build your strategy by segmenting your market, understand the state of technology adoption, and then determine the rate of transition. This can reveal the area for investment and which technology you should invest in. As always, a good mobile strategy is one that is flexible and can adapt based on the market and geography changes. To start defining an international mobile strategy, you must first delve into the underlying mechanism that determines the rate and pace of smartphone and tablet adoption.

Issues Influencing Adoption of Smartphones and Tablets in Emerging Markets

At the end of the day, you will need to have a mobile strategy that takes into consideration your global customer and employee. Emerging markets will see the greatest shift from feature and basic phones to smartphones and tablets. Not every part of the world will be able to move to smartphones and tablets at the same rate. As a result, you need to consider the factors inhibiting adoption of mobile applications. By understanding the inhibitors, it will help you to determine the rate at which your international constituents will shift to smartphones and tablets.

Cost Can Be Too High, but Things Are Changing

The cost of a smartphone can be significantly higher than a feature phone. This may be prohibitive to some who may not have the budget to spend on a smartphone or tablet.

However, cheaper mobile devices are on their way. With a free operating system—Android—and dropping prices of hardware components, smartphones are approaching less than $100 US. The cost of owning a smart mobile device is now becoming possible for a wide segment of the world population.

In addition, you can think of a smartphone as more than just a phone. In many ways, the utility of a smartphone/tablet approaches the computing power and capability of a computer. You can write a document, send an email, watch a movie, and so on. In many ways, the smartphone can save the consumer from having to purchase several different electronic devices. For many individuals in developing countries, the smartphone is their only connection to the Internet. As a result, even at a higher price than a feature phone, the devices may have enough value to justify the higher price.

Network Connectivity Inhibits Use of Mobile App, but There Are Things That Can Help

To gain the benefits of a mobile app, you have to connect to information and data. This means the end user/consumer likely needs a data plan and a 3G network. There may be some locations in the world that lack the network coverage to support a smartphone or tablet. A 3G data plan is needed for an app to send and receive data. Although there may be a means to use SMS as a data transport, or use a local Wi-Fi when a data plan is not available.

As a user interacts with a mobile device in an environment in which there is limited or spotty data network availability, a local data store can help. With a local data store on the device, users can work offline and then after they have access to a reliable network connection, they can synchronize with the back-end system and continue their task. It is important that the local data store be encrypted so that if the device is lost or stolen, the data cannot fall into the wrong hands.

Unreliable or costly data networks might make it a challenge for individuals to adopt the mobile web. Technologies are available to help mitigate network limitations. Proxy browsers such as Operamini work with data cached in the network so that as one browses the web, the performance of the web browsing can be greatly improved.

Complexity of Smartphones Can Be an Inhibitor to Adoption, but This Will Change over Time

As mobile devices approach the power of computers, they also carry a level of complexity. This complexity might be a barrier to adoption for some in some regions of the world.

However, user expectations will likely change over time as people become more accustomed to the user experience of a smartphone and tablet. In many respects, the smartphone and tablet may provide a user experience that has a richer user interface with more visual cues so that those individuals can perform their tasks. In addition, the smartphone or tablet has much greater processing power, so voice commands and gesture interaction might make it much easier for individuals.

Unique Usage Patterns

As you develop your mobile strategy, it is important to consider the unique usage patterns that the customers you serve may have. Some markets may vary by their cell coverage, broad band capacity, and type of phone usage. For example, laying landlines in some countries was cost-prohibitive and difficult to maintain. Cell towers were less expensive to set up and support. As a result, in some regions of the world, there may be a much higher percentage of a population using cell phones than traditional landline phones.

Actually, some individuals may have multiple phones. It is common in some markets to see individuals with multiple phones to optimize carrier in-network fees when calling different friends or families. The premise is that each carrier offers in-network discounts when both individuals are subscribers to the same carrier network. As a result, an individual may own multiple phones with different carriers. When they want to call a friend who belongs to Brasil Telecom, they use their Brasil Telecom phone. If their friend belongs to Telefónica, they would use their Telefónica phone to reduce their rate. This has given rise to the multi-SIM phones. In this way, individuals avoid having multiple phones and can instead switch carriers by switching SIM cards in the phone.

Some markets may also be more advanced in mobile banking or mobile money. In those cases in which traditional bank fees may be too high or the financial infrastructure and local branches may not be in place, the online mobile banking capabilities have flourished in emerging markets as an alternative.

Mobile money has become a necessity in those cases in which a bank may not be available to hold savings. It is not practical to keep all your cash hidden in your home. As a result, systems have been put in place to exchange tokens of value between individuals through their basic wireless phones. This also enables people to more efficiently manage bartering. For example, if one trades a chicken for a goat and the goat has greater value than the chicken, the difference in value can be stored on the mobile device in the form of mobile money. That mobile money token can then be used for other usage such as paying for a bus fair. (Have you ever paid for a bus ride with a portion of a goat?)

There are many examples of mobile device infrastructures providing much-needed financial services to those in need. In South Africa, Wizzit is a virtual bank where customers can use their phones to transfer money, make payments, and prepay utilities. This service is focused on the 16 million South Africans who do not have bank accounts. In Kenya, more than 17 million customers use M-PESA to regularly transfer money from one to another and store cash on their phones. The mobile devices have filled a need that is unique to some parts of the world. By providing simple and secure access to basic financial services to those without bank accounts in the developing world, a critical need has been met. In addition, these technologies have in some way propelled emerging markets into a much more sophisticated solution than may be available in the developed world.[1]

In some cases, the particular region of the world may drive new innovations. For example, there has been a case in which a microfinance organization had to adopt fingerprint readers and retinal scanners to validate the identity of individuals. This was done because the particular tribe in Africa lacked the identity infrastructure (no driver's license, passport, or proof of identity).

What to Consider When Developing a Global Mobile Strategy

When developing a mobile strategy in which your end users may span several countries, you need to consider several key aspects:

- **Every country is different, so understand your target market and adoption rate:** Each country is going to have a different adoption rate for smartphones and tablets. As a result, you need to consider the rate and pass of adoption and when it will approach critical mass (greater than 50 percent adoption). You need to determine when your target market will be mostly smartphones and tablets and what the rate of adoption is. If you determine that the smartphones and tablets will reach 50 percent in the near term, you might want to forgo focus on feature phones and basic phones.

  For example, in South Africa, the penetration of feature phones grew from 20 percent to 50 percent between 2006 and 2009.[2] Therefore, in

3 years, the market reached a tipping point of more than 50 percent. You can then apply that today. Currently, the penetration of smartphones in South Africa is approximately 20 percent.[3] Therefore, you can make the assumption that it will likely take 3 years for there to be at least 50 percent adoption of smartphones in South Africa. However, you also need to consider the implications that the existing feature phone infrastructure will accelerate the adoption rate. The infrastructure and individual learning has already been established. People have gone through the original adoption hurdle of using a wireless device. The carrier billing infrastructure and systems are already in place. The use of the smartphone is much greater. The costs are dropping and the infrastructure is improving. As a result of considering all these factors, you might then conclude that the smartphone adoption within South Africa may be much less than 3 years and may be more like 12–18 months. If your mobile project takes 6–8 months to get out the door, you might want to forgo focusing on the feature phone market and focus just on the smartphone customer set.

■ **Rural versus urban:** The smartphone and tablet adoption may be radically different between the urban versus the rural areas of a country. The urban and city locations may have a sophisticated infrastructure to handle the data traffic in support of the mobile app infrastructure. The disposable income of the customer set within the urban centers may facilitate the ability to purchase smartphones and tablets. Large corporations are more likely to reside in the urban centers and as a result may have issued to their employees mobile smartphones or tablets. On the other hand, the rural areas outside of the cities may have limited infrastructure. Individuals may have limited disposable income.

In the end, you need to consider what your target market is. It may be clear that within urban areas there is a critical mass of end users on smartphones and tablets. The adoption may be more than 50 percent, and your target audience also resides in urban centers. Therefore, you may decide that there is sufficient adoption of smartphones and tablets to make them your primary platform. If your target audience is broader and encompasses rural regions of a country where smartphone adoption is lower, you might want to target both feature/basic phones in addition to smartphones.

■ **Types of apps and disposable income:** The type of app also plays a role in your strategy. If your target market has limited disposable income, it may only download free apps. If your business model relies on end users purchasing your app and they have limited funds, you need to consider if there is a market for the app when disposable income is limited. Apps may need to be more focused and deliver high value (such as banking or commerce apps) instead of casual games. In addition, you need to consider how end users pay for their phone service. It is different in different parts of the world. For example, in places such as India, more than 90 percent of consumers are on prepaid cards, so paying for mobile apps over the phone is not typical.[4] You must consider the market dynamics when defining your mobile monetization strategy and how the different markets pay and use mobile services.

■ **Adoption and usage patterns of smartphones can vary around the world:** There is a wide variety of carrier infrastructure and services that may dictate a wide variety of handset capabilities. Given the infrastructure features and capabilities, devices popular in one area of the world may not be popular in another. Even government regulation can drive unique requirements on handsets and carriers that can shape the device capabilities.

What to Consider When Developing a Dual Strategy for Smartphones and Feature/Basic Phones

If you conclude that you need to develop a strategy that can encompass both smartphones and feature/basic phones, there are some approaches and technology considerations. Your best bet is to consider a technology that spans both the smartphone and feature/basic phones. SMS provides the most promise for a cross platform strategy.

Advantages of SMS

SMS messages can work across almost all mobile OSs, devices, and infrastructures. This includes smartphone/tablets and feature/basic phones. As a result, SMS has a low technology barrier for widespread deployment. Popularity and ease of use of SMS means virtually zero training requirements for mobile users. Growing numbers of mobile phones and availability of SMS capability on all mobile handsets creates wider reach for an SMS-based solution.

SMS-Based Application-to-Person (A2P)

When you are faced with the challenge of delivering a mobile application, yet there is limited network and data infrastructure, instead of building an app, one solution may be an SMS-based application-to-person (A2P) solution. An A2P solution provides a series of menus that interact between your system and the individual. You can deliver an A2P-based application through a series of SMS menus that function as a decision tree. What is helpful with an SMS-based solution is that you can also target smartphones/tablets. This provides a means of protecting investment as your target market migrates over to smartphones. Users can still use the SMS-based solution.

Here is how it works: The end user sends a text that initiates the application interaction. Then the user is sent a text message with a series of options. Each option is associated with a number. The end user then picks an option by texting back a number. After a decision is made, the next menu is sent to the end user via a text message. This continues until the desired interaction is achieved.

Figures 10.1 through 10.10 outline a possible banking app delivered just through SMS messages. This approach can provide an alternative application interface that would be appropriate for feature and basic phones.

Figure 10.1   Initial SMS message to banking SMS system

Figure 10.2   End user enters bank account number and PIN.

Figure 10.3 SMS bank system menu

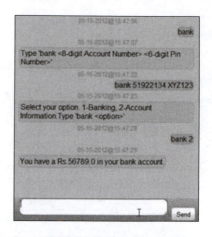

Figure 10.4 SMS bank system provides account balance.

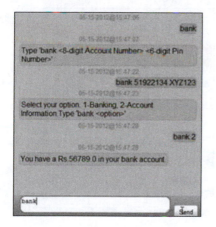

Figure 10.5 SMS bank system main menu

Figure 10.6 End user provides account and pin number.

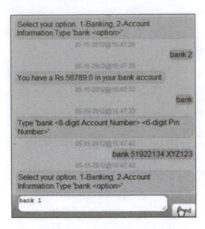

Figure 10.7 End user wants to perform banking function.

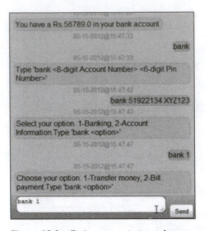

Figure 10.8 End user wants to perform a money transfer.

Figure 10.9 End user enters amount and destination account.

Figure 10.10 SMS bank system verifies money transfer has occurred.

In addition to a banking application, there are several additional use cases for mobile SMS applications, as outlined in Table 10.1.

Table 10.1 Scenarios for SMS-Based Apps

Industry Segment	Use Case
Communications	Mobile content delivery, news, and alerts
Healthcare	Expert advice, registration for public health services, appointment, alerts, and notifications
Government	Traffic updates, complaint monitoring, property tax bills, and warning messages
Financial services	Mobile banking, financial transactions, microfinance, micro-insurance, and information retrieval
Retail	Interactive communication, financial transactions, m-commerce, information update, and location-based services
Utilities	Real-time meter reading, updates, bill payments, and real-time information sharing
Manufacturing	Mobile field force, real-time updates, and low-cost supply chain management
Transportation	Fleet management (real-time updates), mobile ticketing, and schedule updates
Services	Real-time data access, information sharing, mobile content delivery, and stock trading

Summary

A mobile strategy should be comprehensive and should consider your target audience. You should determine if your mobile strategy addresses a global audience. If so, consider the type of mobile device the end user will use. The smartphone and tablet market has been rapidly growing since its inception in 2007 with the launch of the iPhone. However, many parts of the world have not completed the transition to smartphones and tablets. As a result, you need to understand if your target audience uses basic/feature phones or smartphones and tablets. Some parts of the world, particularly in emerging markets, have not adopted smartphones for a variety of reasons. Some have not adopted these new devices because of cost, limited network data infrastructure, or the complexity and sophistication of the smartphones. This will change over time as smartphones decrease in price, network infrastructure gets built out, and users become accustomed to the user experience of smartphones or tablets. In those situations where you need to target devices that are not smartphones and tablets, you must consider an alternative mechanism for delivering your application. One such approach may be to use a common communication format such as SMS. An SMS menu-driven application may deliver a solution that gives you the greatest flexibility in delivering apps while addressing the broadest market.

Endnotes

1 Futureagenda http://www.futureagenda.org/pg/cx/view#339
2 Techcrunch, "In Five Years, Most Africans Will Have Smartphones" http://techcrunch.com/2012/06/09/feature-phones-are-not-the-future/
3 Strategyworx, "Social Media Growth Driven by Smartphones in SA" http://www.strategyworx.co.za/social-media-growth-driven-by-smartphones-in-sa/
4 Gigaohm, "Mobile Apps Are Hot, But Don't Forget Emerging Markets" http://gigaom.com/2010/03/17/mobile-apps-are-hot-but-dont-forget-emerging-markets/

Additional Sources

McKinsey quarterly. "Mobile money: Getting to scale in emerging markets" http://www.mckinseyquarterly.com/Mobile_money_Getting_to_scale_in_emerging_markets_2951

II

Case Studies and Mobile Solutions

Mobile initiatives have come in two phases. In the first phase, companies reacted to the industry and tried to get an app out as fast as possible. Perhaps a competitor had just put an app out in an app store, and to respond, they quickly created an app. Similar to the early years of the Internet in which people felt they just needed to get a site up, people tried to get an app out because they felt they needed to. Now mobile app stores are overcrowded, and many of the apps are of low value. Many found that getting an app up into the app store was the easy part; maintaining and managing the app became the challenge. Their "reactionary app" was created quickly, without the context of a framework or mobile strategy, and now, it is not sustainable within their current development and business processes.

Delivering "transformative apps" is now the goal of the second phase of the mobile app industry. Companies are looking to truly take advantage of what mobile has to offer. They want to extend their systems of record and deliver true systems of engagement. In addition, they are looking for an app strategy that will transform their business by enabling their employees to be more productive and extending the reach to new customers.

Transformative apps bring in historical information, such as buying behavior, from systems of record, and interpret this data to deliver new value. In addition, these apps can be multichannel (working across many different user interfaces such as mobile, PC, and kiosks) and also cross-channel (tying together different systems such as order management, call centers, and transaction systems). They can bring in different capabilities by integrating APIs from business partners and third parties to deliver a 360-degree relationship that can deliver a new level of engagement, transforming the way your business engages with customers and employees. Transformative apps bring together context (information about an individual's environment and identity), intelligence (analyses of the situation at hand), and engagement (easy-and-simple task-specific experiences that integrate into daily lives). In the end, a transformative app can have a significant impact on the bottom line.

Overall, the industry is in a state of transformation. Companies have experimented with mobile and are now realizing they need to deliver something new. They need a platform to deliver mobile applications that allow them to transform their business. Many in the industry have started down this path and offer examples that can help shape a mobile strategy.

When Does an App Fail?

An app can fail when the developer/development team does not think through the process of completely engaging with the end user. User experience is critical; users have high expectations for an easy-to-use and simple mobile app. Your developer needs to make sure that things such as transitions between screens are smooth and responsive and match the experience of the device. Remember, users have experience using mobile apps in their personal lives and have high expectations as they use apps at work.

More important, it becomes critical to think through specific mobile tasks. What are the specific steps involved? Break it down to subatomic tasks to understand the breadth of actions. Avoid adding too much to an app. It needs to be focused on a specific task. How can you simplify the path to the goal? Have you taken advantage of context to help users achieve their goal more efficiently? Have you thought through how it will deliver an omnichannel approach such as web sites, kiosks, mobile devices, and point of sale or through linked multiple channels such as call centers or order center? Have you thought about how to link in third parties so complementary apps and services can be delivered? As you collect information to improve the process for people along their journey, do customers or employees feel comfortable that the data collected is safe and end users get value from the service provided?

For example, a store initiated an incentive program around Quick Response (QR) codes. They developed an app that would enable an individual to bring a QR code to the store. They would show the cashier the QR code, and the cashier would then scan the QR code to get the discount. However, their incentive program failed because the existing point of sale systems were not set up to scan the QR codes.

Another example is a transportation company that sold tickets through a mobile app, but required users to go to their web site to complete the process. This added another step to achieving the goal. The end user would have been better off simply going to the web site and not using the app.

Finally, another example is when trust is violated. A user signs up for a discount at a store and the store sends the discount code as an SMS message. All is well and good, but the end users do not know how to opt out from the continuous stream of SMS messages. They continue to receive SMS messages, causing them to be more and more dissatisfied with the store.

What Makes a Great App?

There are several examples of how companies are transforming their businesses by using mobile to engage their customers and employees in entirely new ways. Successful apps focus on engagement. Because the mobile device is always with the individual, the app has the potential to inject itself into their daily lives and assist them, making their tasks easier by reducing friction in the process or removing steps altogether. For example, you don't want to write down the reading from a weight scale and then type it into a weight management web site application. You want the scale to automatically send the results to the app on your phone. The app can have lots of information and collect lots of data. This can then help predict the next best action. Bringing information to people so that they can better understand the next best step can add significant value to the app.

Now take the simple task of keeping office supplies in the hands of employees. Historically, people went to the supply closet to get the needed office supplies. Next, companies got rid of the supply closet and allowed people to order over the web when they needed something new. Now, you might think that the company should deliver a mobile app that enables their employees to order their supplies on the go through a mobile app; however, this does not truly take advantage of the power of context. What if the mobile app system predicted when you needed the office supply? Perhaps it knows how often you were in the office, your past buying behavior, and what building you frequented. As a result, the app "engaged"; it knew when you needed the next office supply and sent it to you in advance.

The following case studies demonstrate how an app that engages the customer can transform a business.

Air Canada: Innovation Through Customer Experience, Multichannel, and Cross-Channel

Air Canada is a leading air carrier in Canada that runs more than 1,400 daily flights between the United States and Canada.[1] It serves more than 32 million passengers on more than 200 domestic routes. With customers at the center of its business, Air Canada wanted to transform the way it interacts with its customers to deliver a more engaging experience and provide greater customer value. With a changing customer base, Air Canada evaluated customer interactions and experiences to understand what was needed to be competitive in the marketplace. Air Canada already had solutions for self-check-in kiosks in addition to its web site; however, it was clear it needed to expand its reach to mobile. Now, with one app, customers can check flight status and get their electronic boarding pass. It is all integrated across multiple channels due to the way Air Canada built its back-end system. It is a multichannel framework located in one place and is on one platform. The platform presents itself differently depending on who is interacting with the platform and whether it is a kiosk, web, or mobile device. The platform has intelligence and business rules built in, so it can deliver a more comprehensive experience. If your flight is delayed, not only will the platform let you know, it will also provide you with a new flight. All this is real time, so the information is delivered to the mobile device (or kiosk and web) at the same time as it is delivered to the Air Canada agents or employees.

With its multichannel platform, Air Canada reduced its check-in cost by 80 percent. Given the structure of its platform, they can push out new releases within 72 hours (which with their older systems would have taken weeks to do) while also reducing the time of development and test by 50 percent. The Air Canada iPhone App has more than 1.5 million downloads and ranks #1 in the Travel Category (#2 overall) in App Store Canada (see http://tinyurl.com/b99jrlr).[2]

In the end, what makes the Air Canada app transformative is its ability to deliver an integrated multichannel solution across kiosks, web, and mobile.

They can tie together customers, agents, and call centers—adding intelligence so that the app can anticipate the end users' needs before they even ask for it. Finally, the Air Canada app was so successful that it had an impact on its traditional web presence. Air Canada had to rethink the interaction with its customers as a result of designing a mobile app. The mobile interaction had to be broken down into manageable tasks. Efficient use of screen real estate and thoughtful navigation on the mobile front gave it ideas on how to improve the traditional web site. As a result, the traditional web site was improved based on insight from the mobile user experience, and customer satisfaction went up with its corporate web site.

Although airline check-in apps have become ubiquitous, you will see more mobile apps that can predict your next step. They bring together insight about where you are with your journey and update your app interface and interaction based on your current situation. The mobile app understands what you want to accomplish in the moment of need. Then, based on the situation, it predicts the next best action. This might mean changing the UI experience to be more focused on picking up your rental car instead of checking in to your flight. As time goes on, you will see more applications that take advantage of the layout of buildings and landmarks. The airport will be a prime target for future applications that will know exactly where you are and how to get you to the right gate at the right time. Mobile devices will have built-in barometric sensors that understand which floor you are on in a building, giving more accurate information about your location and how best to get you to your appropriate destination to complete your journey.

Visa: Reaching the Right Customer at the Right Time with the Next Best Action

Visa is a global payment technology company with presence in more than 200 countries. Visa was looking for an opportunity to better serve its customers by delivering location-based and time-based offers. Visa developed an app that helps with the buying process by bringing together location-based offers that are based on past buying behavior while assisting with the redemption process at the point of sale. Visa offers this service so individuals can receive offers that match their lifestyle at the moment of need. Customers who join the program have complete flexibility to receive the messages they want in the way they want it, as shown in Figure 11.1.

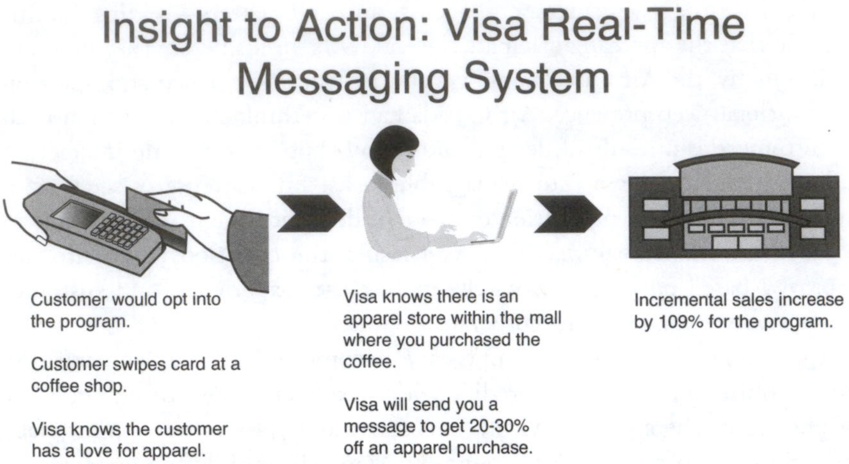

Insight to Action: Visa Real-Time Messaging System

Customer would opt into the program.

Customer swipes card at a coffee shop.

Visa knows the customer has a love for apparel.

Visa knows there is an apparel store within the mall where you purchased the coffee.

Visa will send you a message to get 20-30% off an apparel purchase.

Incremental sales increase by 109% for the program.

Figure 11.1 Visa helps merchants achieve breakthrough marketing effectiveness.[3]

First, the consumer opts into the program. The customer then makes a purchase at a particular retailer such as a coffee shop. Visa would already know buyer behavior information for that consumer and will have already assessed that she has an interest in apparel. Visa knows there is a local apparel store within the mall where the consumer purchased the coffee. Visa would then send a message to the individual with an offer to get 20–30 percent off a purchase at a specific store within the shopping mall. This message is delivered at the moment she makes the transaction in the coffee shop. By linking location, time, past purchase behavior, and partner retail information, Visa can insert its business value at the moment the customer is most likely to make another purchase. Overall, the pilot program was successful driving an incremental sales increase of more than 100 percent. Now Visa is looking to expand to other industries such as travel, dining, and fuel.

TBC Corporation: 360-Degree Customer Experience

TBC Corporation is one of the leaders in automotive service with more than 4,000 retail locations in North America and in 13 other countries. TBC wanted to shift its company's focus to become more of a service company. This meant that TBC had to reinvent its technology and the way it interacted with customers.

The essential element of the TBC strategy was to drive consistency across touch points to establish a comprehensive customer service experience. TBC needed to align all its channels of interaction with the end user. Leveraging open standards and a common code base, it needed a common platform to manage the interaction across multiple touch points: PC, mobile devices, vehicle usage, in-store experience, and employee interaction. TBC wanted to reinvent the consumer experience by providing excellent service throughout the life cycle of the car maintenance process. This would establish trust with customers by engaging in the process of maintaining a vehicle.[4]

TBC realized several key insights about its customers that helped determine its mobile strategy: Many car owners do not understand car maintenance. Most drivers do not remember services received or deferred. Most of the benefits of maintenance are invisible (especially preventative) and are not seen as valuable. Most customers do not typically plan (or save) for car maintenance and repairs. As a result, TBC categorized and prioritized a mobile portfolio of app functionality that would support a variety of devices and individuals (customer, car repair associate, and so on) within the overall customer experience.

The TBC scenario provides a 360-degree experience for customers by connecting them to service experts whenever and wherever they need them. For example, a customer discovers she has a worn tire that needs replacing. The customer searches on the web and finds a local tire company. She finds a tire she is interested in and orders it online, setting up an appointment the next day. The next day, the service rep is ready for her and has all her car information ready through his TBC-developed mobile app. Looking at the auto history through his mobile tablet, he notices that the car is ready for a checkup. The sale associate uses his mobile app to schedule a complimentary service checkup. He then texts her when her car is ready. He also notes that her breaks are worn and need repair in a few thousand miles. She decides to hold off on the maintenance. The car repair associate then makes note of it in the mobile app as a reminder to follow up with an e-mail when the brakes are ready for replacement. When she picks up her car, she realizes she has earned loyalty points toward an oil change. As a result, when she receives her email reminder a month later for the brake pads, she decides to go back to the same company to earn more loyalty points. By providing an easy-to-use mobile experience at each point of engagement, TBC has secured a long-term relationship with their customer.[5]

Waze: Adding Social Insight

Waze is an innovative car navigation app that has taken a nontraditional approach to helping drivers get to their destination. Others in the industry invest heavily in collecting satellite data and proprietary mapping data, and use cars that map street data by continuingly driving the world's roads. This approach can be expensive, and any street indexing must be done frequently to be relevant. However, most players can provide updates only on a quarterly or yearly basis. Accuracy becomes important, so the faster you update, the more value there is to the customer.

This is where the Waze navigation app comes in. Waze is different from traditional GPS navigation apps in that it utilizes crowdsourcing to provide up-to-date route and traffic updates. As members of the Waze community utilize the service, information is collected and fed into the Waze system to improve the map accuracy. Waze can monitor the speed and location of individuals. The speed of the car based on anonymous GPS movement can indicate there may be a traffic jam if many members are traveling 45 mph in a 65 mph section of the highway. As people drive on new roads, Waze can determine that new construction has occurred and can update map data on-the-fly. The Waze community can also report information in real time about accidents, location of speed traps, landmarks, cars parked on shoulder of the highway, traffic, cheap gas, and more (see http://www.waze.com/).

Waze also offers badges and awards for people to participate in the community. The more points received, the higher status an individual can achieve in the community, which then translates into more valuable navigation data for the Waze database. Waze even uses simple games to drive more community participation. Users might see icons (in the shape of cupcakes) on the map and are encouraged to drive over the cupcakes to earn points. As users play the game, they also generate valuable navigation data in the parts of the Waze system that might be lacking data.

Waze has become a huge success. As of July 2012, Waze has 20 million users within its community, doubling from the previous 6 months. Waze has become successful by leveraging a broad community with smart devices to provide a compelling and engaging user experience. This helps users by informing them of the next best action. Waze does this by not having to invest in sophisticated road and traffic data, while instead leveraging the use of individuals to provide real-time data for those users in their moment of need.[6]

Nike+ FuelBand: Enhancing Value
by Extending with APIs

The Nike+ FuelBand is a wristband with a built-in three-axis accelerometer that measures an individual's activity. This activity is then translated into a point system called Nike Fuel that enables users to track their activity in a consistent way. The Nike Fuel amount displays on a set of LEDs on the wristband. Individuals track their progress and goals by tracking their Nike Fuel. Users can upload their Nike Fuel data to the Nike web site to monitor their progress toward a set goal. The Nike+ FuelBand also has a Bluetooth connectivity that enables it to sync with a mobile device (see http://www.nike.com/us/en_us/lp/nikeplus-fuelband).

What is interesting about the Nike+ FuelBand story is that an apparel company has started to become a hardware company by developing and taking to market a smart device. It is also leveraging the smartphone as a data analysis tool. Furthermore, as they expand their ecosystem by releasing APIs and interfaces to their system, Nike becomes, in many respects, a software company.

Nike also has opened up its APIs to developers interested in participating in the Nike+ FuelBand ecosystem. [7] This is the first time Nike has released APIs to third parties. [8] They hope to encourage developers to build companion applications that can create value for the customers, driving more purchases of its shoes and apparel. By opening up the APIs, you can imagine apps that complement the overall exercise experience, such as apps that provide music based on the user location, time of day, or level of exercise. Apps could also easily tie into health management systems or exercise regimens. By extending its application to third parties, Nike can further enhance the task of exercise by leveraging smart devices and monitoring technology and third parties to provide a complete experience for the end user.

Withings: Integrate into the Life Style
to Serve at the Moment of Need

Withings is a consumer electronics company founded in 2008 that has developed a series of Internet connected health and monitoring products. [9] Withings is an example of a company with products that can integrate into the life style of individuals and serve them in their moment of need.

Withings has developed a set of smart products that monitor key aspects of one's health, such as a wireless scale, blood pressure monitor, and baby monitor. All these devices are wirelessly connected and are accompanied with a mobile app.

What becomes interesting about the Withings offering is that it streamlines the process of weight management. It has taken the simple task of stepping on a scale and turned it into an efficient weight program. For example, each time you step on the scale, it automatically is wirelessly captured on your personal weight chart within your app. The app automatically sets realistic goals that can help you to become motivated to reach your desired weight.[10] The Withings WiFi Body Scale can also recognize which person in the family (based on their weight) is on the scale and match them to their particular weight management program (see http://www.withings.com/). Finally, Withings has more than 60 partners that can provide complementary apps that further extend the capabilities of the Withings system with exercise programs, health monitoring programs, running programs, and more.

What makes the Withings WiFI Body Scale so interesting? It has combined smart devices with mobile devices to impact people's lifestyle. It has removed steps from the task of weight management. It made a product that integrates the tasks of an individual. It has tools and resources at users' fingertips at the moment it is needed. It has broken down the activity of weight management into tasks while removing tasks that are not necessary. For example, it removed the task of noting the weight on the scale and then typing it into a mobile app. The wirelessly connected scale does this for you. By aligning with partners it extended the capability of its solution and provides a rich 360-degree experience with the individual. The data analysis gives them insight to action that helps the individual take the best next step.

Tesco's Home Plus: Reducing Steps in Daily Tasks

Tesco's South Korean store chain called Home Plus has developed an innovative way to make it easy for busy South Koreans to do their shopping. Home Plus looked at their customer demographics and saw an opportunity to help their customers improve the process of shopping. Home Plus determined that many of their customers commute on trains. The Home Plus customers work hard and are tired after a long day at work. They have little time to shop. Offering customers the chance to shop while doing something else can help the customers accomplish a task while helping Home Plus sell more products. Home Plus decided to take advantage that its customers are waiting at a train terminal. The train commuters are likely busy but have a few moments as they wait for the train. However, Home Plus could not open up stores in the train terminals, so it turned to mobile devices as a solution.

Home Plus enabled customers to buy products through its mobile device by building virtual aisles on the walls of the train platforms. Home Plus created large beautifully designed images of products in the form of aisles in a grocery store. Each item has a corresponding QR code. Commuters simply go up to the virtual shopping aisle, scan the QR code of the item they want, and then it is placed in the Home Plus shopping cart. The purchased products can then be delivered within a few hours of the order. This enables the products to arrive when they arrive home (see http://www.designboom.com/technology/tesco-virtual-supermarket-in-a-subway-station/).

The Home Plus virtual store delivered successful results. Home Plus online sales increased by 130 percent in 3 months, and the number of registered users increased by 76 percent.[11]

Home Plus delivered an engaging app because they were able to integrate their app into the lifestyle of the individual. They were able to take steps out of the task of grocery shopping by skipping the drive to the store, going to a register, and bringing the groceries home. They were also able to 'time shift' where tasks were moved to a time that was more convenient for them.

Square Wallet

Square is an innovative company founded by Jack Dorsey, cofounder of Twitter, which is revolutionizing the payment industry. You may have seen the square credit card reader at your local farmers' market or craft fair. Square Register is a small white credit card reader that plugs into the audio jack of the mobile phone or tablet. This becomes an alternative to the traditional point of sale and credit card reader from the transaction process. It also reduces the cost to the retailer. At a flat 2.75 percent fee (or $275 per month), retailers now have a much less expensive way of accepting credit cards.[12] It puts the power of a credit card transition in the hands of the masses. And Square enables the transaction to go mobile, happening anytime and anyplace there is a 3G connection. The retailer simply signs up for the program and gets a free square device. Every time there is a transaction, the end user has the option of having the receipt sent to them by email. To conclude the transaction, users simply sign their name on the screen of the smart device with their finger.

This new model revolutionizes the retail experience. Small companies and individuals who accept credit cards had been forced to buy expensive equipment and sign long-term contracts with merchant service providers. This may work for large retailers, but not so much for small businesses.

The Square approach becomes even more interesting with its more recent capability called the Square Wallet—a mobile payment app. The Square Wallet is a retail service with an interesting twist—the Square Wallet has taken yet another step out of the task process in that customers can now make a purchase without even taking their credit card out of their wallet (see https://squareup.com/).

The Square Wallet process is easy and revolutionary. First, a customer downloads the app and then creates an account with name, ID, password, picture, and credit card information. The app can then locate a business near you that can access the Square Wallet. When you enter into the business (within 500 feet) the mobile device knows your GPS location. You then press the Pay Here button on the app that corresponds to the establishment you plan to make a purchase at. You can also set your phone to automatically pay when you come within geographic approximation of the retailer. At the same time, the retailer knows you are in the store on its point of sale register (such as an iPad with a corresponding Square Register app). The cashier checks the photo on the register and validates it is you. After the retailer has matched you with your account and your item of purchase, the transaction takes place against the credit card you registered. Not only that, but you can even leave a tip. Most recently, Starbucks has begun offering support for the Square Wallet in nearly 7,000 stores.[13]

What is interesting about the square approach is that it has greatly simplified the transaction process. First, the Square Register simplifies and reduces the cost for the retailer when accepting a transaction. The Square Wallet then saves the step of actually swiping your credit card. Taking steps out of the task are ways to transform your business through mobile apps. Certainly, the next step is near field communication (NFC) as a way to even further simplify the transaction process. Simply touching your device to an NFC reader would be the ultimate in reducing transaction steps. However, NFC requires standardization of hardware and communication protocols that will likely take time. With that said, the Square Wallet is a revolutionary step that dramatically reduces the steps in the transaction process.

Summary

Engaging mobile apps can transform your business. In the market today you can find examples of mobile apps that are both transforming companies while disrupting the competition. The market is moving from reactionary apps to a new generation of transformative apps. Recall that reactionary apps are often characterized by simply taking a traditional web interface and delivering it in a mobile experience. They often don't take into account the user experience and user expectations that the consumerization of IT brings. Reactionary apps also do not take into account the cross-platform, management, and governance requirements that are so important for the enterprise. In contrast, the transformative app removes and simplifies the steps and tasks that users must take to achieve a goal. It also predicts the next best action so that it can eliminate the thought process or research needed to perform the next task.

In conclusion, the case studies above illustrate how current businesses are leveraging the transformative app to engage their customers and increase business performance. To achieve this, the app must leverage context such as the Visa program that can understand past buying behavior and link it to the context of the card swipe. It needs to leverage cross-channel (such as kiosks, web, and mobile) as in the case of Air Canada. An engaging app needs to use multichannel similar to TBC where the purchase system, appointment process, repair process, retail process, and loyalty program are linked and work together. You must tie in smart devices such as Nike+ fuel does to provide better context and awareness, and link to third-party API and services to deliver a complete experience. Based on what we learned from the Withings strategy, you should think about how to insert the app experience into daily life (personal and work) to engage the user at the moment of need, leveraging smart devices to make tasks more efficient. You need to pull in peers that can help supply information and validation for tasks to help with the next best step and provide a richer insight, such as with the Waze app. Think about how to take steps out of the process, such as the Tesco Home Plus virtual store where South Korean commuters can go shopping with a virtual shopping isle in the train station while they wait for a train. Or how Square eliminates tasks from the credit card transaction process by helping the transaction happen as the customer enters the store.

Endnotes

1   IBM Customer Reference. "Air Canada - Smarter Planet Leadership Series Video": http://www.youtube.com/watch?v=dyXuheNcJDs

2   http://www-01.ibm.com/software/ucd/gallery/aircanada_services_ravereviews.html

3   IBM Customer Reference. "Visa Inc. - IBM Smarter Planet Leadership Series": http://www.youtube.com/watch?v=8M8RoxBvkSY&feature=share

4   IBM Customer Reference. "TBC - IBM client success video": http://www.youtube.com/watch?v=KSIQFSy_4uU

5   IBM Customer Reference. "TBC Customer Success Scenario featuring IBM Worklight": http://www.youtube.com/watch?v=dovM0u0IOZ8

6   Wikipedia. "Waze": http://en.wikipedia.org/wiki/Waze

7   PSFK. "Nike Opens Its Fuel Band API to Developers to Create a More Useful Product": http://www.psfk.com/2012/04/nike-opens-up-fuel-ban-api-to-developers-for-the-first-time.html

8   Wikipedia. "Waze": http://en.wikipedia.org/wiki/Waze

9   Wikipedia. "Withings": http://en.wikipedia.org/wiki/Withings

10 Withings: http://www.withings.com/en/bodyscale

11 Wired. "Tesco brings the supermarket to time-poor commuters in South Korea": http://www.wired.co.uk/news/archive/2011-06/30/tesco-home-plus-billboard-store

12 Square: https://squareup.com/

13 Forbes. "Starbucks Now Accepting Payments With Square Wallet": http://www.forbes.com/sites/kellyclay/2012/11/08/starbucks-now-accepting-payments-with-square-wallet/

Additional Sources

Examples innovative and compelling apps can help inspire new ways of thinking about your own mobile app:

http://gizmodo.com/iphone-apps-of-the-week/

http://www.time.com/time/specials/packages/0,28757,1823107,00.html

http://www.forbes.com/sites/davidkwilliams/2013/01/04/10-mobile-apps-to-make-your-business-more-productive-in-2013/

12

Moving Forward

Mobile will continue to be the dominant way companies interact with their employees and customers. Diversity will continue, and the speed and pace of innovation will not end soon. Features considered to be cutting edge today will be common place tomorrow. New sensors and data capture capabilities will continue to become part of the mobile device, driving deeper and deeper engagement. These sensors will provide more and more insight into the end user behavior enabling richer and richer interaction. All this technology capability advancement will be enabled by greater and greater processing speed matched by improved battery life. The convergence of Social, Cloud, Mobile, and Big Data analytics (SoCloDaMo) will continue to grow in prominence and will become an important platform for building and connecting mobile applications. International dynamics will continue to migrate to the smartphone; however, there will be even greater diversity in device types and capabilities based on the preferences of people in different regions of the world.

Customers will continue to demand the latest mobile device features. These features will collect an increasing amount of data relating to context and behavior. The enterprise will see this flow of data as an opportunity to gain more and more insight into customer behavior that will drive greater opportunity to service their costumers and help their employees become more productive.

The most important trends going forward will be the incorporation of intelligence along with context and engagement in a transformative application. The transformative app will predict the next best action, reduce steps, and streamline how a task gets done. This continued pursuit of delivering value to the end user will be critical to the success of any enterprise going forward. The mobile application has empowered end users with unprecedented information and computing power in the context of their daily lives. Mobile technology has enabled individuals to make the best possible decision or transaction at the moment of need. As mobile technology advances, this shift of power to individuals away from institutions will continue. Those companies with the capability to execute a comprehensive strategy will engage customers and employees at their moment of need; they are the companies that will win against the competition.

What You Have Learned

The key to becoming successful in the new mobile era will be based on executing a comprehensive mobile strategy. As you made your journey through this book, you learned several important aspects of a mobile strategy.

- **Opportunity:** Mobility provides the opportunity to reach customers and help employees in all new ways. Mobility is fundamentally about engagement, such that you can gain a deeper relationship with your customer and greater opportunities to extend your business.

- **Challenges:** Delivering a mobile solution is not without its challenges. Constantly changing technologies, high expectations for speed of execution, unyielding focus on quality, and ubiquitous connectivity will be challenging.

- **Business value:** A mobile strategy needs to be of value to both the end user and the enterprise. To make it effective, a mobile strategy must offer functionality that supports the task the end user wants to perform and contain measurable goals with which to evaluate the success of the project. The linkage between the value proposition of the project and the end user's tasks forms the basis for a framework that defines the tools, infrastructure, and technology needed to deliver on a mobile project.

- **A mobile framework:** To navigate the challenges presented by mobile, you need a framework that defines your core execution plan while allowing for flexibility to incorporate new technologies as the market evolves.

- **Developing mobile applications**: A mobile strategy should address the core imperatives of delivering a quality app with speed and agility, building apps for a diversity of platforms, and connecting data and service to mobile devices.

- **Mobile management and security**: A mobile strategy should address the core imperatives associated with how you manage and secure mobile devices, applications, and networks.

- **Mobile business transformation**: The market is in a massive shift toward mobile. This will lead to a mobile-first priority for enterprises in that systems will be built initially for mobile instead of the PC. This mobile-first priority will drive a focus toward solutions based on context, engagement, and intelligence. Extending existing systems of record to a system of engagement will transform your business.

- **Planning a mobile strategy project**: To deliver a winning mobile strategy, you need a mobile strategy methodology. A methodology must first establish the right organizational structure and leadership. You need to define the appropriate goals for a successful mobile project. You need to define what the end user wants to accomplish and then choose an approach. Study your organization and assess the potential gaps in execution. Are they due to lack of skills, organization, or technology? Define a roadmap for success. Then execute, measure, and adapt.

- **SoCloDaMo**: Social Networking, Cloud, Big Data, and Mobile are synergistic technologies that come together as enabling technologies for a system of engagement. It brings together the behavior and preferences from their peers (social), access, and context (mobile), that will give them insight (big data analytics) in a ubiquitous way (cloud).

- **International**: A mobile strategy should be comprehensive and should consider a global audience. Depending on the market, you may need to consider supporting feature phones, basic phones, and voice-only interaction and SMS.

- **Case studies**: A mobile strategy must consider the best practices and methodology of others. A view of the leading mobile solutions will provide ideas and concepts that can be applied to your own mobile effort. Understanding where the market is heading, even outside your own industry, can help to provide direction for your mobile strategy.

Guiding Principles

As you consider an overall mobile strategy, a set of guiding principles can help shape the direction of your effort. These principles should be your guide posts on your journey to a comprehensive mobile strategy.

- Mobility is one of the most profound changes in technology in our life-time—on the same order of magnitude as the introduction of the main-frame, PCs, and the birth of the Internet.

- Technology change will always be present and will likely accelerate—be flexible to change.

- Comsumerization of IT and BYOD will create pressure on businesses to adopt and use technology that may not be originally designed for the enterprise. Sharing the device between work and personal use will be the norm. In addition, there will be increased pressure to deliver very engaging mobile solutions with very quick turnaround.

- Focus on providing value to the customers and simplifying their task at hand—end user experience trumps all.

- Extending a system of record to a system of engagement is transformative. Focus on how your mobile solution can leverage context, intelligence, and engagement to integrate into the daily activities of your customer and employees. In doing so you can deliver value to your end user but also gain deep insight into the next best services and offerings you can provide them.

- Security will remain a top priority. As adoption of mobile technologies increase so will the type of threats and number of attacks. Devices that are easily lost or stolen will continue to be an important factor driving increase diligence in protecting the enterprise and corporate data. You will need to monitor your security situation and be ready to adapt.

- Privacy will be critical in maintaining the trust relationship between the enterprises and their customers and employees. The more you learn about the end user, the more valuable services you can offer. At the same time, you are entrusted with sensitive personal information that must be used in the appropriate manner.

- You will need to think in terms of an ominchannel approach. Your application needs to support a variety of devices, computing interfaces, and user experiences. People will use a variety of connected smart devices throughout their day (such as a smartphone, TV, wrist watch, PC, thermostat, etc.). As they move from device to device, you will need to deliver a continuous experience.

- The use of open standards will be critical to avoid vendor lock-in and leverage skills that are readily available in the market place.

- Composite applications that chain together a variety of services and integration of apps will enable more dynamic applications that are tailored to a particular end user requirement.

- You should build a strategy that is able to adapt to change. The mobile market is continuously changing and as such you will need to collect data about your customer interaction, analyze the situation, and make course corrections as needed.

- Quality is critical to any mobile strategy. You will need to constantly look for areas where you can improve customer experience by analyzing end user interaction with your company and determining how you can improve the experience. Testing across a variety of devices and environment will be important to ensuring the quality end users expect.

- To get there, you need a framework that not only outlines how you develop mobile apps and manage and secure mobile applications, devices, and networks but also guides you to transforming your business.

- A comprehensive mobile strategy can keep you focused on winning in the market.

Conclusion

At the end of the day, mobile is the biggest technology and business change in a generation. The execution of a solid mobile strategy can enable you to seize the opportunity around mobility. It is not enough to simply build an app and get it in an app store. A knee-jerk reaction to the mobile marketplace can cause more harm than good to a business. A mobile presence can help propel a brand to new heights or (when done poorly) can cause a company's image to be tarnished while wasting countless dollars. The only way to win in the market is to embrace mobile technologies by developing a comprehensive strategy that is based on a solid methodology rooted in customer value.

Index

FREE
Online Edition

 Safari
Books Online

Your purchase of *Mobile Strategy* includes access to a free online edition for 45 days through the **Safari Books Online** subscription service. Nearly every IBM Press book is available online through **Safari Books Online**, along with thousands of books and videos from publishers such as Addison-Wesley Professional, Cisco Press, Exam Cram, O'Reilly Media, Prentice Hall, Que, and Sams.

Safari Books Online is a digital library providing searchable, on-demand access to thousands of technology, digital media, and professional development books and videos from leading publishers. With one monthly or yearly subscription price, you get unlimited access to learning tools and information on topics including mobile app and software development, tips and tricks on using your favorite gadgets, networking, project management, graphic design, and much more.

Activate your FREE Online Edition at
informit.com/safarifree

STEP 1:   Enter the coupon code: MHMAYYG.

STEP 2:   New Safari users, complete the brief registration form.
Safari subscribers, just log in.

If you have difficulty registering on Safari or accessing the online edition,
please e-mail customer-service@safaribooksonline.com

Addison Wesley AdobePress ALPHA Cisco Press FT Press IBM Press Microsoft Press New Riders O'REILLY

Peachpit Press PRENTICE HALL QUE Redbooks SAMS SAS Publishing vmware PRESS WILEY wrox